THE
EXECUTIVE CHALLENGE

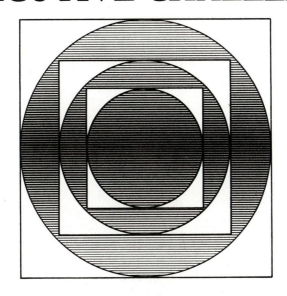

Managing Change
and Ambiguity

THE EXECUTIVE CHALLENGE

Managing Change and Ambiguity

MICHAEL B. McCASKEY
Harvard University

Pitman

Boston · London · Melbourne · Toronto

Pitman Publishing Inc.
1020 Plain Street
Marshfield, Massachusetts 02050

Pitman Books Limited
128 Long Acre
London WC2E 9AN

Associated Companies
Pitman Publishing Pty Ltd., Melbourne
Pitman Publishing New Zealand Ltd., Wellington
Copp Clark Pitman, Toronto

Library of Congress Cataloging in Publication Data

McCaskey, Michael B.
    The executive challenge.

    Includes index.
    1. Executive ability.   2. Management.
3. Organizational change.   I. Title.
HF5500.2.M43   658.4 06   82-628
ISBN 0-273-01846-9   AACR2

Manufactured in the United States of America

10 9 8 7 6 5 4 3 2 1

TO NANCY

Contents

Acknowledgments

Halfway through the research study that forms the basis for this book, I gave a preliminary report to a group of Harvard Business School faculty members. In the ensuing discussion, comments seemed to divide into two camps. One camp was excited by the bold scope of the research—attacking areas clearly at the heart of the general manager's job but complicated, hard to measure, and perhaps intractable for the researcher's art. The other (smaller) camp was angry. Even though the topic was how managers cope with ambiguity and change, they felt that all good research should begin with precise definitions of terms and a carefully programmed plan of attack. In deference to the subject matter, I was engaging in a more directional, more "learn and revise as you go" research mode.

The comments of both camps were helpful and stimulating, though one camp was easier to hear than the other. The polar responses of my colleagues helped me anticipate the likely reactions of readers to this book. Without abandoning my position—that a researcher is foolish to preprogram an attack on ill-defined problems—I have tried to make the going more comfortable and productive for the second camp. Where possible, I present clear definitions; where precise definitions would be premature and misleading, I offer approximations clearly labeled as such.

This book asks the reader to take an active role. Learning to manage change and ambiguity better requires more than just the transfer of concepts. The ideas, guidelines, and ways of thinking, if they are to be useful, must be evaluated by each reader and made one's own. That is not an easy nor a simple process, and it cannot be accomplished without the reader's active involvement with the material.

In that spirit, I often use "we" in the text to indicate that this is a journey of exploration and learning for both author and reader. I have written many of the passages as if I were talking with one of the managers with whom I consult. For other passages, I wrote as if I were talking to a class of MBA students, trying to give them practical ways to think about ambiguity and change in the managerial world.

Footnotes appear for several reasons. The notes acknowledge intellectual debts and help to make connections for readers familiar with the literature being cited. The notes may also serve, along with the Bibliography at the end of the book, to identify further reading on a particular point or topic.

Three permissions to use previously published materials should be acknowledged. An earlier version of Chapter 4, the High Technology Research Project, was published in an article I wrote for *Organizational Dynamics*, Spring 1979. The case is reprinted by permission of the publisher, copyright 1979, by AMACOM, a division of American Management Associations. All rights reserved. The passage quoted in Chapter 8 from *My Years With General Motors* is copyrighted 1963 by Alfred P. Sloan, Jr. and is reprinted by permission of the Harold Matson Company, Inc. The maps of ancient Rome and the New World (Chapter 2) appear through the courtesy of the Research Libraries of the New York Public Library.

I have many people to thank for their help in writing this book. A crucial component of the research is studying managers grappling with change and ambiguity. The officers at BayBanks, especially William Crozier, the citizens and administrators who worked with the San Francisco school system, and the managers and scientists at the "J. Mirl Company" were generous in sharing their time and experience with me. Professor Howard Gruber provided constructive criticism on the Darwin chapter, and Professor James Brian Quinn kindly sent his case on the GM downsizing decision which improved our account in Appendix B. To these and several other managers who allowed me to study and question them about their efforts to master the executive challenge, I am most grateful.

For critical reviews of different chapters I am thankful to splendid colleagues such as John Kotter, Vijay Sathe, Robert Eccles, Robert Tannenbaum, Thomas Lifson, Richard Hammermesh, and Eliza Collins. For encouragement at different points along the way, my thanks go to Paul Lawrence, Raymond Corey, and especially Richard Rosenbloom, who was head of the Division of Research when the study was launched. I wish to thank the Division of Research, Dean John McArthur, and the Harvard Business School for providing time and funding to pursue this research.

I have been fortunate in having E. Mary Lou Balbaky as a research assistant to conduct interviews and to write the first draft of the San Francisco and GM cases. Rita Perloff wrestled the word processor into submission in order to produce numerous drafts. Judy Uhl and Nancy Jackson lent their considerable editorial skills to improving the manuscript.

I would also like to thank my parents, Edward and Virginia McCaskey, for their love and support through the long years of my education, formal and otherwise, and my brothers and sisters who provided the earliest lessons in ambiguity and change. My dad read an earlier draft with the hope of guarding the English language from too obvious discord. His ear for the music of good language improved the text, even if there still remain constructions he would avoid and that I am willing to put up with.

Lastly, I thank my wife Nancy for tough-minded comments on the book and tenderhearted encouragement. She has enriched me and the book in ways beyond what words can say, and so it is to her that the book is dedicated.

THE
EXECUTIVE CHALLENGE

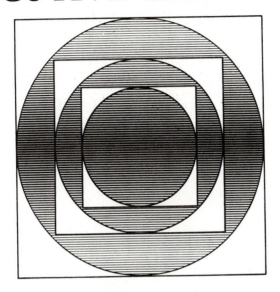

Managing Change
and Ambiguity

Chapter 1

Introduction

Managers today increasingly confront problems whose ambiguities seem to baffle all familiar methods of attack. Even when they rise to the occasion, and invent the new tools they need, the process can be an intensely stressful one. Here's how it might feel:

I'll be glad when this is over—if I survive! For two months now the pressure has been relentless, nothing but work on my mind around the clock. I used to leave office problems at the office. Now I'm coming home at erratic hours, and when home, I'm holed up with reports or on the telephone. The family resents my not being with them and they worry about my health.

Usually I fall asleep rather easily, but lately I find my mind races on—even though the switch has supposedly been turned off. Then, after falling asleep, I might wake up at four a.m. thinking of something else that could go wrong and needs to be checked. My wife's getting grumpy from having her sleep interrupted so frequently, not to mention the tension.

Last week scared the hell out of me. My brain muscle was tightened for too long, and it cramped. On my way to an important meeting I felt dizzy and started seeing double. My mind couldn't sort things out the way it usually does. If there is one thing I am *not,* it is addle-brained. I got scared that the whole thing was going to collapse, or that I would collapse physically. I wondered if I was going crazy.

The others are feeling the stress too. One colleague carries the smell of mounting disaster, hands perspiring, and voice coming out strange. Another treats the rapid shifts of fortune as a vast practical joke. Events wear him down, but a night's sleep revives him. Perils only serve to breed a genial, desperado philosophy in him; momentous changes become part of the general joke.

When I am tired and discouraged, I feel unable to change things, or even seriously disturb the flow of events. We just don't have enough facts, don't understand the sensitivities. Yet if the project fails, they will be looking for someone to blame. In this lightning storm, I'm the one carrying a metal rod. Ambivalent and confused motives abound. What is going on here? My purpose must be to define direction, to inspire confidence even as the lightning cracks around us. I can't let people stay so scared that they refuse to come out of hiding. At times I feel weary and undecided myself, but mainly I'm optimistic that it will work out. I feel the adrenalin pumping. In spite of the dark moments, we are going to solve this thing.

The experience of trying to manage ambiguity is a common one. The monologue presented above, for instance, is based on a composite of my research, interviews with business executives, and reading in the novels of Tolstoy, Melville, and Joseph Heller.[1] These disparate sources yield a common picture of the process of coping with a poorly defined administrative situation. The problems are complex—signal and noise are confused, players have complicated and ambivalent roles, the pressure of work is pervasive. Supported by his own internal strengths, his work team, his family, and others, the successful manager feels he is making progress. Other colleagues, however, may be incapacitated by the stress of high-pressure, high-stakes change. Managing in these situations requires special skills.

Managers increasingly face poorly defined problems that are interdependent, complex, and changing. In such situations information is not as complete nor causal relationships as well understood as managers would like. For the most challenging situations, experts have cloudy crystal balls or strenuously argue contradictory positions. Yet, to be effective, a manager may have to act before the situation is entirely clear, while important elements of the problem can be interpreted in conflicting ways, and while convincing arguments are made for and against different alternatives. In short, a manager must act in the face of ambiguity.

Furthermore, the ambiguity of the manager's world is increasing. We live in an age when old value frameworks are doubted and established patterns for behaving are stretched beyond recognition. Peter Drucker identifies several reasons for the turbulence of our times:

- Rapid inflation distorts and misinforms a manager on how the enterprise is doing.

- The structure and dynamics of the population are changing erratically and unpredictably.
- New modes of economic integration are appearing as goods are produced transnationally, that is, as more goods have components produced in several countries.
- The labor force is fragmented into "labor forces," each with its own needs, expectations, and performance characteristics.
- Business and other institutions are politicized, forcing top managers to spend more time on relations with external constituencies.[2]

To this list one might add sudden shifts in government regulation or deregulation and the destabilizing potential of new technology.

In response to this turbulence managers have been rethinking the way they design an organization to interact with its environment. Buffering out uncertainty in order to keep internal operations stable and continuous, used to be a rational strategy for organizations—but no longer. The ground itself is shifting and many organizations find themselves lying on a fault line. Managers need to build structures that will flex and bend with ground tremors rather than break. Building in flexibility means allowing more uncertainty inside the organization. Practitioners are experimenting with new organizational forms such as the matrix, project management, sharing the responsibilities of the president's office, and dual lines of authority. The increased flexibility is not without its costs. For example, with the matrix form some managers work in its "hot spots," reporting to two bosses and being charged with responsibilities that outstrip their formal authority. The matrix form is appreciated for its flexibility, efficient use of resources, and rapid response to environmental changes, but the matrix "chews up" people. Managers at the hot spots of the organization must endure considerably more ambiguity than managers in more traditional organizations. For members of the organization, these changes mean greater discomfort, less stability, more adventure, and more stress. While some enjoy the excitement, many experience vertigo and fear a loss of control.

These feelings of uncertainty stem from the increasing turbulence and the increasing complexity of organizational life. Researchers who have looked closely at organizational processes have characteristically been impressed by their complexity. Joseph Bower concluded his two-year study of resource allocation in a large multinational corporation by observing:

Perhaps the most striking aspect of the process of resource allocation, as described in this study, is the extent to which it is more complex than most managers seem to believe. It bears little resemblance to the simple portfolio management problem described in traditional financial theory. Moreover, the systems created to control the process sometimes appeared irrelevant to the task. They were based on the fallacious premise that top management made important choices in the finance committee when it approved capital investment proposals. In contrast we have found capital investment to be a process of study, bargaining, persuasion and choice spread over many levels of the organization and over long periods of time.[3]

How resources are allocated, then, is not determined solely at the top; and choices about which projects receive funding are not controlled in any simple, straightforward way. When change and ambiguity are added, the equations become even more complicated.

Given the interdependent problems, shifting values, turbulence, uncertainty, and complexity of a transitional age, managers must become more skillful in dealing with change. Organizations, people, business, and political environments are changing. First order changes, merely rearranging the same basic pieces, will not be sufficient. For the more complex and uncertain challenges they face today, managers must make second order changes, rethinking the patterns connecting the pieces.[4] Such meta-level thinking is more fundamental and demanding, but it opens up correspondingly greater opportunities. Sociologist James Thompson observed that those who can successfully deal with major uncertainties become essential to the organization and gain influence and power.[5] Organizational researcher Melville Dalton argues that the manager who can constructively deal with ambiguity shows the capacities most needed at the top.[6] In short, the present turbulence has created both new dangers and new opportunities for managers.

DEFINING AMBIGUOUS SITUATIONS

Organizational researchers have pointed to several characteristics associated with ambiguous, changing situations. Table 1.1 presents a list of these characteristics. The categories overlap somewhat, and some characteristics might best be described as symptoms of others.

As a first approximation, we might define an ambiguous changing situation as one that exhibits many of the characteristics listed in

TABLE 1.1.   Characteristics of Ambiguous, Changing Situations

Characteristic	Description and Comments
Nature of problem is itself in question	"What the problem is" is unclear and shifting. Managers have only vague, or competing, definitions of the problem. Often any one "problem" is intertwined with other messy problems.
Information (amount and reliability) is problematical	Because the definition of the problem is in doubt, collecting and categorizing information becomes a problem. The information flow threatens either to become overwhelming or to be seriously insufficient. Data may be incomplete and of dubious reliability.
Multiple, conflicting interpretations	For those data that do exist, players develop multiple, and sometimes conflicting, interpretations. The facts and their significance can be read several different ways.
Different value orientations, political/emotional clashes	Without objective criteria, players rely more upon personal and/or professional values to make sense of the situation. The clash of different values often politically and emotionally charges the situation.
Goals are unclear, or multiple and conflicting	Managers do not enjoy the guidance of clearly defined, coherent goals. Either the goals are vague, or they are clearly defined and contradictory.
Time, money, or attention are lacking	A difficult situation is made chaotic by severe shortages of one or more of these items.
Contradictions and paradoxes appear	Situation has seemingly inconsistent features, relationships, or demands.
Roles vague, responsibilities unclear	Players do not have a clearly defined set of activities they are expected to perform. On important issues, the locus of decisionmaking and other responsibilities is vague or in dispute.
Success measures are lacking	People are unsure what success in resolving the situation would mean and/or they have no way of assessing the degree to which they have been successful.
Poor understanding of cause-effect relationships	Players do not understand what causes what in the situation. Even if sure of the effects they desire, they are uncertain how to obtain them.
Symbols and metaphors used	In place of precise definitions or logical arguments, players use symbols or metaphors to express their points of view.
Participation in decisionmaking fluid[7]	Who the key decision-makers and influence holders are changes as players enter and leave the decision arena.

Table 1.1. One aim of this book is to refine our diagnostic powers. In examining different administrative situations, therefore, we will consider which of the catalogued characteristics are most troublesome to managers. By the end of the book we will have a better sense of which features in particular make these situations difficult to manage.

RESISTANCE TO AMBIGUITY

Individuals respond in quite different ways to the appearance of ambiguity. Some managers seem able to tolerate high levels of ambiguity before eventually imposing order. Others seem to actually prefer ambiguity as a way of avoiding unpleasant facts. Still others demand order and control in one area (such as their work or career plans) and allow other areas to be murky (such as their personal feelings and relationships).

For many people, the experience of ambiguity arouses anxiety and the need for more control. To tolerate ambiguity seems to imply some sort of personal failure of understanding or skill. My argument, however, is that ambiguity is a rich, if frustrating, and inevitable part of life. We should not try to ignore, avoid, or rationalize what is fundamentally unclear. To manage the ambiguities of change, we must first allow them to exist. The greater danger is the temptation to deny ambiguity or impose clear meaning on ambiguous events. The experience of U.S. automakers over the last two decades illustrates this managerial pitfall all too clearly.

A Case of Avoiding Ambiguity and Fundamental Change [8]

In 1956 U.S. automobile manufacturers dominated the world auto market. The large Detroit companies had a clear view of their business and their customers, reinforced by decades of success. Prime tenets of this creed were that Americans wanted big, fancy cars; styling, including annual styling changes, was the premier selling feature; and small cars equaled small profits.

Then, during the recession of 1958, something unprecedented occurred. Small, imported cars grabbed 8% of new car sales in the United States. Two new domestic compacts, the Rambler and the Studebaker Lark, also sold well. Detroit executives saw these events through the lens of their beliefs. Their interpretation was that buyers of imported cars were pro-foreign and wanted something unusual and different. Nevertheless, Ford, Chrysler, and General Motors brought out their first generation of compacts and scored an easy victory over the imports, who were hampered by weak distribution and service networks.

With the foreign "invasion" successfully turned back, Detroit executives reached an important choice point. Year by year they increased the size of their once small compacts. Later, in 1969, Henry Ford II commented on the strong tendency of American automakers to increase the size and the cost of their small cars. Ford admitted, "That's the tendency in this business. It's the same old thing we've been through so many times. You'd think we'd learn, but we never do."[9]   As the American cars grew bigger, the sales of imports started growing again.

In the 1960s sales of domestic compacts were also hurt by the charges of Ralph Nader and others. For the first time Congress set safety standards and then air pollution standards for new cars. GM, the largest automobile manufacturer, sustained the most vigorous attacks. Eventually, the company brought in outsiders who broke the previous insularity of their board. Academic and energy experts sensitized executives to the long-term energy shortage and the company began to develop plans for gradually improving the fuel efficiency of their cars. Ford Motor Company, on the other hand, was a recognized leader in the manufacture of smaller cars (a title they were not altogether proud of), and therefore felt less vulnerable. At this time they were selling small, well-built cars in Europe, and could have brought this know-how back to the United States. Ford executives, however, sharply differentiated American from European buyers and saw two completely different markets.

The oil embargo hit suddenly in 1973. Gasoline was in short supply, and prices climbed steeply. Americans refused to buy large "gas guzzling" cars. Again Detroit executives were at a choice point.

Decisions had to be made that would cost billions of dollars and might affect the companies' survival, yet executives lacked hard and reliable information. Significant ambiguity surrounded several crucial issues including:

- changing consumer tastes and fears
- a rapidly shifting economy with wide swings in consumer confidence and purchasing power
- the significance of increasing sales of foreign cars (fad or basic change?)

- government regulations that were obscure, shifting, complex, and expensive and involved unclear technologies and strict deadline pressures
- uncertainty about gasoline availability and the price levels to which comsumers could adjust

The list could be expanded, but the essential point is that ambiguity and uncertainty cloaked many of the elements critical for decision-making. The chairman of GM, Richard Gerstenberg, admitted that "we don't yet have a good fix on what people want."[10] Yet executives could not afford merely to continue the old policies. As Gerstenberg later recalled, "When the embargo came, I was aware that we had to do something drastic, and that we had to do it right away."[11] (A more detailed description of these events can be found in Appendix B.)

The business press was harsh in its criticism of U.S. auto executives. After consumers refused to buy large cars, the press reported that automakers had lost touch with the consumer, were slow to react to the growing demand for fuel efficient cars, and underestimated foreign marketing prowess. But such criticism does not explain why things happened as they did, nor, more importantly, can it suggest how managers might avoid similar mistakes in the future.

With this in mind I began a research study to investigate what happens when managers are confronted with ambiguity, uncertainty, and fundamental change. The times have become turbulent not only for automakers but also for bankers, the telephone companies, health care institutions, and a whole range of enterprises that once operated in more or less predictable environments. In addition, managers of high technology companies and of fast growth companies have long had to cope with rapid change. The study aimed to investigate how managers deal with poorly defined situations and to discover how the challenges of change and ambiguity can be met more effectively.

THE RESEARCH STUDY: QUESTIONS AND DESIGN

The study took four years. My starting point was to differentiate the problem of managing poorly defined, ambiguous situations from that of managing well defined, clearly understood ones. It seemed to me that most textbook and classroom advice for managers was suited for well defined problems. Here was a different and an important class of problems which needed new thinking. Understanding this suggested several questions:

- What are the essential characteristics of ambiguous, poorly defined situations? What particular characteristics make the management of these situations difficult?
- What patterns of behavior are more effective in coping with ambiguity and change? What patterns are less effective?
- Can a person learn to be more tolerant of ambiguity, to be more effective in ambiguous situations? Wouldn't that involve modifying a whole constellation of interconnected personality characteristics, developed over a long period of time, and therefore resistant to change?

Beyond the few studies already cited, little empirical research has addressed these questions. Consequently, the researcher and the manager facing ambiguity share some of the same dilemmas. The process of researching the management of ambiguity has its own ambiguities. From the start, the evolving, multifaceted nature of the topic, combined with sketchy knowledge, recommended close-up in-depth studies.

I chose to study a small number of situations intensively. In each situation, my research aim was to enter the world of participants as fully as possible, and to understand important features much as an anthropologist would. To stretch my thinking I looked at a wide range of settings. This book describes five of these situations in some detail, and highlights of the others are used from time to time to amplify points in discussion. The five primary cases, which are described briefly below, represent very diverse situations, although all involve people coping with disorder. Any patterns that appear in all the cases thus must be robust indeed.

ELECTRONIC BANKING CASE

A bank president wants to move into new forms of electronic banking at a time when the technology, consumer acceptance, and government legislation are largely uncertain. The president forms a study group, pursues alternatives, "decides," forms coalitions, gets a crucial vote, and a new electronic banking system is implemented. Several years later, it looks like a big success.

HIGH TECHNOLOGY RESEARCH PROJECT

In a research laboratory a high technology project appears to have commercial potential. A business manager is appointed to coordinate the effort. For a while enthusiasm is high, but the group fails to win outside funding. The company declines to fund the project, and it eventually withers away.

DESEGREGATING SAN FRANCISCO'S PUBLIC SCHOOLS

A federal court orders the San Francisco school board to prepare plans to desegregate the city's public schools within six weeks. The board and superintendents are occupied with other crises. Staff and consultants try to control the process, but it is taken over by an *ad hoc* citizens' group. Amidst great turmoil they do the planning and their plan is accepted by the board.

CHARLES DARWIN'S CREATIVE PROCESS

As a young man with modest training in science, Darwin undertakes a voyage around the world to collect natural history specimens. Afterwards, in an intense two-year period, he formulates his theory of evolution through natural selection.

GM'S RESPONSE TO CHANGE, 1956-1981

In 1956 General Motors was the pre-eminent automobile manufacturer in the world. Over the next 25 years the firm faced fundamental changes as foreign cars grew to a significant proportion of the market, consumer advocates pressed for safer cars, Congress began legislating standards, the price and availability of fuel became problematical, and consumer values shifted. The case traces how GM executives responded to these changes.

The Darwin case may seem a surprising choice for a management book. But the story of how he developed his radically new understanding of the world provides a remarkable means of studying the creative process, a process which turns out to be critical in responding to change and ambiguity.

At the same time I began to research the cases, I also reviewed various research literatures. Those that seemed potentially most useful were the work on conceptual mapping, the effects of stress on human performance, and conditions that favor creative thinking. If findings from these three areas could be focused managerially, they might supply concepts with which to examine the cases.

The fundamental themes of my investigation, then, can be stated as a set of interconnected observations and questions:

- One way of defining an ambiguous situation is that managers experience some kind of trouble with their conceptual maps of the situation. Their map is blurred, incomplete, or unreliable; or they don't know which of several competing maps to apply. *How does one create and maintain a conceptual map? Why do people hold on so tightly to inadequate and outdated maps?*
- When managers encounter map trouble, they are likely to feel tension and stress. A certain amount of stress can be useful, but if the stakes are high and time is short, the stress can escalate to unproductive levels. *How do people, including managers, cope with the stress caused by ambiguity and change? Can one regulate, and if so how, one's own stress levels?*
- Managers in an ambiguous situation need to create a new map or significantly revise old maps. Given the tendency to hold onto old maps, *what conditions, skills, and personal qualities encourage fresh thinking? How can managers encourage more creative responses when facing ambiguity and change?*

ORGANIZATION OF THE BOOK

In this book I have tried to present both the richness of specific cases and my more general and abstract findings. My organizational approach has been to let the general and the specific interact in a series of three-step dialectics, as illustrated below.

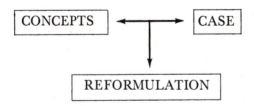

The first step of each dialectic is to synthesize the research findings in a given area into a managerial model or a set of practical guidelines. The second step is to describe a case that illustrates these concepts or principles. But the case may contain both more *and* less than was identified as important in the first step. The third step, then, is to allow the concepts and the case to interact. The theoretical constructs may help explain the specifics of the case. At the same time events of the case may suggest that certain concepts are mistaken or that other concepts need to be added. The interplay shows what is important in the case and what is trustworthy among the concepts. It is in this third step of the dialectic that the implications for the manager are elaborated.

Each of the major themes of the book—mapping, stress, and creativity—is developed in a three-chapter sequence corresponding to the three steps of the dialectic just outlined:

mapping	Chapters 2-4
stress	Chapters 5-7
creativity	Chapters 8-10

A final chapter then looks across all the cases to highlight common patterns and summarize the implications of the research.

One of my objectives in choosing this dialectical organization is to help the reader develop his, or her, own skill in recognizing ambiguous situations. To manage change and ambiguity, one must first learn to recognize what ambiguity looks like and how it is experienced. If you have time, I would strongly recommend that you analyze a case yourself before reading the book's analysis. The models and frameworks, being by definition simplifications, do not convey the idiosyncracies of a specific situation—which is where practical action takes place. The practice of analyzing cases should increase your ability to identify similarities with your own experience.

Ambiguous management problems are not likely to be solved by the mechanical application of simple rules or formulae. Humorist Andy Rooney has captured the problem well:

> I was thinking of installing one of those automatic garage door openers over the weekend. The directions say, "Make certain the garage door is square and straight and that the garage floor is level." Directions always read like that. Is everything in your house straight, square and level? If my house was straight, square and level, I would never have to fix anything. What we all need are directions that tell us what to do when everything is crooked, off-center and all screwed up.[12]

This book is striving for directions in that spirit. Instead of assuming a "greenfield" where the site is clear, flat, and unencumbered, we will assume that the managerial task is enmeshed in regulations and conflicting concerns. We are looking for directions that acknowledge fuzziness and assume that things are *not* all square and straight and level.

To put it another way, the critical aspects of organizational life cannot be successfully handled by applying directions suited to stable conditions—directions as programmed activities or techniques. The real art and significance of managing consists of coping with doubt and uncertainty. Decisions made in that harsh arena necessarily put the manager and the organization at risk, since available knowledge is incomplete and may be contradictory. Such situations call for what psychologist Jerome Bruner has termed "left handed ways of knowing," associating the clumsier left hand with a more intuitive grasp of the problem as a whole.[13] Not that we wish to reject the more precise, rational, and systematic approach of the right hand. The ambiguous situations we are going to study are so demanding that they require both hands to be hard at work, in concert with each other. It would be folly to attack problems with no known solutions with one hand tied behind our backs.

The ground tremors of societal change and the strategy of allowing more ambiguity inside organizations mean that managers will often face problems that do not yield to existing tools. They must move beyond being technicians to being thinkers, leaders, and creators. We need new, more powerful ways of using our minds that involve judgment, risk-taking, experimentation, and the invention of new style directions.

The task is not easy. The difference between the ways of thinking and acting appropriate for well-defined, stable problems and those needed for poorly-defined, shifting problems is as great as the difference between conventional and guerrilla warfare. To learn from this book, then, you may have to operate in a different mode, one that requires patience and a tolerance of ambiguity. It is multifaceted and at times confusing. It is the real world.

Chapter 2

Mapping: Creating, Maintaining, and Relinquishing Conceptual Frameworks

In 1973 William Crozier, a senior vice president of Baystate, a large Massachusetts bank holding company, faced the type of ambiguous, ill-defined problem we are studying. Twelve member banks had tried to centralize computer operations, but a tradition of local autonomy had eventually led to the development of five separate data processing centers. The larger banks vied for dominance. The banks did not cooperate in jointly purchasing or programming systems. Consequently, the systems were inefficient and largely incompatible. Over the years many similar group efforts had fallen apart or produced confusing and frustrating results.

Drawing on his ten years' experience at the bank holding company, Crozier analyzed the problem in a white paper addressed to the board of directors. The current president of the holding company was nearing retirement, and the report amounted to a statement of what Crozier would do if named CEO. He argued that a direct frontal assault on the problem was unwise; that instead one should begin by discussing business strategy and the changing nature of competition in the banking industry. Essentially the report maintained that instead of facing local competition, Baystate banks would have to compete on a regional and perhaps even a statewide basis. Thus, it would become important to coordinate the banks' marketing of financial services and to integrate banking operations, such as data processing. More unified marketing would require greater standardization of services and procedures. The report concluded by recommending that a task force be appointed to work on developing corporate unity and identity among the member banks.

Notice that in this situation the holding company does not face one simple problem. According to Crozier's analysis, computer operations are connected to marketing which in turn is linked to issues of common identity which is tied to the banks' history and tradition. This nested and interconnected quality is typical of the problems we are studying. Also characteristic is the lack of solid, quantitative data on key questions.

Crozier was elected CEO in June 1974. In implementing a new direction for the banks, he and his staff began to investigate forms of electronic banking that might serve as a common product for all the banks to market. At this point, electronic banking was a largely untried new technology for banks in New England. Surveys indicated that customers might resist using machines, no hard data on costs or usage were available, and even a modest pilot program would cost over one million dollars. For a new president, in a year in which the banking industry was suffering, the electronic technology represented a sizable step. The personal stakes were high and information on key issues was incomplete. Crozier later described the period as "extremely tense . . . punctuated by moments of sheer ecstasy."

The details of how Crozier won acceptance for his new concept of the bank holding company's role are presented in Appendix A. Briefly, he curtailed member banks' efforts to innovate electronically and brought several of the brightest and most capable member bank officers into the corporate staff. He hired an outside consulting firm to supply ideas and help carry out staff analysis for a more highly visible and coordinated marketing effort. He appointed those who seemed to have the most to lose—namely the presidents of the largest banks—to a series of holding company task forces to explore the possibility of developing a common product. Crozier was determined that he and his staff should always behave in a cheerful and gentlemanly way toward member banks. One of his staff and an outside consulting firm ran contests among employees to find a new name and generate excitement about the newly defined banking system.

Baystate became BayBanks and successfully introduced a network of automated teller machines (ATMs).

These steps all contributed to a successful transformation carried out over a three-year period. But, the necessary starting point and one of Crozier's most significant contributions, was to create a new way of thinking about the bank's problems. Crozier developed a new perspective that turned the problems of infighting and computer inefficiencies into an opportunity for marketing the holding company's extensive network of locations. The terrain was mapped anew, new connections were drawn, and new possibilities opened up.

Not everyone agreed with this new map. Several bank presidents, especially those in the larger, wealthier banks, already had maps that seemed to work well for them. They said, "We are doing well. Competition among us keeps us healthy. Why should we change?"

The new map or vision of the banks as a more fully coordinated system focused attention upon the need for a product common to all the banks. In spite of previous disappointments, Crozier felt that some form of electronic banking might supply that product. He and several staff members and project teams began to explore this terrain to obtain what solid information they could.

Their efforts convinced them that the potential of ATMs would justify the initial investment costs. With some adroit maneuvering, some coaxing, and some pushing, they were able to get enough agreement from officers of the member banks to proceed. They acted on the new map, and it proved to be a viable picture of what new services bank customers would like to have.

Before Crozier's white paper, the "reality" was that the banks had a problem with lack of coordination and duplication of computer services. Crozier and his staff saw the problem from a more powerful perspective and developed a fuller picture of what was real, and most likely to be important, to the banks and their customers. They therefore changed what they and others saw when looking at their banking landscape.

Crozier's reframing of the problem, what we will call mapping, was a critical step. One of the manager's greatest leverage points in facing ambiguity and change is how he or she *thinks* about the situation.

THE METAPHOR OF MAPPING

We live in conceptual worlds composed of our ideas, images, memories, plans, and knowledge, which inform the way we talk and think about the physical world. Our conceptualizations, or representations, of the parts of reality we have learned to see as meaningful, interesting, and important guide our actions and our work with others. Many researchers have found the idea of a "conceptual map" a helpful metaphor for these conceptual systems that are usually taken for granted and assumed to *be* reality.

At any moment we have only a limited, tangible physical reality around us—the office, the hallway, and the elevator, for example. We see chairs, walls, lights, color, and other people. We have names for, and knowledge about, all of these familiar objects. Most of this knowledge lies in the background of our attention, to be called to the foreground as needed. Our sense of reality, however, is not limited to the world immediately before us. We can visualize buildings, spaces, people, and events beyond our eyes. We can picture current and historical events around the world and use tools to extend our senses. These images, our names, our knowledge of how things fit together and what causes what to happen, constitute our "map." *A map is an interconnected set of understandings, formed by frequently implicit views of what one's interests and concerns are, what is important, and what demands action and what does not. It is a cognitive representation of the world and ourselves in it.*

Each of us has unique maps that have grown out of our experiences and needs. Of course, we also share some maps more or less closely with family, office colleagues, neighbors, members of a political party, and with other groups of which we feel a part.

A complete description of the process of conceptualizing reality would be extremely complex and lies outside the scope of this book. As we consider how managers cope with ambiguity, however, mapping represents a useful *tool* for understanding and exploring our mental representations and their connection to action. Maps come in many sizes, shapes, and degrees of accuracy. Think of a car's glove compartment, filled with road maps of different areas and of the same area drawn to different scales. Another kind of map can be as simple as the sketch a friend draws to show us the way to his house. Maps of the New World drawn during the age of discovery show large unknown areas and coastlines that gradually became more accurate. Maps can also include pictorial representations that uncover new relationships by depicting the known in an unfamiliar way. Like many of these physical maps, mental maps are guides that are not always correct and are subject to revision.

The metaphor of mapping embraces both product and process. Since we are talking about managers operating in poorly mapped terrain, we will emphasize the process of creating new knowledge and extending old knowledge through exploration, study, and action. Horace Freeland Judson, examining the role of physical maps in the history of ideas, likens maps to models. The maps of early explorers reduced the complexity of the world to a model that people could conveniently study. Figure 2.1 shows the new world as mapped by a French priest in 1546. By that time detailed knowledge of the coastline was available, but little was reliably known about the American interior. Maps as models, Judson says, "are ships in which explorers journey into the unknown. They embody what we know and carry us toward what we don't know."[1]

The manager who realizes he is following a conceptual map has taken an important first step toward being able to manage ambiguity. Our maps can be priceless guides, but they can also limit our perceptions, sometimes becoming rigid and confining. Understanding a map as a revisable model generally induces a healthy skepticism as to its infallibility, and engenders more flexible thinking. Mapping and remapping is a fundamental process that a manager facing ambiguity and change must master.

HOW ARE MAPS CREATED AND MAINTAINED?

Ordinarily people think of reality as objective, factual, and as undeniable as the physical world within our reach. What we experience as real are the events that we notice and can make sense of, those that have some significance for our lives and well-being. Reality is what we have become familiar with, and have learned to attend to, through our experience. Yet the recognized and named "world" is complex and ever-changing, and so we need to organize what is important and what is trivial, what is safe and what is dangerous, what is associated with what, and what causes what. The mental process and the product of this *organizing of reality,* this creating and maintaining a frame of reference, is what we call "conceptual mapping."

Imagine, for example, that you are coming out of a building in a foreign country and find the street unexpectedly jammed with people. What is going on? This is *real,* but it doesn't make any sense yet. You haven't related it to anything else. The event needs to be interpreted. Is it a disaster or a celebration? Are people panicky or cheerful? If the crowds are gathering on either side of the street, that usually means a parade and not a riot. If you recall mention of a festival, you have a plausible *reason* for a parade. You begin to map the reality of the crowd in the street. You search your experience and try to find a name for what is happening which will tell you how to act.

People have maps for different domains and for different purposes. Perhaps it helps to think of your head as a chart room full of maps—maps for your personal life, history, work, particular problem areas, routine procedures, and so on. Maps are pulled out according to occasion and purpose, and differ in degree of clarity, reliability, and completeness.

Because our information processing abilities are limited, mapping is selective. On the basis of our values and past experience, we perceive some events as noteworthy, while most features of the world around us are relegated to the background. Otherwise we would be overwhelmed by complexity and change. Out of what is noticed, people build a picture that makes sense to themselves and provides a common base of understanding with others. Although necessary, the selectivity of mapping has its dangers, as illustrated by the recent experience of U.S. automakers cited in Chapter 1. These manufacturers ignored or downplayed the early signals that their business was undergoing fundamental change, since those signals conflicted with the main tenets of their map. While we can never grasp all of reality, what we defend against knowing can hurt us.

Mapping is a dialectic between events and our ideas about those events. Our conceptual maps determine what elements in the turbulence of daily events we focus on and how we interpret them; our experience of events in turn can refine and enlarge our maps. This means that ambiguity resides in the situation, in the mind of the manager, and in the interaction of the two. Like the paradox of Escher's two hands drawing each other, it is both the situation that is perplexing and the manager who is perplexed.

A map becomes increasingly "objective" as more people come to share its view of reality. While one person holds a unique map it is a fragile construction. The map is strengthened as it is transmitted and accepted by more people.[3] Because the coherence of a social group depends upon developing a common map, mapping is heavily influenced by the social setting in which it occurs.

Mapping by a social group is not always a straightforward nor an easy process. Recall the bank presidents. They were concerned with maintaining their traditional autonomy within the holding company. Crozier and the central staff, on the other hand, were eager to realize the potential of closer coordination. Two sociologists who have studied the process of clashing views point out that, "He who has the

FIGURE   2.1.   Desceliers's Map of the Coastline of the New World, 1546.
(Reproduced courtesy of the Research Libraries, The New York Public Library.)

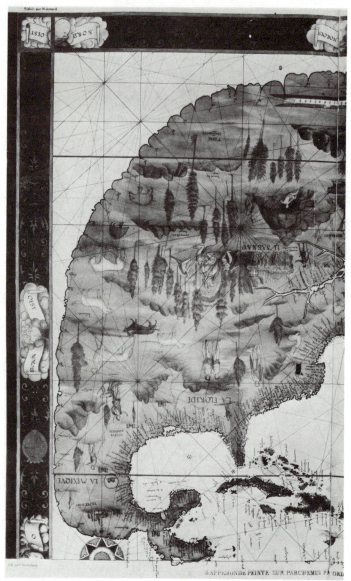

"Desceliers's map was 9 feet by 3 feet, so large that it was designed to be laid out on a table and read from both top and bottom, which is why the lettering in this detail is upside down. Most of the land mass of North America is a blur of speculation inhabited by confident aborigines and nervous Europeans."[2]

bigger stick has the better chance of imposing his definitions of reality.''[4] So it was in the banking case. Crozier had the backing of the majority stockholders and imposed his map on the sometimes reluctant presidents.

In a managerial group the social process of constructing reality this way involves the interaction, perhaps the collision, of several subjective readings (or personal maps) of the surrounding world. The work of a group in its early stages includes forming a publicly held map that is generally agreed to by all members. Once formed, this version of reality is treated as real; it *is real* for group members and is slow to change. The map guides a member's daily decisions about what to notice, what to do, and how to interact with others.

When a map is more completely drawn and begins to make the surrounding landscape of events intelligible, group members often pressure each other to conform to using the group's map. The group has a range of punishments and inducements which few can withstand and still remain a group member in good standing. During a recent strike by Chicago firefighters, for example, most men refused a federal court order to return to work. A television news report captured the dynamics of the situation by focusing on one fireman who had been working, but then decided to rejoin his fellows amidst much cheering and backslapping. The firefighters' map of what was fair and what was legal obviously differed from the maps held by the mayor and the courts, and the firefighters were able to enforce the norms implied by their map on most of their fellows.

Groups and individuals use maps in such a way that the existing maps tend to be reconfirmed. Argyris and Schon have called this the "self-sealing" quality of some systems or models.[5] Since a map points out what is to be noticed and valued among the plethora of events in each day, those events that do not jibe with the map tend to be ignored, or called aberrations, and thus forgotten. Discrepant events can create anxiety or, more rarely, wonder. If the discrepancy is too great, the map holder is likely to defend against seeing or appreciating the event. If the discrepancy is not too great, and individuals vary widely on this, the event provides an opportunity to redefine one's understanding of reality.

The same territory can be mapped in different ways. The map of the Roman empire presented in Figure 2.2, for example, reflects the needs, strengths, and worries of its inhabitants. The land masses where Roman armies operated are given proportionately more space than are the seas on which the enemy, Carthage, operated her superior navy. And just as the territory can be depicted politically, topo-

FIGURE 2.2. Map of Ancient Rome and Italy. (Reproduced courtesy of The Research Libraries, The New York Public Library.)

"Roman road maps distorted sea and land masses in order to fit the imperial road system into a confined space . . . The center strip is Italy; the Adriatic and Mediterranean are attenuated into mere rivers. Across from Rome and her harbor lies Carthage."[6]

graphically, or geographically, organizations or groups will map their worlds in distinctive ways. The more the maps of groups diverge, the more problematic communication becomes.

Finally, mapping is so natural a dimension of our everyday lives that large parts of our own maps are created outside our awareness. Mapping organizes what is put in the foreground and is often itself unnoticed. Frequently, a map and its embedded assumptions only become visible when they fail to provide a suitable basis for action. Only after its demise in 1969 were the top managers of the old *Saturday Evening Post* able to see that they had been wrong in expecting increased circulation to improve profitability.[7] Managers must search for ways to make maps visible before they break down. Some specific suggestions on what to do when maps are weak are presented later in this chapter.

MAPS AND AMBIGUITY: IMPOSING ORDER ON CHAOS

One way of defining an ambiguous situation is to say it is one in which none of your maps works well. Events are puzzling, confusing, and don't fit with what you know. The world seems baffling when events outpace ideas. Remember how frightening the initial outbreak of Legionnaire's Disease was? Many of those attending a Philadelphia convention mysteriously fell ill, no one knew why, and several died. People were deeply shaken by an occurrence that seemed to expose the limits of modern medicine.

Crisis situations like this expose the transient quality of any map. A messy problem disrupts the map's ability to explain the everyday activities of members of a group. Members may have differing ways of stating what the problem is, but no one way appears adequate to solve the problem or compels widespread agreement. Since the ambiguous problem cannot be adequately defined, people do not respond to it in predictable, dependable ways. Because familiar routines and patterns are disrupted, group members feel increased stress. As the consensus about what is real breaks down, individuals are thrown upon more subjective and idiosyncratic interpretations and tend to want to withdraw from the situation. Without an adequate and commonly shared way to define the problem, communication and coordination become problematic.

Half a century ago John Dewey clearly pointed out how ill at ease we tend to be when nature is indeterminate. We greatly dislike confusion, disorder, obscurity, and indeterminateness, but "nature is characterized by a constant mixture of the precarious and stable."[8] Our reaction sometimes is to think and take intelligent action, but more often we settle for a feeling or an illusion of order. (In Chapter 5 we will examine how people deal with the stress of ambiguity.) People want "to do something at once; there is impatience with suspense, and lust for immediate action."[9] We invent theories, rituals, or superstitions to make what was uncertain and confused into something clear and stable.

Dewey's observations on human nature are strongly supported by a review of work in cognitive psychology during the last several decades. Steinbruner found that, while researchers might disagree at the frontiers of knowledge about how the mind works, there was general agreement on five basic principles.[10] Researchers found:

1. The mind is an inference machine that actively imposes order on highly ambiguous situations.
2. The mind works to keep internal core beliefs consistent and unchallenged. (The stress literature also shows that the mind will deny, distort, or ignore signals that contradict core beliefs.)
3. The mind prefers simplicity.
4. The mind is constrained by reality (here the objective side of reality) in important ways.
5. The mind prefers stable and enduring relationships among its core beliefs.

These five principles are all of interest to managers facing ambiguity but the first is perhaps the most important; the others can all be gathered into it. *The mind is an inference machine that strives mightily to bring order, simplicity, consistency, and stability to the world it encounters. In other words, where nature is ambiguous, people develop strong beliefs and act upon them.* People tend to simplify complexity and make the inconsistent seem consistent. These tendencies are heightened when we perceive a threat to our identity, safety, security, or status. Generally speaking, we dislike disorder especially in areas where we are invested.

Mapping is affected by the mind's very active, interpretive quality. Our cognitive faculties operate ahead of conscious awareness, sorting through a wealth of potential information. Our mental processes make rapid estimates of what is valuable to notice and what can be treated as background. The mind takes fragments and makes something that fits existing organizing schemes. In the felicitous apothegm of Norwood Russell Hanson, "There is more to seeing than meets the eyeball."[11] Everywhere we look, we see with theory-laden vision.

HOLDING ON TO MAPS AND "LITTLE DYING"

Perhaps because maps are so hard-won and so necessary for orderly interaction with others, people are very reluctant to change them. In fact, people fight to retain their maps. They want to hold onto that order, and suffer a little death if they have to relinquish it. "Little dying" is Keleman's term for the painful letting-go of any of the major anchors of our life: separation from a loved one, moving from the home town, leaving a successful position in a company. "Big dying" is biological death.[12]

Little deaths compel the acknowledgement of our finiteness; we see that we cannot do or be everything we value, and that forces exist outside of us that have their own power. Acknowledgement of such hard facts is difficult and often avoided. Little dying involves giving up something central and important in our map.

In a thought-provoking paper that is the basis for this section of the chapter, Robert Tannenbaum has urged that more attention be paid to the process of little dying and holding on in organizational change.[13] Organization development specialists and managers often underestimate the need for people in a system to maintain continuity and to hold onto what they know has worked in the past. Tannenbaum argues for a balance in attending to the *yin* of stability and the *yang* of change. An organizational unit may have to die in order to clear the ground for something new to grow or for the unit, phoenix-like, to be reborn into new vitality. Each person undergoing such change faces the prospect of a little death and can be expected to try to maintain the existing map.

Other researchers have seen parallels to something like little dying on the organizational level. Fink, Beak, and Taddeo have identified four phases in an organization's response to a crisis:

1. *Shock*—organizational members become aware of a threat to existing structures
2. *Defensive retreat*—holding onto the old map
3. *Acknowledgement*—giving up the old map
4. *Adaptation and change*—establishing a new structure and a sense of worth.[14]

The process resembles that seen by psychiatrist Elisabeth Kubler-Ross in her studies of the terminally ill. She finds that patients pass through the following stages in coming to terms with their own deaths:

1. *Denial and isolation*—the patient is shocked and disbelieves, puts off, or forgets
2. *Anger*—also rage, resentment, and envy—"Why me?"
3. *Bargaining*—an extension of time is sought to complete unfinished business
4. *Depression and grief*—two phases: mourning what has already been lost and then mourning losses that lie in the future
5. *Acceptance*—accompanied by an inner and outer peace.[15]

These two models trace through the responses of an organization and an individual to a threatening disruption. When the disruption is perceived to be life-threatening, human systems at both levels feel shocked, deny the disruption, and strenuously attempt to hold on to old maps. This phase gives way to feelings of anger and resentment and eventually to a period of mourning that looks backward and then toward the future. Only after grieving can the past be relinquished. Leaving one safe spot becomes easier when the next is in sight. Individuals create new meanings and definitions—a new or revised map—for what is happening. We have seen that our perceived reality is at least partly a social construct, and the transition to the acceptance phase of the sequence can be greatly facilitated by the help of friends and others who have undergone the pain of mourning and renewal.

MAINTAINING ORDER BY DYNAMIC CONSERVATISM

How powerful the need is to hold onto familiar ways of knowing can be seen in Elting Morison's history of the adoption of continuous-aim firing in the United States Navy.[16] First devised by an English officer in 1898, this system allowed a ship's gun to be continuously aimed and readjusted as it was being fired. (Technically, this was achieved by altering the gear ratio in a battery's elevating gear so that the gun could adjust to the inertial roll of the ship and mounting a telescopic sight away from the recoil of the gun barrel.) A U.S. Navy lieutenant stationed in China, William Sims, learned about the system from its originator, Percy Scott of the British Royal Navy.

With Scott's assistance, Sims had the system installed on an American ship and trained a crew to use it. After a few months, the American crew showed the same remarkable improvement in accuracy as British crews had. Sims wrote 13 official reports, complete with great masses of data, to naval officers in Washington arguing the merits of the new system.

At first Washington officials made no response. According to their conceptual maps of naval gunnery, Sims's claims simply were not credible. As Sims became deliberately challenging and shocking in his reports, officials began to rebut the claims. They argued that existing American equipment was as good as British equipment and that any deficiencies must lie in the training of the men. They also conducted gunnery practice *on dry land* where, deprived of the benefits of the inertial movement, their results *proved* that the new system could not work as Sims claimed. They called Sims a "crack-brain egoist" and accused him of deliberately falsifying evidence.

Not to be denied, Sims, who had the combative personality of a bantam rooster, circulated news of the new gunnery system among his fellow officers in the fleet. Finally in 1902, he took the bold step of writing directly to President Theodore Roosevelt. Roosevelt brought Sims back from China and forced change upon the Navy by installing Sims as Inspector of Target Practice.

In his analysis of the events, Morison points out that the Navy had its own reasons for resisting the technological innovation. The officers in Washington identified strongly with the existing equipment and their instinctive desire was to protect the established pecking order of the Navy. Intuitively they realized that the Navy's social system was organized around its major weapons systems and that a change would significantly disrupt the existing hierarchy of status. Indeed, the chaos of subsequent events proved this fear justified. In the terms of our discussion, the Washington officers sought to protect their map and the culture in which it was embedded. They held onto the map as long as possible and only let go when forced to do so by greater, outside authority.

Commenting on the same case, Donald Schon uses the term "dynamic conservatism" to describe the tendency to fight to remain the same. He goes on to depict a social system as a set of concentric rings.[17] Change is more readily accommodated in the outer rings — that is, in the more superficially held elements of the system. But toward the center are core values and ideas whose change would necessarily induce a large-scale restructuring of the whole system. Here human systems fight hardest to conserve their sense of identity and reality. Maintaining a map becomes a fight to protect what is familiar and known—and to maintain identity, status, income, and standing.

COMPARISON WITH SCIENTIFIC COMMUNITIES

The same conserving tendency can be observed in the social systems of scientific communities. To be sure, groups in the scientific community also show some significant differences from military or business groups in how they operate. Both the differences and the similarities are instructive.

Thomas Kuhn, a historian and philosopher of science, has characterized the scientific enterprise as consisting of long periods of steady development, infrequently broken by revolutionary periods. The steady development of "normal science" is made possible by a culture of shared values and norms, and by the existence of exemplary "paradigms."[18]

Paradigms in this sense are models for solving important problems in a given scientific field; these models embody what scientists know, but cannot verbalize. The tacit knowledge of these paradigms directs scientists to seek out and devote themselves to solving puzzles that contribute to the steady advancement of the field. According to Kuhn, a scientist working on a puzzle can be assured that, if he or she is clever enough, the puzzle can be solved. Because of the guidance and knowledge that paradigms offer, a group of scientists is very reluctant to give them up. Mitroff's study of "moon scientists" showed that those whose theories of the moon's geology were contradicted by the first examination of moon rocks were more willing to dismiss the rocks than change their theories.[19] The rare revolutionary breaks in the steady development of normal science come when a scientist becomes dissatisfied with a paradigm's ability to suggest simple and accurate explanations for what is observed in nature. Kuhn cites Darwin, Copernicus, and Newton as examples of the extraordinary scientific work that involves shifting to a new paradigm.

In business and government, managers and administrators have maps that are based on some knowledge, but are much less complete than the exemplary paradigms of scientists. So managers more often face situations in which their maps are vague or may need to be reconstituted. In comparison to scientific problems, the situations faced by managers are also less general. In the example that began this chapter, the president of the bank holding company was not trying to solve everyone's electronic banking problem. He was trying to solve *his* electronic banking problem, as it existed in 1974.

Scientists doing normal science are puzzle-solvers; managers facing ambiguity are problem-attackers. Kuhn notes that large pressing problems, such as finding a design for world peace, are characteristically perceived as having no solution. Consequently, not much scientific work, and none of what he calls normal science, is directed toward solving such problems. Managers and administrators, on the other hand, often do not have the option of avoiding seemingly unsolvable problems. External circumstances commonly force them to try to do something to attack the problem, even though prospects for solving it are dim.

WHAT TO DO WHEN MAPS ARE WEAK

When the terrain is poorly mapped, what can managers do? Researchers of business and public administration have made several suggestions. In such situations managers often shift from optimizing to "satisficing."[20] Instead of trying to perform a complete analysis that will identify the *best* course of action, they settle for taking the first *satisfactory* alternative that comes along. This represents an important shift in outlook and captures an attitude of mind more likely to be effective in moving through uncharted territory. However, it is not, and is not meant to be, a detailed method for dealing with a particular problem.

Lindblom comes closer to describing a method. Government administrators, he observes, regularly muddle through poorly mapped problems.[21] They make limited comparisons with the recent past and take circumscribed steps into the future that conform to past trends. Administrators, he says, should accept their limited ability to foresee or plan for the long term and should advance by small, often uncoordinated steps. There is no room for revolutions here, and thus such an approach will not work well in a crisis that demands a complete shift in paradigm.

Christenson argues that when the terrain is poorly mapped managers should turn to "negative thinking."[22] Negative thinking proceeds more by refuting errors than by positively and conclusively proving a case. According to this view, managers confronting a poorly defined problem should not seek conclusive evidence and argument. They should instead treat contradictions as opportunities and aspire only to reasoning in terms of sufficient rather than necessary causes. Learning to recognize errors and avoid an associated course of action is the more important logical operation for advancing into unknown territory.

Barnard would, I think, agree with Christenson. As decision materials become more speculative, Barnard argues, the balance of a manager's mental operations should move toward nonlogical processes, thoughts that cannot be expressed in words, and which derive from judgment, intuition, and the grasp of an overall pattern.[23] Barnard is uncertain, however, about how to enhance these qualities in managers, or how to judge them except after the fact, on the basis of performance.

In an earlier work, I also advocated more explicit use of metaphorical and intuitive processes.[24] I suggest an alternative to goal setting, one that employs a more holistic sensing of the situation. When goals cannot be specified with confidence, as when the terrain is poorly mapped, you can shift your focus away from goals and toward influencing the domain in which you are working and the direction in which you are heading. March has also argued that managers should not always wait to act until goals are clear; rather, in some situations they should act in order to discover what their goals are.[25] Among other provocative recommendations, he urges that we treat memory as an enemy that preserves too many past answers that no longer work, and that we view a plan more as a summary of past decisions than as a program for future use.

Mason and Mitroff describe how to attack ill-structured organizational problems through a dialectical process.[26] Central to this method, the assumptions made in framing the problem must be brought to the surface. Two groups are put to work, one using the original assumptions, the other using directly opposite assumptions. Both groups go through a cycle of searching out relevant data and building a strategy. Since what one sees depends on one's theory, the second group should uncover new facts unnoticed by the first group. Under conditions designed to prevent premature compromise, the two groups meet and argue their positions. Out of this dialectic a new pool of assumptions is created from which a strategy is drawn.

These various suggestions for dealing with weak maps each have some value. They can best be tested by using them to explore the specifics of a case and we will turn to that task in the following chapter.

In closing let us look at one final example of how a different way of mapping can reveal new features in what might seem familiar.

FIGURE 2.3.

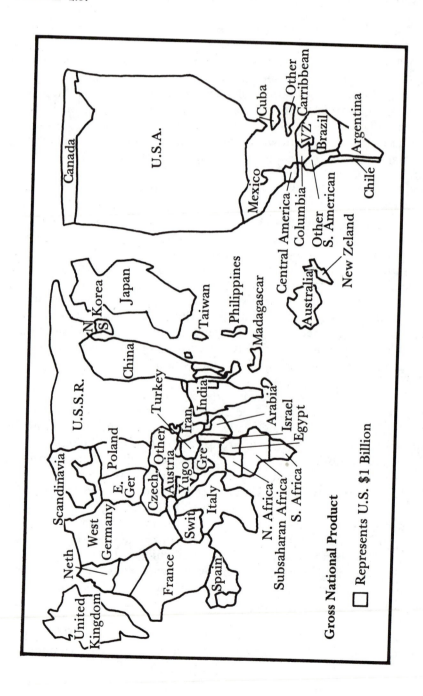

Figure 2.3 shows a map of the world constructed under new rules, with countries sized in proportion to their gross national product. This particular way of representing the territory highlights relationships that perhaps not everyone has recognized before.

Chapter **3**

High Technology Research Project (VIS Case)

Now that we have reviewed the process of conceptual mapping, the second step of the dialectic is to test those ideas against the events of a specific case. The case we will examine takes place in the research laboratory of a large aerospace company. I chose this situation because I thought that scientists working on the frontiers of knowledge would face a great deal of uncertainty and ambiguity. Since the nature of scientific investigation is to explore new areas, its outcome can never be predicted precisely.

Over the period of a year, my research assistant and I visited the site roughly once every two or three weeks. We would visit more often when more was happening. We were able to talk with everyone connected with the project and had full access to the files. The aim of our research was to capture how scientists and managers perceived events, choices, and problems as they were occurring. Because we were actually there as the events unfolded, this case is an especially appropriate one for a study of mapping.

A word of caution: since maps are subtle and have an everyday, taken-for-granted quality, a managerial case about maps is not likely to be dramatic. As we have already seen, however, mapping is important precisely because it is not dramatic and so often occurs without much conscious attention.

There are several things to watch for in the management of this ambiguous situation:

- Where do ambiguities arise in this project? Which characteristics of Table 1.1 are most troublesome for managers in the situation?
- How does the project manager go about trying to build a common map? How successful is he?
- What beliefs and values embodied in the company's map have an impact on this project?
- When confronted with events that are out of joint with their map, how do different group members respond?

The reader is encouraged to make notes on his or her answers to these questions before reading the case analysis in Chapter 4. Names in the case have been disguised. A brief chronology of events follows the case.

1963-1972: BACKGROUND AND HISTORY

In 1963, a young Ph.D. named Edward Gordon joined the J. Mirl Company, a large aerospace firm on the West Coast. Gordon was a lively, enthusiastic person with an owlish and playful manner. One of his first assignments involved lasers, a new and largely unexplored technology. Working part-time on lasers over the next five years, Gordon and two senior scientists achieved significant scientific and technical advances. In 1969, however, the new Nixon administration reduced federal funding for basic research. Like other aerospace companies, J. Mirl dismissed thousands of workers and pressured scientists to focus on practical applications of their research.

These pressures, combined with a growing feeling that the original effort had spent its promise, led Gordon to reconsider the direction of the laser project. Working after-hours and on weekends to test its feasibility, he eventually decided to investigate the technology's potential for storing information. Over the next three years, internal company funding for Gordon's VIS (videographic information storage) project increased modestly until he was spending one-fourth of his time on it.

Under the research lab's matrix structure, scientists were pulled by dual lines of authority—market-based project managers on the one side, and a research management structure on the other. Decisions by either line of authority could cause scientists to shift or redesign their work. Of course, having two bosses sometimes placed a strain on the scientists. A rough diagram of how these reporting relationships, stemming from two autonomous divisions, affected a scientist looked like this:

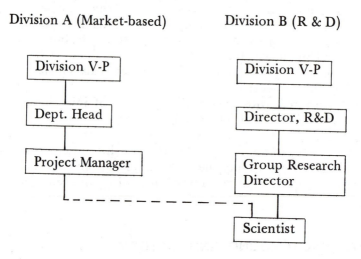

Division A (Market-based)   Division B (R & D)

After several unsuccessful marketing attempts, Gordon secured a small Navy contract. Internal funding also increased, so that in 1972 he and two other scientists were working nearly full time on the project. Gordon wanted to build a large-scale mass memory system, but the market for a large system was uncertain. The scientists' contacts with customers were largely unsystematic and, perhaps as a consequence, they lacked specific customer requirements. To protect the project from the vagaries of shifting customer desires, Gordon formulated some design objectives and shifted into engineering-oriented work for a year.

During this period technical work on VIS achieved outstanding results. The researchers developed a working model to demonstrate how lasers and videographic technology could efficiently store large amounts of data. The flashy hardware attracted the attention of many people, including the company's president, who appreciated the growing need for systems with such capabilities.

By the end of the year, Ed Gordon was spending more and more time promoting and administering the project. Although these were important activities, they pulled him away from what Gordon considered the most valuable use of his time—working in the lab. Through patents and scientific papers, he was developing a reputation as a creative and able scientist. His immediate superior tried to interest him in playing a more managerial role for the project, but Gordon resisted.

At this point, Earl Gatsby began to take an active interest in helping Gordon obtain outside support for development. Gatsby had recently become a group research director, responsible for overseeing about 30 projects. He was enthusiastic about the prospects of the videographic project, but he noted:

> Most R & D efforts are not commercial successes, and the project casualty ratio is usually pretty high. The good potential for commercial and specific hardware outcomes (as opposed to reports or analyses of data) are what make the project atypical.

Gatsby was a placid, quiet person as long as he felt things were going smoothly, but he could become a fierce fighter if his research group were threatened from outside. He believed that scientists should maintain a somewhat independent status and be free to explore.

Gatsby sometimes had to fight because the top management of the company was ambivalent about the charter of the research lab. On the one hand, the president, the annual report, and company training materials extolled the possibilities for transferring research projects from the lab to other company divisions. On the other hand, Fred Salt, director of R & D, reported that twice a year he was called to a meeting where top management would ask one of two questions: (1) Is the R & D group's work really relevant to company activities, and should we continue to subsidize the group at current levels ; or (2) Are we putting too much pressure on the R & D group to be relevant to our known interests—maybe they should be able to explore the frontiers more? Salt rarely knew ahead of time which question would be asked.

JANUARY–JULY 1973: EXCITEMENT ABOUT PRACTICAL APPLICATIONS FOR THE RESEARCH

In 1973 another J. Mirl group committed funds to the VIS project and the Navy awarded it a second small contract. Although total funding was still modest, enthusiasm about the future of the VIS project increased dramatically.

The hardware was attractively housed in two tabletop units linked to a small computer. The system consisted of a laser beam hooked to optical readers, which converted stored images into electronic digital impulses. These were read into a computer and converted through a series of programs so they could be read out on a cathode-ray tube or printer. The system, if developed on a bigger scale, offered significant advantages over existing technologies in terms of compactness, durability, and light weight. As envisaged by Gordon and Gatsby, potential customers for such a system included libraries, insurance companies, retail credit systems, the military, and government agencies.

By April 1973, after much urging, Gordon and Gatsby finally succeeded in interesting a marketer, Z.K. French, in actively promoting the system. The marketer added an important skill to the project. Scientists were reluctant to press potential customers very hard about how much money they could spend on a project. But, both the customer and the scientists expected the marketer to be brash and to inquire directly about money and funding. French also brought some conflict to the situation, because he believed the project should be sold as a piece of hardware, while Gordon felt it was not far enough advanced to be sold in that way. He thought French often promised the customer greater systems capabilities than could be safely guaranteed.

French, Gordon, and another scientist toured government agencies in Washington, D.C., setting up and demonstrating the model on people's desks. These "dog and pony shows" elicited some interest, but the men did not consistently follow up with potential customers. Gordon had enough to do on technical development, and French had 19 other programs to sell.

After a VIP tour through the lab in May 1973, Bill Rodgers, a corporate vice president at J. Mirl headquarters, saw a possible use of the videographic technology for handling the records of his business. He discussed this with the president of the company. Together, they then asked Frank Coyne, a corporate vice president located near the research lab, to investigate. Coyne and his staff found the technical development well under way, but there was no business development plan for the work. Coyne requested that the research group prepare a thorough and detailed business plan. Until now the plans were largely in Ed Gordon's head, intuitively derived, and others were informed on a "need to know" basis.

The director of the R & D lab, Fred Salt, and the R & D business manager, Alex Rouhas, were not enthusiastic about putting together a business plan at this stage. Salt regarded the extensive documentation and detail of formal planning as unrealistic and a waste of time for the R & D group:

> You generally have some scheme in mind that you can write up in three or four pages. Beyond that length, the mental gyrations and detail are

in order to get the plan signed off by management. The next day a customer calls and his specifications don't fit your plan. So you drop the plan and write up a new proposal.

As Rouhas put it, "We'll put together a lot of motherhood and enough information to be palatable, and kicking and screaming all the way, we'll come in with two armloads of view graphs and hand-outs."

To develop a formal business plan, everyone agreed that a full-time project manager was necessary. Gordon was steadfast about not wanting to leave his scientific work. So he and Gatsby began searching J. Mirl for the right person.

AUGUST 1973: A PROJECT MANAGER APPOINTED

August marked the beginning of a new phase in the videographic project with the appointment of Patrick Miles as project manager. Miles was strongly recommended by French, who had worked closely with him on previous programs; the two men enjoyed "running to-gether on projects." Everyone involved was enthusiastic about his selection and felt that he could quickly develop a VIS business plan. Although Miles was still working on another project, he would spend 25–30 hours a week on the videographic mass-memory effort. With the addition of Miles, the reporting relationships could be sketched as follows:

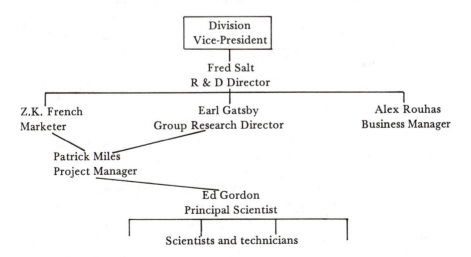

Patrick Miles was a dynamic, aggressive person whose background included work in physics and a proven track record for managing projects at J. Mirl. He had begun and successfully run several small businesses of his own. In explaining his working style, he good-humoredly remarked that "these scientists are murder—always another refinement." He then drew the following graph:

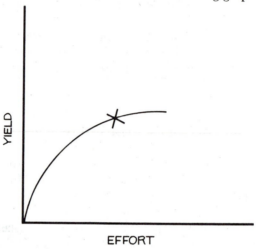

Marking an X on the curve, he said, "I like to get off here. Payoff after this point is very small for the hassle. Fine-tuning is not my bag." Miles described his role as "adding a sense of direction to the program—in the interest of all parties in the program." He felt that the VIS project was in an embryonic stage, a laboratory curiosity with good potential. His key activity would be to orchestrate the team and to sort out what goals to pursue and in which order.

Unlike most of the others involved in the project, Miles was uneasy about the follow-up contract with the Navy. He figured that their hesitation in signing up for 1974 boded ill for the project. Moreover, he regarded the equipment's cost competitiveness and reliability as complete uncertainties at this point. The proprietary aspects of the project were critical, he thought, since its greatest potential would be in the commercial market. Miles hoped that J. Mirl would fund the development and then take over production.

Over the next two months, Miles attempted to complete the business development plan for which he and Gatsby were jointly responsible. But he was not progressing as fast as he would have liked. "Scientists," Miles explained, "are inclined to drink the beer they sell. But when held to a specific performance objective on any system parameter, they back off and are reluctant to make a definite commitment." After three iterations on a matrix of design objectives, Miles was able to define system parameters and performance requirements that the scientists felt they could live with and aim for. While Gordon preferred to keep his estimates verbal and conservative, Miles was trying to push him further, in order to have a basis for talking internally and externally about a larger-scale project.

Gordon and Miles had complementary abilities. Gordon recognized Miles's strengths in pursuing customers and knowing how to make the bureaucracy work for him. For his part, Miles said, "One of the most enjoyable things I do is to sit with Ed Gordon and talk with him and draw things up." He felt that their working relationship was excellent. "If we really had the money," he said, "we might be dangerous."

French and Miles were anxious to offer the customer a high-performance, "guaranteed" system that could be quickly delivered, thus making the sale easier. Gordon would have preferred a research contract to continue his activities. Since research money was hard to come by, he felt compelled to go along with French and Miles. Gordon continually cautioned Miles about the technical risks in selling hardware and felt that Miles appreciated the scientist's plight. French, however, discounted the technical risks in the program, treating it instead as a "standard" job that could be turned over to an engineering group for a speedy and economic completion. Gordon viewed this expectation as extremely naive.

Tension was building between French and Gordon. Previously French had sold very expensive, one-of-a-kind hardware systems, and he was not comfortable selling research programs. His performance was evaluated against a sales quota measured in dollars. A videographic hardware system might bring in $1 million, while a videographic research program might cost about $80,000. Furthermore, the same brashness that worked so well with customers rubbed the scientist the wrong way. Gordon was torn between wanting to see his brainchild grow and his scientific conservatism. His ambivalence was exacerbated by French's seemingly unsympathetic and sometimes cavalier manner.

Miles estimated that it would take from $750,000 to $1 million to complete the hardware development effort. Although he still preferred internal company funding, the company was not accustomed to spending such sums on internal project development. Commercial companies were also not likely to commit that much, so marketing plans were oriented toward government agencies and other divisions within J. Mirl.

SEPTEMBER–DECEMBER 1973: A NEW CUSTOMER AND A MEETING WITH TOP MANAGEMENT

In September, a new potential customer emerged. SECOM, a newly created federal agency, would be required to process an enormous amount of meteorological information every day, and was not sure how best to handle such data loads. Miles, Gordon, and French tried to sell them on the storage capacity, compactness, and reliability of a videographic system, and SECOM seemed responsive. However, officials at SECOM pointed out that if data were stored with very high density, their many users would spend much of their time accessing. If each user had to wait for the system to run through a lot of data to find the location of the data they wanted, the line of users waiting to enter the system could grow long. This might make swift random access an important capability for the system and could represent a significant interface problem. Miles was not absolutely convinced that SECOM needed random access, since the agency asked that the work be priced according to different-size work packages, including one without random access. He speculated that there was disagreement within SECOM on this point.

The scientists had always favored dense storage of information. The implicit guideline had always been, "the denser the better." Among many design choices, this one had seemed trivial, a "no-brainer." Now, however, it appeared that densely storing information could adversely affect access time.

On the basis of a September 1973 meeting, Miles wrote SECOM's requirements into the VIS technical plan for 1974. Since SECOM could not afford to buy the whole system, he reorganized the development plans toward a system that could be developed and purchased in modules.

At the same time Miles and Gatsby strongly disagreed about the business development plan they would present to top management at J. Mirl. To enhance flexibility, Gatsby wanted to offer a "menu" of what could be done at different levels of funding. He believed they should draw up several plans differentiated by financial source, amount of support, and potential market.

Miles was holding out for one total-system plan that requested $500,000 internal support from J. Mirl. He felt that at a lower level of funding nothing significant could be accomplished and J. Mirl's proprietary position would suffer considerably. Moreover, if patents were not built into a large system, it would be vulnerable to copying by competitors. After 10 or 12 iterations, the business plan still had not left Gatsby's office. In Rouhas's opinion, "The people who now have control of the business plan (Gatsby) are unwilling to let go and are smothering it." The October deadline for obtaining internal funding through regular channels passed without submission of a plan.

Salt did not force the issue. His management style was to guide the research group with a loose rein and fatherly concern, encouraging what he thought were the most promising developments. When conflicts arose, he would often let the course of events and the force of personalities settle the matter. This laissez-faire style was possible because his scientific work had won him enormous prestige in the company.

Gordon was alarmed that support was slipping away, but his and other's enthusiasm for VIS and its commercial possibilities was still fairly high in November 1973. During the last months of the year, the Arab oil embargo, fuel shortages, and the danger of a longer-run energy shortage created a new sense of national priorities. The federal government began to reallocate research and development spending toward the development of alternative sources of energy.

Gatsby called a meeting for December in which the chief people on the videographic project would discuss their progress with members of division and corporate management. To some extent, the meeting was a response to corporate vice president Frank Coyne's request for a business plan. At first Miles prepared 30 pages of "bullet charts"—simplified charts and figures—but Gatsby and Salt told him that was the wrong approach. Gatsby and Miles still had not resolved their differences about how to develop the project. Miles said, "My underlying emotion is that I want a commitment from management now. They should know how much it is going to cost them over two years. I don't want to keep going back for small bits. They get disenchanted when that happens." Gatsby favored a lower profile. He wanted to get a foot in the door, and gradually build the size of the project. Funding for the original videographics effort had begun this way, and such an approach fit the research nature of the project.

The two men differed greatly in their personal style and in their sense of the purpose of the meeting. Gatsby was prudent and cautious, interested in keeping corporate management informed about his efforts to sell an $80,000 research program. Miles was bold and daring, wanting to challenge top management to take on a

$500,000 hardware program. They had very different ideas about the potential of the videographic project, and about what would appeal to top management.

For the meeting, Gatsby and Miles agreed to a pseudo-compromise. The plan would have a big price tag up front with itemized costs for packages of work in the back. Miles would stress the futility of buying just one of the packages and show that it did not make sense to do any of the packages alone.

The meeting was held in a conference room near Gatsby's office. It was informal in style and lasted two hours. Attending were Coyne and two members of his staff, the division vice president and his staff, Salt, Rouhas, Gatsby, Gordon, French, and Miles.

Miles began by outlining the cost to get into the business, the potential dollar volume of the market, and the likely potential customers in government and industry. Early in the meeting he sensed corporate management's negative reaction to the plan's high cost, and switched the emphasis of his presentation to the possibility of winning a contract from SECOM. Reading their nonverbal behavior and the trend of their questions, Miles guessed that if this group were forced to recommend whether the company should fund the project, they would turn it down. Thus, the December gathering became an information-passing session to keep higher management posted on the videographic memory project. No specific decision or action step was taken. Top management was content not to declare a position on a potentially valuable, but highly vulnerable, research project.

Rouhas and Salt were depressed by the lack of top management enthusiasm and afterwards explained that "we are finally facing up to the fact that we aren't in the videographic memory business." They felt that the company would not try to compete in the commercial market against large, established data processing firms which were strongly suspected to be working on a videographic or similar type of memory system. Members of the R & D group had hoped that another part of the company would be interested in developing or taking over the project. Salt commented,

> We began kidding each other, saying that if the Navy did the development work then we could "cheapen it up" and go to regular manufacturing techniques. Then reality sets in and we gradually realize that maybe we won't get the Navy contract, that the internal capability for mass manufacturing isn't that good, and that it would cost an awful lot of money.

Salt and Rouhas felt that even if the project received some outside funding, it would be "the last dying gasp."

Miles recognized there were major problems in gaining internal support. "If I were representing the best interest of J. Mirl," he said, "I'd probably shut the job down. However, my job is to keep Gatsby and Gordon happy, and I intend to continue marketing this inside and outside J. Mirl." Z.K. French was more determined than ever to obtain support for the project. Because of their friendship, he felt a strong personal obligation to help Patrick Miles.

JANUARY–APRIL 1974: RESPONSES TO THE REDUCTION IN FUNDING

By late January, Salt had moved completely away from the videographic mass-memory project, and Rouhas was left to clear up any remaining problems. Sometime that same month, French and Miles realized that Salt and Rouhas had decided against the project. Serious problems with Miles's other project occupied most of his time during December and January, leaving the VIS project with no consistent planning or marketing effort. In February, Miles came down with pneumonia.

Gordon and Gatsby believed that a basic core of internal support remained. They discounted Rouhas's statement that internal funding would not be granted. Gordon did not believe that Rouhas knew enough about the VIS project to make a valid judgment about its continuation. For 1974, he planned to concentrate on developing a high-speed recorder for the system.

After his recovery, Miles journeyed with French to Washington, D.C., intending to spend a week meeting with SECOM. They returned two days early, and Miles appeared crushed. Although he had been sure that SECOM would fund development work, the agency had refused to do so. "Send us one when you develop it," said SECOM. Miles began writing himself out of the videographic project.

Everyone was worried that Gordon would find it difficult to let the videographic work die. Rouhas was concerned that he might even leave the company. Gordon's original enthusiasm had evolved into a grim determination that the project had value and should continue. He had another R & D program to complete in 1974 and intended to work in the lab on his normal routine. He continued technical planning for the project, but admitted the pace of work had slowed considerably.

In April 1974 those connected with the videographic memory

effort held differing views on the present state of the project, on what should be done, and on what would be done. Salt considered the project to be shut off and had immersed himself in the problems of researching alternative sources of energy. Rouhas said the Washington trip to SECOM was "the last-gasp marketing trip." Gatsby thought the project would revert to technical exploration at low levels of funding. French had not given up hope of selling the program, possibly to SECOM. Miles was developing other work projects. Gordon wanted very much to continue work on his brainchild, and still received several calls and visitors weekly, asking him about videographic data storage. Top management never made a clear declaration. In April 1974 the project had reached no final resolution.

OCTOBER 1974: THE PARTICIPANTS LOOK BACK

Six months later I asked the participants to meet to discuss the project. While earlier meetings with these men had been lively, their tone was now almost funereal. They were reluctant to go back over the death of a cherished hope. From hard experience, the men knew that the odds against successfully transferring high technology to the marketplace were staggering. Yet they were drawn by the challenge of possibly pulling off such a coup. In discussion they interrupted each other with gallows humor that brought laughter to cover their disappointment.

Once discussion got under way, all agreed that the project was scientifically a success. Technical breakthroughs had been achieved, and a working model constructed. As a research program, the project added to the company's expertise in an important area of technology. Turning to other criteria for evaluating the project provoked the following discussion:

Miles: I think the successful thing about it was—

French: It's like the operation was a success, but the patient died. (laughter)

Gordon: No, the operation was a success, but the patient didn't pay his bill. (laughter)

Miles: I think it was successful in the sense that it got top management to make a commitment.

French: Even though it was a negative commitment.

Miles: Even though . . . Well, we put the burden of commitment on top management, and they really backed away from it. When they did, I know I did, and I think Z.K. and Fred did. And what they really meant is that instead of pumping $125,000 into that program this year, and putting another $60,000 in next year and phasing it out over a two-year period, they may have saved $100,00.

Rouhas: The project was successful in the sense that it got a lot of valuable people interested in something worth doing. In an R & D organization it is extremely important to have projects that keep good people committed.

Interestingly enough, some team members felt a decision had been made in the December meeting, while many others were unsure or felt no decision had been made:

Miles: They told us, "We don't really want to be in that business." At least, they told us something and I interpreted it as, "We don't want to be in that business."

Salt: Maybe what they told you was, "We don't want to be in that business at the price we see it would take to get into that business. We would really have to start a whole new division. We aren't prepared to do that, and we don't know if the risk will be worth it."

Rouhas: I think a lot of the decisions that were made on this project were not made by the "company." They were made by people who were deeply involved in it.

Looking back on a project that had evoked considerable enthusiasm in some participants, they reflected on the value of such excitement about a project's potential:

Salt: I guess the point was it wasn't really managed from the beginning and planned for in the sense of setting out, knowing what we wanted to do, laying out a budget . . . What I keep having to remind myself is every time somebody comes up with a new and clever idea and we get enthusiastic about it, chances are that you're not going to suddenly break open the market. I mean Z.K. and Pat and I have had some other experiences where we thought we were going to crack the thing open and you get carried away. You really think you're going to do something.

French: But unless you're enthusiastic you don't have a chance to do anything. You've got to have that enthusiasm.

Salt: There are a couple of other things going on right now where you look at them and think, boy, if that works out . . .

French: But most of the programs around here move on emotion anyway.

Rouhas: That's why they come to a shuddering halt.

French: No, I don't know. Some of them are quite successful.

Rouhas: Yeah, but the ones that are successful are usually the ones that are relevant to the type of business that the company is in in the first place. And that kind of detached assessment was never made (on the videographic project). Before you get started, before you start getting carried away by—

French: Oh, I don't know. I think if we want to try building this business again, we'd get that kind of assessment pretty quick. (laughter)

Here too, the participants saw different lessons to be learned from the project.

BRIEF CHRONOLOGY OF EVENTS

1963–1969	Edward Gordon joined J. Mirl Company and worked part time on videographic technology.
1969–1972	Gordon developed his own research project to use videographics to store information.
January–July 1973	Working model developed. Some marketing trips to Washington. Corporate VP visited the lab and became interested.
August 1973	Patrick Miles appointed business manager.

September–December 1973	SECOM emerged as a potential customer. Miles had trouble developing a business plan with Gatsby. They missed the October deadline for internal funding. The meeting with top management was held in December.
January–April 1974	Funding was reduced. Project team members reacted differently.
October 1974	Meeting of participants to review the project.

Chapter **4**

Commentary on the High Technology Case

The case presented in Chapter 3 is a story familiar to those who manage research and technology. An exciting new technology attracts the interest of a few researchers in an aerospace company. After several years of apprenticeship, a bright young scientist carves out his own research project for exploring a commercial application of the new technology. During four years of part-time work, the project shows more and more promise, and eventually a business manager is appointed to develop a business plan. The project team knocks on doors to find a customer, but they cannot obtain funding. The company declines to spend the large amount of money required to commercialize the project, and the program shrinks. The scientists still hold on; the business manager, the marketer, and others move on to other projects.

This case presents the opportunity to test the ideas on maps and mapping that were developed in Chapter 2. Because the ideas of Chapter 2 are themselves a way of framing a set of problems, discordant evidence from the case is likely to lead to a revision of the ideas of Chapter 2, rather than an outright rejection. Therefore, the appropriate test is not whether the ideas of Chapter 2 completely explain the VIS case, but whether they are useful for understanding what happened. Do the concepts highlight features of the case that are important for managing ambiguity and which might otherwise be overlooked?

We begin by examining the sources of ambiguity in the VIS case. I had chosen to look at a high technology research lab because it seemed that scientists working on the frontiers of knowledge would face considerable ambiguity in goals and technology. Surprisingly, however, the scientific aspects of the case were less ambiguous than others. The principal scientist spent most of his waking hours, and some of his sleeping hours, thinking about how videographics could be used to store information. With Edward Gordon's considerable expertise and creativity, the scientific frontier was thoroughly explored. Gordon was able to significantly improve the mapping of how lasers could be used to store information.

The ambiguity in the VIS project derived from other areas. Table 4.1 briefly discusses how each of the twelve characteristics of ambiguous situations defined in Chapter 1 applies to this case, and shows my rating of how troublesome each one proved to be for VIS project participants.

Items 4 and 5 were perhaps the most significant sources of difficulty. Forceful personalities had quite different values and therefore pushed in opposing directions in defining what VIS was and how it should be sold. Contributing to the confusion, and perhaps sustaining it, top management was ambivalent about the basic mission; the laboratory director's laissez-faire style allowed pursuit of multiple and conflicting goals; and the players' different value orientations clashed repeatedly without achieving any resolution.

Another major difficulty, not captured by the list, was the marketing of the project. Who would be the first customer? There were many possibilities, but no one was willing to step forward and be number one. In addition, the most promising customer, SECOM, sent mixed signals. Could they, and would they, fund development? Did they really need the random access feature? Which of the several representatives with whom project members spoke had real influence within SECOM?

MAJOR PROPOSITIONS ABOUT MAPPING

We may now test the major propositions about mapping developed in Chapter 2 against the evidence of the VIS case. First, the notion of conceptual maps implies that *reality is a product of social interaction*. That is, as discussed in Chapter 2, our sense of the world develops as we compare and calibrate our conceptual maps with

TABLE 4.1.   Sources of Ambiguity in the High Technology Research Project

Characteristic	Presence in the Case	How Key or Troublesome
1. Nature of problem is itself in question	Was the project research or hardware? There were two different camps. If either alternative had been chosen, the nature of the problem would have been clear. But strong personalities for both sides kept the choice from being made.	**
2. Information (amount and reliability) is problematical	The greatest difficulty was not knowing what information was reliable. Examples: who spoke for SECOM and how interested was top management in this project.	**
3. Multiple, conflicting interpretations	Top management needs to be challenged to start a new business *versus* they will support research but not commercialization.	**
4. Different value orientations, political/emotional clashes	Marketer and business manager value commercial profits, while scientist and research group director value advancing the state of the art.	***
5. Goals are unclear, or multiple and conflicting	The mission of research lab was ambivalent. Two very different conceptions of the essential nature of their work.	***
6. Time, money, or attention lacking	How much money was top management willing to invest? Most key players were not full-time.	**

7.	Contradictions and paradoxes appear	Scientists should be free to explore, but the company needs to make a profit. "Moonlighting" is not officially sanctioned but is an important source of new ideas.	**
8.	Roles vague, responsibilities unclear	People's roles were clear, but they did not have enough time to carry them out although having two bosses did cause some ambiguities for the principal scientist.	*
9.	Success measures are lacking	Good measures of success were available: patents, winning contracts, being funded by the company, interest of fellow scientists at conferences, etc.	*
10.	Poor understanding of cause–effect relationships	The big problem—who would be the first customer?—was not a cause-effect problem.	*
11.	Symbols and metaphor used	Symbols included: obtaining patent protection, winning a Navy contract and commitment from another division, interest of president and vice presidents.	*
12.	Participation in decision-making fluid	For this case changing participation was not a very noticeable feature. Potential customers came and went, but a base of important players in the company was established and maintained.	*

***=very troublesome **=moderately troublesome *=slightly troublesome those of others. If you find the idea of a socially constructed reality unsettling, you are probably now experiencing some of the defensive reactions of dynamic conservatism—again, as discussed in Chapter 2. But try to hold those reactions in abeyance, and consider the events of the VIS case.

Take the "decision" at the December meeting. Neither then, nor later, did top management ever deliver a clear-cut "no" to the videographic project. Instead, as Chapter 2 suggested might happen, much of the important communication took place through nonverbal channels. Top management was in a difficult spot. The project team had invested a lot of effort in the project, top management had encouraged them, and the company often proclaimed its willingness to commercialize promising research projects. On the other hand, the capital outlay and organizational commitment that would be required did not seem justified in view of the risks. So top management displayed their uneasiness and said nothing definite, instead using highly ambiguous nonverbal signals which could be read differently by different people.

Immediately after the meeting, some project members, like Gordon and Gatsby, did not think that top management had reached a decision on the future of the project. The others believed that top management was unenthusiastic and negative about the likely future of the project. Some were depressed, grieving, and getting ready to let go; others were more determined than ever to find the customer who would sign a contract and save the project. As the months went by, it began to look more and more as if a negative decision had been made in December. At the conference meeting held in October 1974 to review the project, Miles put it aptly:

> They told us, "We don't really want to be in that business." At least, they told us something and I interpreted it as, "We don't want to be in that business."

The December meeting turned out to be a pivotal event in the life of the project, and yet in December and January its meaning was fuzzy. Only in the light of subsequent events did opinions on the meeting's implications converge. As support for the project shrank, the December meeting came to be seen as having delivered a negative decision. Project members developed a plausible explanation for what happened.

The mind prefers simplicity. Events in the later months of the VIS case were confusing: Why is the project receiving so little funding? Why is the project manager working on other projects? Why has the project team dispersed? Team members found an explanation: "Top management decided against funding the project internally, and we couldn't find funding elsewhere." This version of what happened is easy to accept, because it conforms to the widespread notion that decisions are choices made at one point in time, and that top managers are the ones who make such decisions. So history is rewritten in light of subsequent events to simplify and give meaning to an ambiguous stream of events. The "reality" of the December meeting was elaborated in a gradual, social process.

One should not infer that top management was weak or evasive in leaving matters unsettled at the December meeting. *Ambiguity can have positive uses.* First, ambiguity can serve to keep decision-making in the hands of the people most knowledgeable about the technology and its prospects. As Rouhas said:

> I think a lot of the decisions that were made on this project were *not* made by the "company." They were made by people who were deeply involved in it.

Especially in matters of high technology or arcane specialties, top managers may not have the expertise to make informed decisions. So they react as a judicial court sometimes does when presented with an extraordinarily difficult case. The legal wisdom is that "hard cases make bad law." To avoid committing itself to a precedent, for example, the Supreme Court may refuse to hear a thorny case, base its ruling on very narrow technical grounds, or express itself in fecund phrases such as "with all deliberate speed" that can be interpreted in light of subsequent events. Similarly, when top managers lack the relevant technical expertise, they may prefer to leave a business decision to the hands-on team. They turn to nonverbal channels and/or use metaphors to widen the field for interpretation and to encourage others to make their own meaning out of the situation.

Second, deliberate ambiguity can allow people to sidestep important tensions or contradictions that are inevitably part of complex systems. For example, researchers need independence and the freedom to pursue their interests; at the same time research projects should be relevant to the company's business. A clear-cut decision in December might have short-circuited the creative tension between the two sides of this truthful contradiction. So, for the moment, all sides were willing indirectly to indicate which side of the polarity they were leaning toward. Those at the meeting took a reading on others' apparent positions, thereby changing the decision context, if not the decision. The possibility of internal funding grew dim, and project members began to focus all their attention toward potential customers outside the firm. Ambiguity in this instance allowed an important contradiction to stand.

Third, ambiguity can allow people time to disengage themselves emotionally from the decision. Scientists and others on the VIS project were valuable resources to the company. Having invested heavily in the project, they might need time to let go of their hopes and dreams. Ambiguity allows for individual variation in how quickly people want to face their little dying.

Viewing reality as a social construct makes it easier to understand several important features of managing an ambiguous situation like the VIS project. If one presumes a stable, "out there" reality, several features of the VIS project are puzzling, to say the least. If reality is objective and fixed, why didn't top management render a clear-cut decision? How does one explain the evolving interpretation of the December meeting? Why does the company remain ambivalent about the mission of its R & D group? The other alternative is to force clarity upon these questions by saying, for example, that top management was cowardly or inept for not clearly deciding. But such a view does violence to the uncertainties of incomplete information and to the wisdom of tolerating the sometimes ambiguous nature of managing. Whether consciously chosen or not, management's use of ambiguity in the December meeting allowed later events and the people involved to clarify the best course of action.

Chapter 2 argued that *the mind is an inference machine, sorting through the flood of experience in advance of conscious attention and imposing order upon fuzziness.* This sort of proposition is very difficult to test in a field situation and seems to require the controlled conditions of laboratory experiments. Nevertheless, it is worth looking at the events of the VIS case to see whether they support this view of the mind or suggest refinements in the concept.

In several instances, participants in the VIS project made inferential leaps and, on the basis of skimpy evidence, formed beliefs that shaped their actions. One such belief was that patents would protect the company's proprietary position in the new technology. There is considerable evidence, however, that the protection afforded by patents is largely an illusion, although having patents may increase the confidence of management.[1] A second belief was the myth that "the company will commercialize promising research projects." Rhetoric in speeches and brochures made this claim, but the hard facts were that the company had never successfully moved a project from the lab to mass production because it lacked the necessary production capabilities. Still the belief sustained Miles in his clashes with Gatsby. Only later and temporarily would some members see the hard facts and recognize where they had been kidding themselves. A final example of an influential belief based on scant hard information was the suspicion prevalent among members of the VIS project that competitors were actively pursuing the development of videographics. Beliefs and myths were created and sustained on very thin evidence. In most instances they seemed to provide a feeling of protection and order in a vulnerable and ill-defined situation.

The retrospective decision of the December meeting is a further example of minds at work bringing order to fuzziness. The ambiguities in the December meeting were considerable, and people devised meaning according to their own lights. But there were significant differences in individuals' needs to impose order on fuzziness. The principal scientist was happy to leave large parts of the project loosely defined and to guide the project intuitively. The marketer and the corporate staff, on the other hand, were anxious to impose order. The marketer wanted to sell a proven hardware system. Corporate staff members, perhaps hoping to protect themselves and their boss from later recriminations, wanted a well-defined, detailed business plan for the project. In an intermediate position was the business manager, who understood the predilections of individuals on either side of him. That there should be individual differences in tolerance for ambiguity is entirely consonant with the large body of psychological research on human information processing and ego development.[2] The VIS case indicates that such differences can be important, and should be recognized in our model of how groups of human beings behave in ambiguous situations.

Chapter 2 also argued that *we see with theory-laden vision.* What we see is influenced by who we are, what is important to us, and how we think the world around us operates. Influences on perception can include one's organizational position and stake in the matter at hand. In the VIS case, the participants' different perceptions led them to develop competing ideas of what VIS was and how it should be sold.

The marketer saw an expensive hardware system that was almost ready to be sold off the shelf. A $1 million sale would help him meet his sales quota and justify the amount of time required to sell a unique new product. On the other hand, the scientist saw in VIS an exciting new technology with *potential* to be developed into an off-the-shelf item. But he was acutely aware of the many features of the system that were unknown and yet to be invented. Considering his role and stakes, the caution of the scientist seems natural. Similarly with the other participants;   each looks at VIS, the December meeting, and the selling task through the filter of his own theories about the world.

The maps most likely to be of interest to managers are created by groups in a process that *involves the interaction and perhaps the collision of individuals' personal maps*. Although Chapter 2 acknowledged that the process of creating a public map may not be smooth, it assumed that a map would usually be created. The events of the VIS case do not entirely support this assumption. Not every collection of individuals called together becomes a group capable of developing a common map. This is especially important to remember in ambiguous situations. The only full-time members of the VIS project team, for example, were the scientists. Everyone else had to divide his attention between two or more projects. The VIS team members struggled valiantly to create a group map, but they never succeeded. In November 1973, for example, Miles, Gatsby, French, and others had very different maps of what VIS was and how to sell it to top management in an impending meeting.

Had the project continued longer, the flow of events and force of personalities would probably have eventually resulted in a commonly held map—or team membership would have changed. But, the crucial point here is that the creation of a common map is more problematical than the discussion in Chapter 2 suggested. This means that we should pay more attention to the steps involved in, the possible aids to, and the pitfalls of map making in a newly commissioned team.

Chapter 2 surveyed the literature for ideas on how to proceed when maps are weak. Table 4.2 outlines how those recommendations fared against the events of the VIS case.

IMPLICATIONS FOR MANAGING AMBIGUITY

Our discussion of maps and mapping has covered a lot of ground, and a summary of the major implications may be helpful:

1. Consciously attend to the mapping process. Do not let maps be generated and applied automatically. The formation of a map is a leverage point—and quite often a source of authority—for a manager facing a messy and ambiguous problem. Appreciating the deep-felt need for a map and the "lust for action," managers

TABLE 4.2.   Recommendations on Mapping and Case Events

Recommendation	Upheld by the Events of the VIS Case?
Satisfice and muddle through	No, the level of money required forces the issue. Lowering expectations is not enough to see participants intelligently through this mess.
Negative thinking	Unclear. We don't have enough detail on the thinking processes that participants used. The requirement for business planning may represent a failed attempt to *prove* the argument, to use positive thinking.
Nonlogical processes	Certainly the scientists used nonlogical as well as logical thought. The request for a business plan pushes the balance toward logical processes.
Don't tightly specify goals	Evidence on both sides. In early years, no choice but to plan in terms of a generalized sense of domain and direction. Yet the year of engineering in 1972 was guided by specific design objectives and made possible some important advances. How you read the denouement of the project depends upon your guess about whether the winter of 1973–74 was the right time to force the issue.
Dialectic	Yes, this is the most strongly supported recommendation. Players didn't use it, and it could have clarified the nature of the project and associated pitfalls earlier on.

should resist immediately taking action when first presented with an ambiguous problem. Time should be spent at the start carefully constructing a map that identifies the right problem.

To slow down the impulse to act, one suggestion is to generate sketches of two very different ways of mapping the problem. Try to make one map as distinctively different as the GNP map in Chapter 2. Other suggestions for creating a new map will be developed in Chapters 8–10 on the creative process.

2. Root out and examine embedded assumptions. A manager's limited time is better spent on problem formulation at the outset, when the direction and context for subsequent steps are determined, than on fine-grained analysis of alternatives at later stages. The manager of ambiguity knows the limits of such analysis and the seriousness of solving the wrong problem.

Barnard points out that tacit knowledge and taken-for-granted assumptions are the most vulnerable links in a chain of logical reasoning.[3] The dialectical procedure outlined in Chapter 1 is a means of discovering and examining these assumptions. Similarly, conflict and disagreement can be very useful in ambiguous situations. More attention should be directed toward the constructive and creative use of conflict, and we shall do so in Chapters 8–10. One should not have to wait for maps to fail before testing their soft spots.

3. Actively guide the social process of constructing reality. Managers should consider seriously how maps are socially constructed and continually ratified by a group. Since the formation of a group map is very much influenced by the similarities and dissimilarities between members, several important choices for managers can be identified. What people are chosen for the group and how diverse are they? How should new members be socialized into the group? Should a currently staid group be renewed by the timely introduction of new members holding quite different personal maps?

    Managers should also guide the group in deciding which parts of the map should be clearly defined and which should be more metaphorical. Language and types of conceptual order can vary. Managers should be skeptical of the cultural value that the most clearly defined maps or models are always the best. When the world is messy and discontinuous, wisely chosen ambiguity can better guide action!

4. Communicate face-to-face and develop skill in nonverbal communication. The breakdown of a map or a clash between competing maps creates confusion. In such a situation, no map seems to provide an adequate explanation of the events that are occurring and thus participants do not have a good sense of what to do. Yet, like the automakers, they may have to act before a map can be fully developed and sufficient evidence accumulated to clarify entirely the meaning of events.

    Without a common map and language to objectify reality, subjectivity becomes more important in attacking a messy problem. Since disorder cannot be named, formal and explicit language, which is the sign of a highly objectified situation, cannot be used. The language most appropriate to convey messiness is metaphorical and nonverbal.[4] Managers coping with an ill-defined problem are generating hunches, intuitions, and judgments that are crucial for building group agreement about direction, but which are frequently difficult to express in words, especially written words. Because of a general cultural bias toward tough-mindedness and logical argumentation, intuitive messages tend to be sent through nonverbal, rather than verbal, channels. Nonverbal messages are themselves more ambiguous and, very importantly, can be disowned. The use of an ambiguous channel of communication can help a manager convey the subjectivity and nuance of meaning that are crucial in an ambiguous situation.[5]

A lower-level task force trying to communicate its reading of an ambiguous situation to top management faces a difficult problem if it can only express itself through impersonal means such as memos or reports, since these cannot convey tacit knowledge and subjectivity. Yet those best suited to make decisions and to decide upon action steps are typically the task group members. Top management must either be in frequent face-to-face contact with this group or be willing to delegate the most important decisions to the group.

5. After careful examination of assumptions, begin to act before all the causal connections are completely and definitively drawn. Accumulate evidence if you can, but don't expect that evidence to be completely trustworthy or to clarify entirely what action should be taken. Do not expect that collecting evidence will entirely resolve the ambiguity of the situation. The methods of specifying goals, using logical programs, and accumulating evidence are the methods of the regular army fighting a traditional war on well mapped terrain. But ambiguous problems are like poorly mapped jungle terrain and respond best to a guerrilla style of coping. Without jettisoning rationality, managers should embrace contradiction and paradox to see what can be made of them. Dialectical processes may help you use contradictions and conflicts creatively, to find new facts and more trustworthy assumptions. Negative thinking, metaphors, intuition, and judgment may take you farther than a doggedly systematic approach.

6. In a major crisis, pay careful attention to the difference between map and territory. As Korzybski has pointed out, the map is not the territory, and people can have different maps of the same territory.[6] In a sense, each person lives in his own world, although we ordinarily assume that we all share the same reality. When major disagreements come to light, regarding map and territory as synonymous and assuming that everyone lives in the same world can exacerbate misunderstandings. In such situations one must pay tediously close attention to differences in the referents of people's maps.

7. In an ambiguous situation, allow time for people to relinquish

their old maps. People fight to retain their maps because identity and security are wrapped up in familiar and known ways of doing things. Organizations will more readily change on matters of marginal importance, and will fight tenaciously to conserve more central beliefs and values. If you see a need for change, or if change is thrust upon your organization, you should attend to the need for grieving over the loss of old and familiar ways. Some time must be spent in letting go of the old map and preparing to accept a new one. Instead of trying to devise ways to overcome resistance to change, managers in an organization approaching transition may find it more useful to seek ways of satisfying people's need for continuity.

SUMMING UP

Managers have a lot more flexibility in how they conceptualize a problem than they commonly realize. The chance to map a problem is an opportunity of enormous potential for managing ambiguity and change, but unfortunately it is often carelessly used. Chapters 2-4 have offered several ideas for better understanding and conducting the process. Mapping is always important, and it becomes crucial when change and ambiguity characterize the work.

The evidence so far indicates that contradictions and conflicts are inescapable components in trying to map a complex situation. In subsequent chapters we take up the question of how a manager can regulate the stress of dealing with contradictions and how he might use those contradictions creatively.

The concluding point about mapping is well-expressed in a review of the 1979 New York City subway map. The author briefly compares the new map to the previous edition and goes on to say:

> The new map, by contrast, is a model of naturalism—composed to scale, showing the exact routes taken by the trains and indicating streets, points of interest and neighborhoods, Water is blue, parks are green . . .

> This appears to be a noble effort. Yet in truth it is not only quixotic and doomed to failure, but seriously misguided. The subway system is not a rational phenomenon; it is mythic, uncanny, reason-defying. Trying to describe it with the tools of realism is like sending a newspaper reporter to cover the Last Judgment.

> Indeed, this map resolutely ignores the poetry of the subways.[7]

Chapter 5

The Stress of Ambiguity

Managing ambiguity and fundamental change is stressful and exacts physical, emotional, and psychological tolls. Yet change can also be exhilarating. Officers at the bank described in Chapter 2 compared the introduction of electronic banking to the elation of winning an election, and those connected with the VIS project spoke of the need to be seduced into behaving heroically. Without assuming, then, that stress is always harmful, we need to learn how it affects human performance. Chapters 5–7 examine how people try to cope with the stress that results from ambiguity and change.

Researchers from psychology, anthropology, sociology, medicine, and psychiatry have studied people under stress: soldiers in combat, prisoners in concentration camps, surgery patients, victims of hurricanes and floods, people with highly dangerous jobs (like the Mercury astronauts), managers on the firing line, and students about to take exams. We will not attempt a comprehensive review of this literature, but will focus on observations relevant to a manager trying to deal with the stress of managing a messy, ambiguous situation.[1] The main questions addressed in these chapters are:

- How does severe stress affect human performance?
- How do individuals differ in the way they respond to stress? Why do ambiguity and stress seem challenging and invigorating to one person, while another person in the same situation feels threatened and anxious?

- What happens to groups under pressure?
- What conditions, personality characteristics, and attitudes favor productive responses to the stress of ambiguity?
- How can technical training affect one's response to ambiguity and pressure?

In short, we will be looking at the stress literature through a pragmatic and managerial lens. In the area of foreign policy, Henry Kissinger has made the point succinctly: "What is relevant for policy depends not only on academic truth but also on what can be implemented under stress."[2]

HUMAN PERFORMANCE UNDER SEVERE STRESS

We turn first to an especially important aspect of coping with stress: what happens to human performance under conditions of severe stress. There are ambiguities in the research, but the general pattern of response seems clear. High stress attacks the whole organism, which tries to respond in various ways. The physical manifestations differ among individuals and include sweaty hands, cold sweats, gastrointestinal disturbances, violent pounding of the heart, loss of appetite, diarrhea, irritability, and increased consumption of alcohol.[3] Some people become physically agitated, unable to sit still, their nervousness communicated in jerky, discontinuous movement; others shift into slow motion, making easy and normal movements at a much reduced pace, as if they were painting a picture of the perfect way to perform.

The emotional response to severe stress has similar characteristics. People often experience roller-coaster swings from elation to depression as their feelings become more pronounced and more erratic. For example, soldiers who remain in battle too long can become trigger-happy and fire at shadows. Under severe stress, the need for the emotional reassurance of one's group becomes paramount. Soldiers in World War II left hospitals while injured and sometimes refused promotions to avoid separation from their combat units.[4] People look for others who share their plight, are sympathetic, and might help them control their anxiety.

Under severe stress, cognitive operations are impaired. Scanning flits from clue to clue, backtracks, becomes erratic and inefficient. People seek out less novelty and reject fearful and unpleasant messages. They also see fewer connections between their ideas and observations. People under severe stress tend to think more primitively, using either/or dichotomies, and losing an appreciation for nuance and complexity. They also tend to fixate on a single approach to the situation and become more rigid in their thinking.

Behaviorally, groups and organizations under high stress try to increase structure and control. In a severe economic downturn, accounting and control functions gain influence, as the system tightens up on spending. Those at the top tend to make more unilateral decisions which enhances their sense of control, but decreases the sense of control for those lower in the organization.[5] Under severe stress a group often emphasizes loyalty and good feelings over problem-solving efforts. I have observed that loyalty is enforced unless the group is so thoroughly threatened that it breaks apart and reverts to being a collection of individuals, each looking out for himself.

The impact of severe stress on human performance thus poses an important dilemma for managers. Just when one needs more flexibility, complexity, and sophistication of thought, severe stress engenders the opposite reaction. How can one keep cool under pressure? A closer examination of how individuals respond to stress offers some possibilities for hope.

STRESS RESPONSES ARE IDIOSYNCRATIC

Stress is a product of the interaction between a particular person and a particular situation. The problem that makes one person feel severely stressed may be only moderately stressful to another. Individual identity, beliefs, values, and prior experience with similar situations all influence how a person will perceive the present problem. How one perceives a situation and what the situation is determine the level of stress. The implications for managers are powerful: to some extent, people's level of stress can be regulated by changing how they perceive the situation.

How stress is perceived significantly influences one's performance, according to a hypothesis proposed by Janis and Leventhal. Based on a review of the literature, and upon an idea first formulated as Yerkes-Dodson's Law, they hypothesize that performance is curvilinearly related to stress.[6]   Figure 5.1 describes the inverted-U relationship between intellectual/motor performance and level of perceived stress.

The exact shape of the curve would vary according to the type of performance and stress under investigation. In every case, however,

FIGURE 5.1.   Relationship Between Performance and Stress

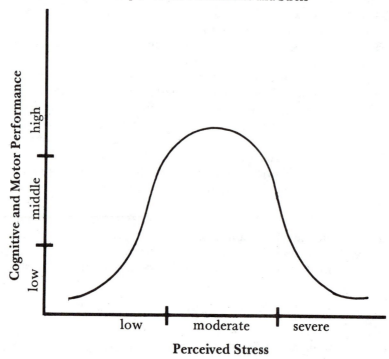

Perceived Stress

performance is optimal at some point in the middle range of perceived stress and falls as stress becomes too low or too high. The
same U-shaped function was observed by Schroder and his colleagues
in their research on how people cope with increasing environmental
complexity. Again cognitive performance was optimal at moderate
levels of environmental complexity, and declined toward either
extreme of the range.[7]

   Each individual responds in characteristic ways to various kinds
of stress. That is, he has a set of stress curves that vary by type of
situation. In addition, researchers have found that family and ethnic
backgrounds influence response to stress. For example, Zborowski
studied male patients in a Veterans Administration hospital in New
York City. He found that Jewish and Italian patients emphasized
their pain, openly sought support from others, and had less confidence in doctors. In contrast, patients of Anglo-Saxon and Irish
ancestry tended to downplay pain, withdrew from others, and expressed confidence in the skill of doctors.[8] A study by Zaleznik and
his colleagues found similar patterns for other cultural groups.[9]

Prior success in coping with difficulties also seems to affect one's present ability to cope. Studying the recovery of severely burned patients, Andreasen and his colleagues found that poor adjustment (severe depression and violent behavior) occurred frequently among patients who had had difficulty coping with life prior to the accident.[10] Those who showed good adjustment, about 50% of the sample, had developed coping patterns that worked well for them in previous difficulties. Thus, coping ability may, to some extent, be a learned and enduring capacity of people. This suggests the importance of training and conditioning to strengthen one's personal resources for dealing with unexpected threats. In training for space flight, the astronauts were frequently put through routines designed to simulate as closely as possible what would happen during the flight. The first launch revealed that moving the gantry aside was unfamiliar and potentially frightening, so that activity was added to the training program. The same idea underlies crisis training in flight simulators, which accustoms commercial airplane pilots to calamities that might occur and conditions their responses. Such training increases the chances that, if a real-life crisis occurs, the pilot will find it at least somewhat familiar and thus it will fall in the moderate stress range where his performance is optimal, and he will be more likely to handle the situation effectively.

A study of 93 owners of small businesses that were severly damaged by hurricane floods provides additional evidence for the central role played by the *perception* of the stressful event. Psychologist Carl Anderson found that the severity of actual financial loss did not account for how well the owners coped with the disaster. Rather, successful recovery depended more on how the stress was perceived. As predicted by the curvilinear hypothesis, the best recovery efforts were made by those who perceived their stress to be in a middle range. Those who felt low stress made fewer recovery efforts and their performance was relatively poor. Interestingly, those with the highest perceived stress showed *average* organizational performance— that is, did better than the low-stress business owners.[11] The study supports the hypothesis that stress is affected by the interaction of the person and the situation, and especially by how the individual reads or appraises the situation.

A MODEL OF THE EXCITEMENT/STRESS OF AMBIGUITY

We can now look more closely at how individuals respond to ambiguity—a lack of clarity in the environmental display—and uncertainty—an internal mental confusion about the display's meaning.[12] In some cases the environmental display is clear, but the person is nevertheless uncertain. Conversely, a person may impose a clear meaning on an ambiguous set of events. This way of looking at the problem recalls our emphasis in Chapter 2 on the subjective and objective faces of reality. Here we are especially concerned with the stress resulting from poorly defined events.

Each person's mind is constantly skimming through a great deal of data, working ahead of conscious attention, to identify what may be of importance to that individual. Much of the flood of experience is channeled into familiar categories and habitual patterns of activity are evoked. If the scanning operation encounters ambiguous stimuli, the mind actively imposes order. A person shapes, distorts, selects, and neglects information so that a small and stable set of beliefs can be maintained. As we stated it in Chapter 2, the mind is an inference machine that strives to bring order, simplicity, consistency, and stability to the world it encounters.

A stressful episode begins when scanning turns up a disruption or a break in one's map. Some event occurs for which the individual has no readily available category, or which evokes multiple and possibly contradictory categories. According to Berkeley psychologist Richard Lazarus, the mind makes a preliminary appraisal of the disruption through cognitive and emotional operations. Then the individual makes a coping response which may or may not involve action. This response very often prompts a reappraisal of the disruption. New events occur, and the entire process continues through further cycles of reappraisal, coping responses, and appraisals of new stimuli.[13]

Lazarus's model says that these several processes are continuous and more or less rapid, and that they regulate each other. Stress and excitement reside neither in the situation nor in the person, but in the interaction of the two. If a potential disruption occurs but is not perceived, there is no stress/excitement reaction. As we shall see, the model (which will be modified somewhat) highlights cognitive operations but does not neglect emotional accompaniments. We will look in turn at the processes that constitute the model: scanning and categorizing, disrupting event or events, appraisal, coping responses, reappraisal, and additional coping efforts.

Essentially, scanning and categorizing involve applying one's maps to the flow of events. Each individual has a set of beliefs that influence his perception of the situation and guide his choice of strategy and tactics. Since the mind can only take note of a very small proportion of the information it receives, most information is relegated to "not significant" or "not pressing" categories. To render the fast-flowing river of events intelligible is such a massive under-taking that the mind must rely on habit, routine, and rapid guesses. In self-defense, the scanning mind often skips over what is novel.

However, some events bring the usual categorization process to a halt, either because they loom so large or because the individual is particularly alert. The person stops for a short while, feeling slightly confused. In business, a manager might puzzle over the erosion of market share, a competitor's failure to follow a needed price in-crease, or a sudden shortage of raw materials. In one's personal life disrupting events include getting married, changing careers, and having a baby. In these situations, the habits that have conducted a person through most days do not apply. Routines are thrown askew by the need to behave differently and to see new possibilities in the future. What is familiar and predictable is likely to be changed in ways that are not fully known, and this raises stress/excitement for the individual. In the electronic banking example, disrupting events included losses from bad loans, shrinkage of deposits, competition from NOW accounts, and the prospect that electronic transactions might replace paper transactions. These events, like most such clues, were ambiguous. Some of the disruptions were not clearly recognized as disruptions by all.

As bank officers interpreted these events, they entered what the model describes as the appraisal phase. Each person appraising a dis-rupting event first crudely classifies it as either a threat or a challenge. A threatening event is expected to bring harm to the individual or the system, and such an appraisal is accompanied by feelings of anxi-ety. A challenging event is expected to bring overall positive benefit and evokes feelings of excitement.

This distinction of threat and challenge illuminates the inverted-U curve pattern of performance described above. High perceived stress is threatening, while moderate stress is challenging. Since perfor-mance decreases rapidly as stress becomes threatening, a key question for managers is what determines whether a disruption is seen as threatening or challenging. We should remember, of course, that ap-praisals are subjective, and the shape of the inverted-U curve differs significantly from one person and situation to another.

Professor Lazarus's examination of the appraisal process high-lights the importance of how an individual reads *the balance of power* between his own resources and what the situation demands. If the individual feels his abilities and other resources give him a fighting chance to master the situation, the disruption is more likely to be experienced as challenging. On the other hand, if the situation is seen as overwhelming and the individual feels he has little control over this type of problem, the disruption is likely to be experienced as threatening. An essential point for managers is that this balance-of-power reading can change over time, as individuals develop the requisite skills and feel more able—and *are* more able—to perform well. As their level of stress moves from extreme to moderate, their appraisal changes from threatening to challenging.

It is not the actual balance of power but one's *perceptions* of the balance of power that affect appraisal. People whose experience has taught them that they will never be able to do anything mechanical, for example, find themselves unable to cope with a car breakdown. On the other hand, people who might seem to lack any power, like prisoners in a concentration camp, sometimes fight to develop control over at least a small part of their lives. In Solzhenitsyn's *One Day in the Life of Ivan Denisovich*, a prisoner supplies favors to other prisoners by taking the risks of being a camp entrepreneur. McDonough points out how Ivan Denisovich prides himself on controlling his own liking for cigarettes and never asking for these limited goods, always waiting for the other person to offer.[14] By these measures and others, Denisovich maintains his sense of dignity and develops control over part of his life. He is therefore better able to survive the horrors of imprisonment in a Stalinist concentration camp.

In the hierarchical organization structures of business, studies by Zaleznik and others show that top managers experience less stress than middle managers do.[15] Zaleznik attributes the difference to the top managers' greater control over organizational resources, including a better understanding of power relationships, and their greater confidence that they can act upon the environment. In short, top managers perceive the external–internal balance of power as relatively favorable.

When the disrupting event is ambiguous, the latitude for interpretation is widest. Lazarus argues that:

> Ambiguity by itself does not always result in threat and will in fact not do so unless there is present some other cue which leads the individual to anticipate harm or the disposition exists (as in Frenkel-Brunswick's analysis) to be easily threatened by such ambiguity. . . . The more ambiguous are the stimulus cues concerning the nature of the anticipated confrontation, the more important are general belief systems in determining the appraisal process.[16]

Those who are intolerant of ambiguity or chronically anxious are predisposed to appraise a disrupting event as threatening. Others can read the balance of power as favorable and appraise the same event as challenging. Which appraisal is made depends very much on one's general beliefs and personality structure and on the presence of others who might be predisposed to react one way or the other.

Among general beliefs, one's sense of potency, or mastery, in transactions with the environment is particularly important for the appraisal process. The self-confident manager who has successfully coped with past disruptions is more likely to appraise events as challenges than threats and to have a better chance of coping. On the other hand, chronically anxious managers lack confidence and have inferred from past experiences that they are often powerless about things that matter.

A person's values and motives also influence how he or she appraises potentially threatening events. Astronauts in the Mercury program were able to deal with the potential dangers of their mission because they had confidence in their abilities and training. In addition, according to the psychologists who studied them, they found the possibility of failing to perform even more threatening than the threat of death.[17] Writer Tom Wolfe, who interviewed the astronauts and their families, put it vividly. According to him, their constant prayer was "Please, dear Lord, don't let me fuck up!"[18]

In summary, appraisal is a cognitive and emotional process, a large part of which probably occurs outside conscious awareness. The process is complex and multistranded, and depends heavily upon previous experience and on personal characteristics, including values and general beliefs. The initial appraisal is tentative and awaits the results of further processes, namely coping responses and additional disruptions.

How do people cope with disruptions of their maps? How do they respond to signals of possible danger? In *War and Peace*, Tolstoy records how residents of Moscow responded as Napoleon's army advanced toward the capital, pushing the Russian army back at every battle.

> As the enemy drew nearer to Moscow, instead of the Muscovites' view of their situation growing more serious, it became more frivolous, as is always the case with people who see a great danger approaching. At the threat of danger there are always two voices that speak with equal power in the human soul: one quite reasonably tells a man to consider the nature of the danger and the means of averting it; the other, still

more reasonably, says that it is too depressing and painful to think of the danger, since it is not in man's power to foresee everything and escape from the general march of events, and it is therefore better to disregard what is painful till it comes, and to think about what is pleasant. In solitude a man generally yields to the first voice; in society to the second. So it was now with the inhabitants of Moscow. It was a long time since there had been as much gaiety in Moscow as that year.[19]

Most of the psychological literature agrees with this twofold division of responses. Typically the two responses are described in terms like "attack versus avoid" or "vigilance versus withdrawal." But such terms have evaluative connotations that are contradicted by more recent research. So we will use the terms "engage" and "not engage," arguing that at times both can be healthy and functional responses.

Psychologists have researched the various ways people will *not engage* a problem—how they will deny, avoid, distort, and create myths and illusions to defend against hearing bad news. A classic case of denial and avoidance occurred at Pearl Harbor in 1941. Admiral Kimmel, commander in chief of the Pacific fleet, ignored or reinterpreted several signals that the Japanese might be preparing to attack Pearl Harbor. Certain of the base's invulnerability, he was reluctant to upset the training programs and other procedures he had in place. He thought that any Japanese attack would come further west, at the Philippines, Guam, or Malaysia. Kimmel and his staff clung to their beliefs and denied and distorted several warning signals that were inconsistent with these beliefs.[20] The same mechanisms are at work when smokers discount information that heavy smoking causes cancer.[21]

The other major choice in responding to a disrupting event is to engage the problem—by increasing vigilance, by gathering more information, or by direct action. In a previous example, the prospect of electronic funds transfer led the bank president and his staff to gather information from a variety of sources, including equipment vendors, banking conferences, and industry and consulting reports. The staff spent a great deal of time gathering, sifting, and analyzing this intelligence, trying to match it to capabilities their own banks had, or could, develop. Eventually they acted by marketing the bank network in a new way and by installing new automated teller machines. This case illustrates how an active attack on a multifaceted problem can be successful, and the point is refined by research on the range of surgery patients' coping responses.

Yale psychologist Irving Janis conducted a series of studies on how surgery patients cope with pain, the threat to bodily integrity, and the severe stress of major surgery. He observed three general patterns of emotional response and adjustment defined by a patient's level of anticipatory fear:

- **High fear.** These patients had extreme feelings of vulnerability. They were anxiety-ridden and worried about everything. They showed the poorest adjustment to surgery.

- **Moderate fear.** These patients sought out realistic information and mentally rehearsed the pain and feeling they would undergo. They prepared themselves so they would suffer no unpleasant surprises. They made the best adjustment to surgery.

- **Low fear.** Before surgery these patients were constantly cheerful, able to sleep well, and socially pleasant. They thought of themselves as personally invulnerable. After the operation they were more likely to display anger and resentment toward the staff. They took longer to recover and stayed in the hospital longer.[22]

These patterns are reminiscent of the inverted-U curves discussed earlier. A limited avoidance may be helpful, but the patient has to do some advance thinking to prepare for disruption. This "work of worrying" seems analogous to the grief work Kubler-Ross describes as a necessary stage in coming to terms with death (Chapter 2). The chief lesson is that it helps to be a part-time worrier. By extension, Janis's work helps explain why managers don't like surprises and reinforces the wisdom of not hiding significant problems from your boss. He or she has to do some worrying ahead of the event.

Active coping responses also seem to play a helpful role in regulating one's own emotional turmoil. Gal and Lazarus studied the different stress reactions of fighter pilots and radar operators in two-person fighter planes. Those in the less active role—radar operators—were more anxious and suffered more somatic complaints than the pilots. (How similar to the different stress levels of the auto passenger and driver in hazardous traffic!) The researchers offer several possible explanations for the calming effects of activity. Activity can provide a sense of mastery and control (thereby affecting the balance of power), it can divert attention, and it can discharge "nervous" energy. They argue that "being engaged in activity—rather than remaining passive—is preferable for most individuals in stressful situations."[23] Taking some action seems to help people regulate their emotional state.

I have seen this effort to establish some sense of control in MBA students facing an important exam or presentation. Some create lists of things to be done, carefully indicating the appropriate sequence of tasks. Others will wage a small campaign to clean up and order their physical surroundings before starting into the intellectual work. The physical ordering has a calming effect and helps them to reduce high stress to more moderate and productive levels.

Coping efforts often create new information to be appraised, and new events in the environment may further disrupt the individual's map. The first appraisal may, thus, be changed or reconfirmed.

As pointed out in Chapter 2, people tend to self seal theories, that is they notice data that confirms their theory and downplay or ignore data which is inconsistent with their map. This self sealing tendency can create a downward spiral. The response of domestic automakers to the first wave of smaller imported automobiles is a clear illustration of this dynamic. In examining the causes of organizational decline, Whettan finds that such negative loops can prevent managers from clearly focusing on the problem and the full range of choices available to them. He quotes Forrester as a possible explanation for such a downward spiral:

> Our first insights into complex social systems came from our corporate work. Time after time we have gone into a corporation which is having severe and well-known difficulties . . . . the known and intended practices of the organization are fully sufficient to create the difficulty, regardless of what happens outside the company or in the marketplace. In fact, a downward spiral develops in which the presumed solution makes the difficulty worse and thereby causes redoubling of the presumed solution.[24]

The downward spiral is not inevitable, however. In some cases, a threatening disruption first leads to feelings of depression as large map shifts are contemplated, but then prompts information-gathering and a reappraisal that highlights opportunities. To cite an example, a large regional trucking company was hit by deregulation of the trucking industry, wildcat strikes, fuel shortages, and a doubling of fuel costs—all within eight months. The typical reaction might have been to lay off workers, sell equipment, and try to ride out the storm. Instead, top managers decided to double their marketing force, and consequently added new customers. They used the crisis as a basis for talks with the drivers, who responded by rescheduling vacations, studying techniques for conserving fuel, and getting involved in making sales calls. Instead of a disaster, the disrupting events turned out to be an occasion for reexamining and revitalizing old ways of doing business. Because these managers and workers were able to exert some control over the stressful situation, a positive, upward spiral developed.

Our model of how managers respond to the stress and excitement of ambiguity is presented in Figure 5.2. Scanning and categorizing proceed, routinely applying maps to the flow of events until a disruption occurs. The disruption is appraised as primarily threatening or challenging according to personal beliefs, predispositions, and one's sense of whether his or her personal resources are adequate to the demands of the disruption. The appraisal, which is only partly conscious, influences how the person responds. Coping efforts involve either engaging or not engaging the problem. The pattern of coping creates loops into which the individual fits new events and consequences of action. Since the cues received from the environment are ambiguous, one may maintain these loops, whether functional or not, long past the best opportunities for change.

FIGURE 5.2. Model of the Stress/Excitement of Ambiguity and Change

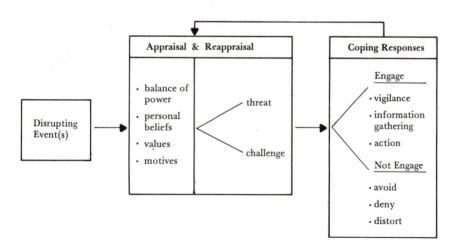

The model and our brief review of the literature highlight a dilemma for managers facing ambiguity and change. Just when you most need flexibility and complexity of thought, a severe stress reaction can provoke the opposite cognitive responses. Fortunately, it is not the disrupting event itself, but how it is perceived that determines the stress people feel. To cope effectively with the stress and experience the excitement of ambiguity, managers must know how their people respond to different types of stress. As we have seen, individuals vary greatly in their response to the same disrupting event. Thus the manager may have to tailor his approach to individual differences as he tries to help his people function under stress. By providing encouragement, the manager can bolster the individual's sense of a favorable balance of power vis-à-vis the demands of the situation. This will increase the chances that the worker can keep cool under pressure and operate in the middle range of stress. In particular, the manager must keep his people confident in situations where they are learning—that is, trying out behavior in which they are likely to make mistakes.

The model highlights the relation between the cognitive operation of mapping and the stress/excitement of ambiguity. A manager can project a great deal onto the opaque screen of an ambiguous problem. What is projected—how much threat and how much challenge—depends upon core beliefs, past experience, and values. Research has not yet determined how much these very personal processes can be consciously influenced. The stress literature suggests that stress can be regulated to some extent *if* managers know the right levers to pull at the right time. Thinking in terms of the model proposed here may help managers make better use of the potential for excitement and challenge inherent in ambiguity.

Chapter **6**

Desegregating
San Francisco's Schools

This chapter describes the desegregation planning process in the San Francisco Unified School District. The case provides an opportunity to test the usefulness of our model of stress in analyzing and suggesting action alternatives in an administrative situation. (A brief chronology of events in the case can be found at the end of the chapter.)

The 1960s saw clamorous struggles over desegregation of the San Francisco public schools. In 1971 a federal judge warned the school district that they should begin preparing plans for desegregation of the schools. Several months later, he issued the order to prepare plans and set a six-week deadline for their completion. Because of the complexity of the task, the potentially explosive issues involved, and the short time available, the stress on the participants was enormous—and ambiguities were a considerable part of the problem.

As the case was written eight years after the events, participants' accounts may reflect their efforts to render prior confusions sensible in light of subsequent events. Newspaper accounts and documents written at the time provide some corrective triangulations. We are also fortunate that a dissertation on these events was written a year later by Stephen S. Weiner at Stanford.[1] My research assistant and I conducted interviews with many of the participants and found them eager to talk. For many, this experience had been a high point of their lives, and they remembered events with unusual vividness.

THE SCHOOL DISTRICT IN 1970-71

In 1970-71 the San Francisco Unified School District (SFUSD) was besieged with problems and crises. For the past decade, the SFUSD had been struggling with increasing pressures to desegregate the public schools and with violent opposition to desegregation. Vitally interested and determined community groups were active on both sides of the issue.

In September 1970 the district took a major step toward desegregation by opening the Richmond Complex, a group of 12 racially mixed schools serving over 5,000 students, or roughly 20 percent of the elementary school students in the district. About half of the students were to be bused to school. Various quality programs such as individualized tutoring, diagnostic reading, bilingual education, and day care were included to encourage integration. Although there had been frustrating delays and setbacks, the citizens' group that had planned the Complex and the board of education which had supported them were enthusiastic.

"We did the thing just the way it was supposed to be done!" said Zuretti Goosby, a black school board member. "We did it voluntarily and the teachers were charged up. It was innovative, creative . . . . People were anxious to put their children in public schools. We were going to try to sell the Richmond Complex plan to the city and do it in an exemplary fashion, and get rid of all the fears of fights and antisocial behavior. We were going to go year by year and spread it through the city."

However, Mayor Joseph Alioto was strong and public in his opposition to busing. "He felt he really had an issue," said Goosby. "And he exploited it to the fullest."[2]   At first, Alioto asked the board to delay implementing the Richmond Complex. Then he harassed and criticized the city board of supervisors, and finally the mayor urged parents to sue the board of education to prevent busing. "We will never allow busing in San Francisco!" was his media claim. The mayor's public threats, together with a delay in opening the second complex, represented the last straw to an impatient NAACP. They pressed forward with a suit already filed against the school district, demanding immediate desegregation of all the elementary schools in the city.

Even before the suit, the district was engaged in an administrative changeover. A few months before the Richmond Complex was scheduled to open, the superintendent of schools resigned. Out of hundreds of applications, the board of education picked Thomas

Shaheen to be the new superintendent. Shaheen had a reputation as a risk-taking, change-oriented administrator with a commitment to minorities and desegregation. He was brought in for the express purpose of furthering desegregation. Shaheen was very much aware of the limited tenure of school superintendents of large school districts, and of the fact that "he who desegregates is not around to integrate."

Shaheen, 53 years old, had most recently been superintendent of schools in Rockford, Illinois, where his busing program had been attacked as "too progressive." A newcomer to San Francisco, he was stepping into a troubled, politically complicated spot. One of the San Francisco newspapers, in reporting his appointment, described the situation:

> Never in the history of U.S. public education has the position of School Superintendent been fraught with such obstacles. Gone are the days when Superintendent was considered a position of reasonable security and tranquility.
>
> The single item of "equal education" has been the culprit that has brought on all this turmoil. Superintendents across the country have become targets for all kinds of severe harassments, vehement attacks by other public officials, and, in some cases, targets for violent threats and abuses.
>
> Therefore, it is imperative that this important position be filled with men of strength who can take such abuse and still remain objective and above all the din of public noises when it comes to making decisions that will affect the future of a school system.
>
> The San Francisco Board of Education believes, when it appointed Thomas A. Shaheen, that it has a man of such character. The test of his strength and educational wisdom will come in September when San Francisco schools begin to operate under the highly controversial "School Complex" program.[3]

As a new arrival, Shaheen had to get to know some 300 staff members and influential members of the community. Adding to the stress was the personal difficulty of going through a divorce. Still, the swearing-in ceremony was graced by music, felicitous words, and high hopes.

In August, federal judge Stanley Weigel met with attorneys from both sides in the NAACP suit. He urged them to work together to develop a plan for desegregating the schools starting in September 1971. "If the parties can work together," he said, "this is the best way to get these things done." As the *San Francisco Chronicle* reported, "And then he strongly hinted that, if they could not agree, he would not hesitate to order the desegregation . . . . But he stopped, deliberately and vaguely, short of saying he would order desegregation."[4]

Board members, even staunch desegregationists such as the board's president, Alan Nichols, argued for more time. He said, "I'd rather see many more people involved and a little longer time for phasing in such a massive program." When the attorney for the NAACP was told of the president's statement, he replied, "I have only two words for Mr. Nichols. The first begins with an 'F.' The second begins with an 'H.' "[5] A few days later the school board attorney reported that the district was financially "too broke" to integrate the schools by 1971.

The Richmond Complex opened in an atmosphere of relative calm, although a number of students and parents refused to comply with the new assignments and urged a boycott of the schools.

On September 22, 1970, Judge Weigel ruled in favor of the NAACP suit. He commented that if the Supreme Court authorized the use of busing—a decision that was expected the following spring—he would most likely order the desegregation of *all* the city's elementary schools for the following school year. Weigel stressed that the absence of a definitive ruling should not be misinterpreted, and he warned the board of education to prepare a student assignment plan that would racially balance the elementary schools.

The judge's warning was addressed to the two top policy-making bodies in the school district, the board of education and the school superintendents. Although desegregation and the movement of more than half the system's 85,000 students was likely to be a vital issue, the two groups did virtually nothing about it for the next three months.

The only top official who actively responded to the judge's warning was the head of the business department, Associate Superintendent Edgar Egly. Egly realized that any desegregation plan would require substantially more data on students' backgrounds and abilities and on the racial, ethnic, and social composition of the city than the district currently possessed. In fact, the school district's data files on students and staff were less adequate than almost anyone guessed. "We didn't even know how many teachers and staff we had," Tom Shaheen stated later.[6] Egly was interested in building up the district's electronic data processing capabilities, and this combined nicely with the need to collect data and develop plans for desegregation. He contacted Dr. David Bradwell, a planning consultant who had experience with the logistics of student files but no background in desegregation problems.

Bradwell, finding the existing data woefully inadequate, proposed extensive data collection and the formulation of quantitative operating criteria as first steps. Then, based on the data, alternative plans could be developed and submitted to the community and the school board. They could choose one plan and design implementation steps, while Bradwell would design evaluation procedures. Three months passed, and still the board took no action on desegregation.

At its mid-December meeting the board was swamped by crises and demands. There were antibusing boycotts, many schools were physically deteriorating, and a school bond issue had just been defeated at the polls. Teachers in the new complex protested a lack of funds for the promised "quality" programs. Discussion of desegregation planning did not begin until after midnight. Twelve civil rights groups including the NAACP demanded that the board finally begin planning for desegregation. They also demanded the immediate appointment of a citizens' advisory committee similar to the one that had planned the Richmond Complex. The board concurred and directed Superintendent Shaheen to prepare specific proposals for desegregation and "to report on January 14 on formation of a citizens' advisory committee to work with the administrators on planning."[7]

In late December, Superintendent Shaheen appointed Donald Johnson, planning officer for the Richmond Complex, to the new post of director of desegregation. Johnson was an integrationist and a competent administrator. Shaheen trusted Johnson to do a good job and didn't feel he needed to check on every detail. As he described it later:

> In my discussion with Don all the way through planning desegregation he led me to believe it made sense. I didn't have to go through reading the 50–60 pages, whatever was involved in this . . . My general pattern with good people is that I let them run with something until I have evidence to the contrary.[8]

Johnson was not relieved of his other duties and his staff consisted of one secretary. Furthermore, despite his protests, his budget was largely allocated to funding the electronic data processing work that Bradwell had begun. Johnson had a heavy load to pull but was given few horses.

In January, three committees were formed to work with Johnson. The first two, central staff and teachers, never played an active role. The third group, the Citizens' Advisory Committee (CAC), was composed of 46 citizens chosen by board members and Donald Johnson. Figure 6.1 diagrams relationships among the various individuals and groups in the school district who were working on desegregation. Although racially mixed, the CAC did not reflect the racial makeup of the city's schools. The CAC overrode Johnson's warnings about the shortness of time, dissolved itself, and asked the school board to reconstitute the committee to reflect the racial makeup of the schools. The appointees to the reconstituted committee tended to be friends of board members and of Johnson, and many had been prime movers in the fight for minority rights and desegregation during the 1960s. The more intransigent opponents of busing were not included in the reconstructed committee. Lacking a sense of urgency, the new advisory committee did not meet until March 15.

FIGURE 6.1. Partial Diagram of San Francisco School Administration, May 1971.

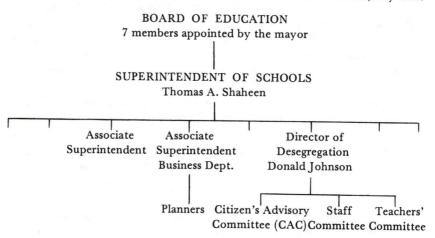

Note that not all the lines represent formal reporting relationships.
Donald Johnson, for example, could hardly be said to "control" the CAC.

At all levels in the school district hierarchy, very few people believed that the judge would order the schools to be desegregated in 1971. The time seemed impossibly short to do the detailed planning and careful implementation necessary for such a potentially explosive change. A state consultant called in to aid the planning process noted an air of unreality about the court order. "They couldn't believe that this was it." Nor did he sense any eagerness on the part of the staff to take on the responsibility for desegregation planning. "We discovered . . . that basic assumptions relative to goals, objectives, or guiding principles were only vaguely understood and not a part of the board's policy or the superintendent's directives for staff work."[9]

When the 67 members of the CAC met in March, their planning efforts lacked focus. Many members had a goal of integrating rather than simply desegregating the schools. To accomplish this, they were willing to consider many problems not intrinsically related to the court suit. For example, the committee discussed the possible use of educational innovations such as educational parks, magnet schools, individualized instruction, and so on. In addition, Chicano and Chinese parents wanted bilingual programs, and others wanted to integrate the school children along ethnic and socioeconomic as well as racial lines. Over the next five weeks the CAC met only five times and set no target dates for completing plans.

Reverend Donald Kuhn, a close associate of several board members and an accomplished group facilitator, was elected chairman of the CAC. His style in conducting meetings was to help discussion move in productive directions and to ensure that everyone had the chance to be heard. To cope with the demands and stresses of working in a public arena on issues such as busing, neighborhood schools, and racism, Rev. Kuhn sought the help of a close friend, the wife of a psychiatrist. She agreed to be his aide, attending daytime and nighttime meetings, helping with all the details, and offering support.

At the beginning of the year the swirls of crisis deepened around the school board administrators. In January, they learned that the district faced its most extreme financial crisis since the Depression, a $6.7 million budget deficit, without counting the money needed for busing and necessary school rehabilitation. In February the buildings and grounds department declared that as many as 62 schools might not meet earthquake standards. Since the district had often pleaded financial hardship in years past, many were skeptical of the urgency of the present financial crisis. In fact, the controller had so often cried wolf in past negotiations, only inexplicably to find millions afterwards, that the newspapers took to calling him "Goldfinger." In early 1971, teachers continued to demand higher salaries and smaller class sizes; parents called for rehabilitation of schools and new programs; and some desegregation planners continued to assume that integration would be achieved by educationally innovative but expensive programs.

In February, Shaheen began an attempt to reform the administrative structure of the district. On the basis of current and substantial anticipated drops in student enrollment, he saw a need to reduce staff and teachers. In March he proposed to demote or transfer more than 200 school administrators in what Jim Wood, education writer for the *San Francisco Examiner* called "the biggest shakeup in the district's history."[10] Administrators were stunned, and then reacted angrily through an attorney, threatening a legal challenge. The attorney added, "I have never seen a successful general who spent so much time attacking his lieutenants and sergeants."[11] Arguing that "the extra weight of administrative deadwood in the system is unwholesome, but Shaheen's approach is too abrupt," an editorial urged going slower and reducing staff through attrition.[12]

In rapid succession followed threats from the teachers' union of litigation over the proposed demotions, administrative resignations, and demands for hearings. Shaheen was forced to prepare an extremely austere budget for the district, mediate a teachers' strike that had two-thirds of the students and teachers out of school, and testify at the state hearings on the administrative tenure issue. "I've never been so exhausted in my life," he said.[13]

THE JUDGE'S RULING

On April 20, the Supreme Court approved the use of busing to achieve desegregation, and Judge Weigel announced that he would soon issue a desegregation order for September 1971. On April 28, Weigel ruled that the board of education should submit by June 10 a comprehensive plan for desegregation of the elementary schools. In case that plan proved unacceptable, he also asked the NAACP to submit a desegregation plan by the same date. The race had begun! The school district had six weeks to plan for a complex and potentially explosive undertaking.

Eleven days later, the *San Francisco Examiner and Chronicle* published an article by Jim Wood entitled "The Reason for Weigel's Ambiguity." Wood reported that school district officials were protesting that the judge's decision was ambiguous. Board of education representatives met with Weigel, but he refused to spell out in detail what he would require the schools to do. He said his job was not to run the school district, but to see that it headed in the proper direction. "It can be said authoritatively," Wood wrote, "that Weigel's refusal to detail what he expects is no accident. The judge ... believes that the schools themselves should have a chance to work out their own solution to integrating the district. . . . He has ruled that schools must have substantially the same proportion of black students, but again here is a deliberate blurring, leaving it up to the schools to come up with a satisfactory plan."[14]

The article went on to suggest, as an example, that the district might adopt the state's guideline for desegregation. The state of California had defined as racially imbalanced any school whose racial composition differed more than 15 percent from district-wide averages. But the judge did not require the adoption of this standard. Board members were highly discomforted by this ambiguity.

Because of the extraordinarily bad state of the district's files (in addition to the sheer lack of data, many files contained false information), Bradwell and the data processing staff were far behind schedule. According to the "rules" of rational planning, they could not begin to develop plans without a reliable data base on which to build, and clear guidelines for the work. The citizens' group felt no such constraints. Under the spur of the judge's order, the planning effort of the citizens' advisory group began in earnest despite the lack of formal data. "We turned into a 'do-business' outfit overnight," one of the members reported.[15]

A CORE GROUP FORMS

Early in its life the CAC had emphasized ethnic representation and equal access to the planning process. With the imposition of the June deadline, however, it became clear that time was short and the need for expert knowledge of the neighborhoods pressing.

In response, a small group of very active participants took command of the planning process and began meeting every day. The group included Donald Johnson, members of the staff committee and the data processing staff, and several white, middle- and upper-middle-class women. The women knew the city's neighborhoods and leaders intimately from years of civic efforts, and they could rearrange their family commitments to make a maximum amount of time available. Ironically, the minority members of the CAC were pushed to the background by the dominant experience, determination, and stamina of the white women. One minority woman explained:

> Their knowledge of the system was overwhelming. No matter how much you know you can't compete with them. They can read things ten times faster than anyone else. I consider myself one of the few minority people with a knowledge of the schools but next to them I'm a dum-dum.[16]

In the unstructured atmosphere of the core group those individuals who already had preferences and solutions, or rudimentary models of student assignment plans, were able to take the initiative. They gained control by acting in spite of the lack of formal data. "We just started working," said Naomi Lauter, one of the nucleus group that emerged. "I'm an organized kind of person and I see things spacially. . . . I just sat down and started figuring numbers. Myra Kopf did the same. And so we'd actually come to meetings with maps and figures."[17]

Members of the core group knew the city well and went forward on the basis of rough estimates. They began drawing maps of different zone configurations for schools, and in this way established the assumption that the city was to be divided into zones with no busing across zones. As new data appeared, they revised their maps accordingly. When information was needed, they would jump in a car and trace out a proposed bus route, or telephone personal contacts and acquaintances in the area in question. Members frequently met for breakfast in each other's homes during this period, and they kept up frequent, informal contacts with board members. "They were totally confident," said Donald Johnson, "because they knew as much as it was possible for anyone to know, and they knew that no one was going to drop a bunch of facts on them!"[18]

As the group devolved to a highly active few, they shed issues such as bilingual education, integrating with suburban schools, and educational innovations which were not essential to solving the desegregation problem. Core group members' intense immersion in the day-to-day problems of map-drawing further sharpened their knowledge and intuitive expertise in everything from the attitudes toward busing in various neighborhoods to the kinds of physical facilities in each school. They also became highly sensitive to the subtle differences between alternative desegregation plans.

Two basic approaches to desegregation began to emerge in the CAC. The school-complex approach stressed the creation of small contiguous zones that would decrease busing and preserve neighborhood schools. People supporting this approach were not concerned with meeting a numerical standard for desegregation, but with producing a plan that would be accepted without violence. A fear of "white flight" underlay most of their discussion but was rarely acknowledged explicitly, lest such a position be confused with racism. Most of the women in the core group and Donald Johnson favored this approach.

The second, more radical approach was favored by the technical staff people, state and federal professional planners, and most of the black members of the CAC. Their city-wide approach would create a few large zones, rely more on busing, and achieve greater ethnic and socioeconomic desegregation. Backers of this approach were less concerned with public acceptability of the plan than with achieving the maximum numerical desegregation.

The numerical standard by which it would be judged whether a school was desegregated was a continuous source of troublesome debate. The state guideline was reluctantly adopted by the CAC, but some felt that the 15 percent rule should be adhered to strictly or considered a minimum level of desegregation, while others thought it should be considered a rule of thumb to be altered if the "spirit of the law" were being followed. Naomi Lauter called a friend who had been on the state commission that formulated the guideline and asked if any research or educational theory lay behind it. "No," her friend told her, "it was completely arbitrary."[19]

Another split in the planning group was less clearly defined for the participants but contributed to misperceptions, polarized the group, and caused a rancorous explosion of feelings at the end of the planning process. The split was between what David Bradwell called technical or rational methods and personal or political ones. Bradwell felt that his programming approach, in which a computer assigned students according to certain broad general criteria, was technically and economically the most efficient method. He also felt it would produce the best racial and socioeconomic mix in the schools. The idea of a computer-generated solution had a rational, "in-control" flavor, and seemed to promise that decisions would be made impartially and "objectively."

What Bradwell needed for his computer approach were broadly applicable criteria and guidelines by which all the assignments would be made. But the core group of citizens refused to articulate or accept a criterion until its impact on different neighborhoods could be ascertained. Core group members were antagonistic to simply "putting people into computers." They believed in individualized decisions, responsive to the unique needs of different groups. "We were dealing with people, not numbers!" said Myra Kopf. "We dealt with the political reality of what was mixable and what wasn't. . . . It took people who understood the mechanics of putting together the *feelings* of the different communities to come up with a plan. . . . We were mainly concerned with acceptance on the part of the community."[20]

During the month of May the core group created and worked

over two dozen different desegregation plans. The data processing staff and Bradwell supplied actual block counts of students so that the exact racial/ethnic distributions for the proposed zones could be determined. The authors of the various plans would submit proposed changes in zone boundaries and the computer would process each plan modification and report new zone totals in about 45 minutes. Computer runs were frequently made at night, and in the morning the printouts would be compared and a new modification tried. To varying degrees, each author was trying to bring his or her plan within the state guidelines, trying to preserve the existing complexes, decrease the size of zones, increase socioeconomic integration, minimize busing, and respect the political factors associated with certain neighborhood boundaries.

David Bradwell's programming approach, however, was running into severe troubles. First, the data collection effort had absorbed most of the data processing staff's time. In addition, it was technically formidable, if not impossible, to write a program that incorporated all the idiosyncratic details of San Francisco's hilly geography and multiethnic politics. Worst of all, some of the objectives that the program attempted to include, such as minimization of busing and socioeconomic integration, were contradictory. The computer began spewing forth senseless assignments.

Len Hanlock of the data processing staff explained what happened next:

> We were able to allocate a certain percentage of students at which point the program just went into a loop and wasn't able to work its way out. It was starting to assign students in a very unrealistic manner at random which mathematically would make sense but in a real life situation wouldn't make any sense at all. It would produce the shortest distance and the most desegregated program, sure, but you could have a situation where you would have *one* kid from one block going to a different school from the kid across the street. It generated results where there would be discontiguous blocks from all over the city going in all different directions so we had to say, "At this point we have not achieved the ability to use the computer to make the assignments directly." So we abandoned that approach. We finally did the assignments visually and used judgment.[21]

PUBLIC MEETINGS ON THE PLANS

On May 18 seven plans were presented to the full 67-member CAC for review. Discussion was heated and at times angry. To avoid emotional overtones in the designations of the plans, they were given names drawn from California history. Naomi Lauter's "Sequoia" plan maintained the integrity of ethnic communities and minimized busing. But it was attacked because several of its attendance zones failed to meet the 15 percent guideline. Myra Kopf's "Horseshoe" plan divided the city into seven zones and included her son's school in a second complex—to be designed like the Richmond Complex. This was one of the issues that had brought her into the planning work. Like Sequoia, Horseshoe was attacked for failing to meet the state guideline. Saul Barnett of the staff presented "Poker Flat," which was unique in specifying only four basic zones. This made it possible for each zone to represent a racial and ethnic mix close to city-wide averages, but it required more busing. No agreement was reached on which plan to recommend to the board of education, and the committee eventually voted to recommend three plans at this time.

A resolution to integrate the secondary schools along with the elementary schools was discussed but dropped as unrealistic, given the time constraints. Once again, the committee jettisoned an issue as the deadline approached. "The time for abstractions was over," one member of the CAC observed. Len Hanlock commented:

> As we got closer and closer to reality, we had to concede on some of (our) ideals, still keeping in mind that we were supposed to develop an *integrated* school system. There were a lot of words, a lot of discussion about how we were going to integrate teachers, how we were going to develop educational programs, but when it got down to the bottom line it was moving students . . . just really trying to get the numbers to work out . . . that was the *big* problem, and that was the total emphases, as far as I could see.[22]

From May 18 until the end of the month, the core group members began to work around the clock—six to seven days per week, 14 to 16 hours a day. A night telephone line was installed in the planning room at the central district office. Busy days blended into nights filled with long meetings, in which CAC members presented their ideas and tried to assuage the fears of the community. Emotions built up as exhaustion set in. On one occasion, after working all day and evening, Bradwell was remonstrated for "leaving early." It was then 4 a.m. Meetings, discussions, phone calls, ideas, review sessions—a fever of activity encompassed the lives of the handful of full-time participants who stayed with the task. The data were inadequate, the resistance from the public—particularly the Chinese community—was becoming tangible, criteria for the plans were fuzzy and subject to change, communication with the board, staff and other CAC members was episodic, and families were becoming irritated.

The school district appealed to the court for more time to develop desegregation plans more carefully and to settle some additional problems that affected the district's ability to plan. The newspapers summarized the situation as follows:

> The district last August and September was warned by Judge Weigel to prepare for city-wide integration, but no serious effort was made until late this spring.
>
> As a result, the district now finds itself in a terrible bind.
>
> It has appropriated no adequate amount of money to integrate next September (the cost is estimated at $2.5 million, and the district will be lucky to come up with $500,000).
>
> There is doubt that buses will be available to carry out an integration order. Planning is stalled because schools which do not meet earthquake standards may be closed, thus disrupting any plan for pupil assignment.
>
> For a district that takes months to carry out the simplest actions (the radiators are still at winter full-blast in the district's headquarters), it seems an almost impossible deadline.[23]

During the last week of May, David Bradwell developed a new approach. His plan was considered radical because it created three large zones and required extensive cross-town busing in order to provide a more thorough socioeconomic mix than any of the other plans. "Tri-Star" combined into the same zone blocks from the heart of the four most volatile areas—Chinatown, the Chicano district, a black ghetto area, and the white community most resistant to busing. The combination was directly contrary to the conventional wisdom about how to sell a desegregation plan to the public in San Francisco.

The response to the Tri-Star plan clearly delineated the splits in the small planning group and the larger CAC. Tri-Star was attractive to the computer technicians because fewer and better-balanced zones would make individual school assignments an easier task. The state and federal planners clearly favored it because it made it possible to meet the state guidelines more precisely, and it did not insist on preserving the neighborhood school. The majority of the white women in the core group and Johnson were outraged with the Bradwell plan. They resented the fact that a technical consultant for the district had become an advocate for a particular plan; worse yet, his plan ignored all that they had been working to achieve in terms of community cooperation. Johnson commented:

> The day before my staff was going to make a recommendation . . . Bradwell walked up with his own plan and said, "This is better than yours because we're going to have more desegregation, better racial balance in the schools!" I said, "That's dumb. You will have more desegregation *assuming* that everybody goes where you assign them to go. But everyone is *not* going to go on the basis of the mass busing of kids. It's just not going to fly, David, forget it." We ignored his plan and went on with our own plans, and the next time we heard from him was in court.[24]

A group of federal consultants appeared in San Francisco on May 24 as a result of a request by Shaheen for extra federal money. They were unable to gain access to the planning and decision making process, which was already well advanced, and considered their visit "a waste of time."

On May 27, at the major CAC meeting for selecting the final plan to submit to the board, 500 angry protestors declared that the Chinese members of the CAC did not represent the Chinese community and that all the plans so far devised were unacceptable. After the protestors departed seven plans were distributed to the CAC for review, including four that were specifically recommended by the core group—Myra Kopf's Horseshoe plan (their first choice), Columbia, Poker Flat, and Monterey. Horseshoe created small contiguous zones and required relatively little busing but had serious problems in meeting state guidelines in one zone. Figure 6.2 shows a map of the Horseshoe zones. Advisory committee members wanted more time to understand what actual student assignments to specific schools would look like under each plan. The representative from data processing said that this was physically impossible at this time. Johnson added that there was only enough time to program the computer for one plan, if the CAC were to have a plan ready for the board by early June. The members adjourned at 1 a.m. without making a decision.

The CAC met again on the evening of June 1 for a final debate. The four plans recommended by the core group and the Tri-Star plan were presented by their authors. Naomi Lauter's Sequoia plan was also placed in the running because it had strong Chinese support. The debate was heated. Several black CAC members spoke in favor of Tri-Star because it was the most "drastic" plan. Others thought it was a ridiculous plan and would cut off community participation in

FIGURE 6.2. Busing Zones of the Horseshoe Plan

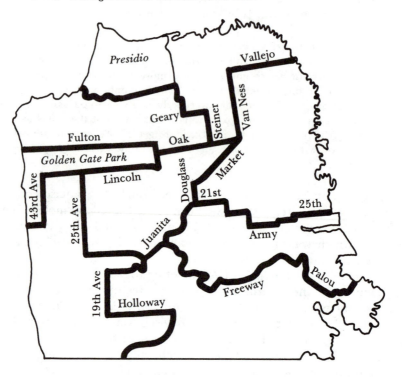

the schools. Paper ballots were passed out late in the evening, and the CAC members were asked to rank the plans in order of their preference for submission to the board of education. The Horseshoe plan received 16 first-place votes, Tri-Star 11, Sequoia 9, and Monterey 2. These four plans were approved and sent on to the board. The Horseshoe plan was seen as the compromise plan.

The board of education met on the evening of June 3, 1971, to consider publicly the recommendations of the Citizen's Advisory Committee amid the booing, shouting, and foot-stomping of 600 Chinese-American parents. Despite the commotion, which lasted until 11:30 p.m., Kuhn and Johnson presented the CAC recommendations concerning the four plans and the recommendations of the various subcommittees. Len Hanlock informed them that the data processing staff needed an immediate decision as to which plan was to be put into final form if they were to meet the deadline, six days away.

It was then 1:40 a.m. and the board had been meeting for a

marathon eight and one-half hours, three hours in the late afternoon and five and one-half hours after dinner. Claire Lilienthal of the board moved that the Horseshoe plan be submitted to the court with the stipulation that further adjustments would be made. Laurel Glass of the board agreed. "It was far from perfect," she said, "but there was no time left."[25]

The board's resolution was ambiguous. It did not approve a specific set of zone boundaries, but only the continued modification of the Horseshoe plan. Nor did the board adopt any of the CAC sub-committee reports (on personnel, bilingual education, etc.) that accompanied the Horseshoe plan. Fearing that the reports had been excluded, members of the CAC notified Judge Weigel's clerk that the court might not have received the subcommittee reports, and Weigel's office requested them.

In accordance with Judge Weigel's April 28 directive, the NAACP also prepared a plan for desegregation. Two Rhode Island educators, Myrl Herman and Howard Munzer, were retained by the NAACP and within three weeks completed their report, by June 14. The development of the NAACP plan (named the "Freedom" plan) involved no community participation. Munzer only visited San Francisco for 48 hours—and talked with Donald Kuhn, Donald Johnson, and the NAACP committee. Herman and Munzer had none of the block data that became available to the CAC in late May and instead used school attendance data collected in the fall of 1970 and the 1960 census tract data. The resulting plan was similar to the Tri-Star plan but adopted a much tighter standard for desegregation than the 15 percent state guideline. The total enrollment within each zone for each ethnic group was within 5 percent of the city-wide average.

Judge Weigel held a private session on June 21, 1971, to review the district plan and the NAACP plan. He expressed dissatisfaction with the board of education for "having done very little until after April 28 to get ready for the various contingencies that were foreseen and foreseeable . . . plainly foreseeable last September." Of himself he said, "I feel a sense of harassment by the tremendous number of problems on which I feel I have no grasp or expertise."[26]

The NAACP lawyer attacked the Horseshoe plan for barely meeting the state guideline and for the deficiencies in socioeconomic integration. The judge responded that he was concerned with racial balance, not socioeconomic balance. Another NAACP representative attacked the special treatment given the West Portal school. David Bradwell testified against the Horseshoe plan, thus greatly incensing several members of the core group.

At the end of the meeting Judge Weigel said that the NAACP plan was clearly better in terms of racial percentages, but he continued to press for changes in the Horseshoe plan. The Horseshoe plan went back to the drawing board. In particular, racial imbalance in one zone resulted from one core group member's insistence that children at the West Portal School, including her child, be assigned to the Park South Complex in another zone. Johnson directed the data processing staff to split the West Portal school attendance zone and make changes in other zones as well to improve the percentages. The altered Horseshoe plan was submitted to the judge on July 1.

On July 9, Judge Weigel issued his final judgment that both the Horseshoe plan and the NAACP plan were acceptable and the final choice was left to the board. He said that he and the SFUSD regarded Horseshoe as an "evolving" plan. The board chose the Horseshoe plan and proceeded to implement it on an emergency basis.

The Horseshoe plan did indeed evolve, but not in the way the judge or the board had hoped. When the schools opened in September 1971, white and Chinese parents refused to comply with even limited busing. Enrollment dropped by 6,000 students, and thousands more were applying for exemptions. As a result, in December 1971, 38 of the district's elementary schools failed to meet the state guideline.

BRIEF CHRONOLOGY

August 1970	Thomas Shaheen appointed Superintendent of Schools.
September 1970	Judge Weigel warns school district to begin planning for desegregation.
November 1970	David Bradwell is hired as a planning and computer consultant.
December 1970	Bradwell proposes computer model. Donald Johnson appointed director of desegregation.
January 1971	Superintendent names three committees including CAC, Citizen's Advisory Committee.
February 1971	CAC dissolves itself.
March 1971	New CAC has wide-ranging discussions.

April 1, 1971	Teachers' strike settled.
April 28, 1971	Judge Weigel orders school district and NAACP to prepare desegregation plans by June 10, 1971.
May 1971	Core group works intensely.
June 10, 1971	The judge's deadline for receiving plans.
July 9, 1971	Judge rules on plans.

Chapter **7**

Commentary on the San Francisco Case

Stress was abundant as the San Francisco school board tried to develop plans for desegregating its elementary schools. Goals were in conflict, information was inadequate, and participants were swamped with other crises. Although the boundaries of authority and power were clear at the beginning of the process, they soon became muddled as a deadline was imposed and requirements for participation changed.

As a first step in seeing how our theoretical understanding of ambiguity and stress applies to the San Francisco case, it may be helpful to refer back to the list in Chapter 1 of characteristics of ambiguous situations. Table 7.1 rates how troublesome each factor was for the participants in the desegregation planning process in the period before the judge issued his ruling. Ratings for the six-week period after the ruling would shift somewhat, reflecting a more clearly delimited and focused problem, the shedding of some goals, more time and attention made available, forced choices on standards, and even greater emotional turbulence.

Many of the twelve characteristics played an important role in the San Francisco case, as witnessed by the proliferation of three-star ratings in Table 7.1. In this highly political situation, the participants had to weigh and compare incommensurables in an emotionally charged atmosphere. Among the most troublesome problems were uncertainty as to the problem itself: what exactly were they trying or required to do; the clash of different value orientations on such an important issue as children; the shortage of time, attention and perhaps money; and contradictory demands flowing from the different value positions. In addition, communication problems arose from the tendency of school board members, the mayor, representatives of community groups and others to use the mass media to send messages and seek support. It was often hard to know who was communicating what to whom, what was real and what was said for effect.

REACTIONS OF THREE GROUPS

Not everyone reacted to this ambiguous, important, and stressful situation in the same way. The top administrators, the professional planners, and the citizens' group each tended to take a distinct approach to the problem, as summarized in Table 7.2.

The seven board of education members and the 12 school superintendents constituted the district's two highest policy-making bodies. Planning and implementing the desegregation of the schools was their responsibility. Two psychologists who evaluated the role of the school officials concluded:

> The pattern of response on the part of the bureaucrats appeared to be essentially a form of defensive avoidance based on feelings of hopelessness about arriving at a solution that would be satisfactory to all interested parties in the community. They permitted a power gap to develop by taking no active interest in the desegregation policy planning despite mounting signs that a deadline crisis would soon be at hand.[1]

This seems too harsh. The administrators did not despair of finding a solution, and several board members maintained *informal* contact with the citizen activists. With civil rights groups, newspaper writers, and the judge involved, the administrators could not simply ignore the problem even if they had wanted to. From their perspective the top administrators took action by delegating the problem—the board to superintendent of schools Shaheen, and Shaheen to director of desegregation Johnson. But they did not provide enough direction and resources, nor shield the process from attack.[2] In short, top administrators did not sufficiently engage a serious and urgent problem.

TABLE 7.1. Sources of Ambiguity in the San Francisco Case

Characteristic	Presence in Case	How Key or Troublesome?
1. Nature of problem is in question.	Densely interconnected mesh of problems that could be defined many different ways. Desegregation was itself an ambiguous term susceptible to many interpretations. What did it mean to desegregate? Did it include, or should it include, socioeconomic and ethnic mixing? Should it include the high schools as well as the elementary schools? The suburbs as well as the city? How did desegreation relate to integration? Were teachers, staff, and students all to be integrated?	***
2. Information (amount and reliability) is problematical.	Information about students and school facilities was outdated and unreliable. Planners did not think they could begin planning without much more reliable information.	**
3. Multiple, conflicting interpretations.	What did integration and desegregation mean? What was the proper standard for a desegregated school? These questions were discussed, but until a deadline was set, resolving these questions seemed less pressing.	*
4. Different value orientations, political/ emotional.	Issues balkanized city into warring camps. Demonstrations, threats of violence, yelling, and screaming charged the discussion.	***
5. Goals unclear, or multiple and conflicting.	Was the primary goal desegregation or integration or completing an *acceptable* plan? Must the plans be acceptable to the community, to the judge, to the NAACP, to the professionals, to all of these? In case of conflicts, what had priority?	**

6.	Time, money, or attention lacking.	How real was the $6.7 million deficit? How long did the school system have to plan? Would the judge set a deadline or not? What aspects of desegregation had priority?	***
7.	Contradictions and paradoxes appear.	Contradictory demands, urgently pressed, from Chinese, Hispanic, black, and white groups.	***
8.	Roles vague, responsibilities unclear.	The Board wanted to be heard but not seen. Was the basic responsibility for the plan Shaheen's or the other superintendents? Who had the power to make things move?	**
9.	Measures of success lacking.	Was success getting a plan done on time, getting a plan implemented without violence, or meeting the state guidelines precisely or in the spirit of the law? Was it desegregating or integrating the schools?	***
10.	Poor understanding of cause-effect relationships.	School officials, board members, and parents could not be sure of connections between special quality programs, extent of busing, and white and Chinese flight from the public schools.	**
11.	Symbols and metaphors used.	Desegregation came to have powerful symbolic meaning for racial and ethnic groups. For example, for some blacks, busing seemed to become a symbolic punishment due those who had committed past injustices.	**
12.	Participation in decisionmaking is fluid.	Before the deadline was set, many different actors or groups were popping up trying to influence events. After the deadline was set, stiff barriers to effective participation were erected.	**

***=greatly troublesome, **=moderately troublesome, *=slightly troublesome

TABLE 7.2.   Reactions of Three Groups to Desegregation Problem

Top Administrators (board and supervisors)	Professional Planners (Bradwell and others)	Citizens' Group (core group)
Largely ignored problem	Took rational systems approach on assumption that careful planning would produce a plan requiring little revision	Took flexible approach, which employed reason and intuition and readily accepted frequent revisions
Swamped by so many other problems, hoped this one would go away or could be delayed	Preferred to delay planning until accurate, comprehensive data base and careful measurements were available, i.e. preferred step-by-step orderly operation of reason	Began planning based on limited, out-of-date information and on personal impressions or knowledge; i.e., based on mixture of reason, intuition, experience
Believed in delegating the problem; appointed Johnson desegregation director		
Gave general support and encouragement, avoided getting into the details	Articulated general principles to inform planning process; their principles and implementation were separated	Suspicious of accepting general principles until they saw impact on neighborhoods; principles and implementation were intertwined
	Believed in being objective, fair—"go by the numbers"—and not considering acceptability of the solution as part of the problem (people *should* obey)	Believed in taking subjective passions and political realities into account in order to broaden acceptance

During the period covered by the case, Shaheen was preoccupied by a major battle over administrative reform. Many observers agreed that the school district was overburdened with administrators, and

Shaheen thought that he had been hired in large part to reform the structure. He was to some extent caught up in his own personal and professional myth of being a crusader, struggling against inept bureaucracy on behalf of the kids and minorities. With some pride he avoided politicking and currying favor with interest groups and powerful figures. Pragmatically, however, he may have been unwise to threaten the job security of so many central staffers at a time when teachers were talking of striking, and a great deal of staff help was needed to plan for desegregation.

Because they were caught up in other battles, administrators did not give desegregation planning sufficient attention. In some important ways, they avoided the problem.

The second group, the professional planners, suffered from constricted vision. Trapped by the blind spots of their professional training, they set up a large, intricate operation that required very substantial resources, long lead times, and a smooth environment. Yet the problem had none of these characteristics. In effect, they drew up plans for a racing Ferrari, when what they needed was a Land Rover. An all-terrain vehicle with four-wheel drive would have been less sleek and not one-quarter as fast on a smooth track, but it would have had a better chance of traversing the hilly terrain of the San Francisco desegregation problem.

The professional planners thought they needed a substantial data base before they could begin work. They abstracted the problem from its emotional and messy human context in order to deal with it technically. "Going by the numbers" and letting the computer make assignments "objectively" offered a certain appealing purity. For the planners the 15 percent standard was sacred, and they would gain professional satisfaction if their numbers could better that standard. They systematically set aside the political considerations and community passions that the citizens thought must be dealt with if a workable plan was to be devised. As planners defined the problem, acceptability to the community was not an issue. According to them, people *should* accept the solution that was right, fair, and objectively arrived at. Thanks to their efforts and those of the data processing staff, the citizens' committee acquired data invaluable for their planning. The professional planners had little influence, however, and were bewildered, frustrated, and ultimately embittered by the way events unfolded.

Of the three parties, the one that coped with stress and ambiguity most effectively was the core members of the citizens' group. The 67–member committee devolved down to seven to ten highly active participants. Core group members were drawn to each other by symmetries in background, personal philosophy, and their dreams for the city and its public schools. They were quite confident; and in a situation where responsibility was ambiguous they *took* the responsibility to plan for desegregation.

The core group operated in a largely democratic fashion. No one leader emerged although several strongly opinionated members made themselves heard. Major issues were confronted, and minor ones smoothed over. Unlike the planners, the citizens began working with the data on hand, even though it had serious shortcomings. To fill in gaps and correct the inadequacy of the data, core group members made inspection trips themselves, called acquaintances in the relevant neighborhoods, or approximated on the basis of judgment and good sense. They were remarkably adept at winning other people's help and at quickly revising their maps on the basis of new information. Born in a power vacuum, the core group became quite influential and in fact developed the plan eventually adopted.

Thus there were distinct differences in how people reacted to this messy situation, defined the problem, and began to plan. Of the three groups, only the core citizen committee felt more excitement than stress from the ambiguities of desegregation planning. Our model may suggest reasons for these differences.

USING THE STRESS MODEL

The model says that a stress episode begins with the interaction of a person and a disrupting event in the environment. For most important problems, clues about the appearance of a disrupting event come more than one at a time, awash in a sea of other alarms and noise. The judge's warning in September 1970 was just one in a long series of clues for the school administration including the NAACP suit, racial troubles in other big city school systems, and parental and student demonstrations. But, for the most part, dealing with such clues was postponed for a later time.

According to the model, the appraisal process determines whether a disruption is seen as largely threatening or challenging. Already strained to put the Richmond Complex into operation, people found the judge's September 1970 warning a potential last straw. Desegregating the whole school system at that time seemed too overwhelming a task to consider seriously. Most simply dismissed the idea. Interestingly, the one person who did respond to the judge's warning was a superintendent who saw the chance to realize a long-held plan of enlarging his data processing unit.

The administrators saw the April order as threatening because of their highly vulnerable position. The majority of parents opposed busing, and a powerful mayor was leading the attack. The citizens' group, on the other hand, found the judge's order challenging and displayed confidence, high energy, and commitment. For the professional planners, the desegregation planning process was mainly a time of frustration, since they favored a technical solution to the threat/challenge and could not persuade the power holders to accept this view.

The third element of the model is the response stage, at which people either engage, or do not engage, the problem. The top administrators' first response was essentially one of avoidance. Their failure to deal with the September warning provoked the NAACP to apply more pressure, directly and through other civil rights groups. The planners engaged *part* of the problem, having put on their professional blinders to define the problem technically. The citizens began in leisurely fashion to engage the situation. To say they "attacked" the problem would be an overstatement.

In response to the judge's April order, the administrators let the desegregation director and the citizens handle the problem. They encouraged the director's efforts, but did not deal either with details or policy. The citizens attacked the problem with a will, and the planners who stayed with the process became part of the citizens' effort.

Overall, the stress model in the San Francisco case helps explicate the stress/excitement of ambiguity. It is difficult, of course, to apply any model to the complexity and ambiguity of a real-life situation in a clean-cut way. If one remains faithful to the richness of the case, the lines that can be drawn are not definitive ones. Instead, one sees estimations and tendencies that the model helps identify, but which must be defined flexibly because the events themselves are not unalloyed. The case shows that appraisals can be mixtures of threat and challenge, and responses can be ambivalent combinations of engaging and not engaging the problem.

In Chapter 5 several specific findings about human performance under conditions of high stress were related to the model. Keeping in mind the inverted-U curve relationship between stress and performance, let us examine how these findings hold up in the San Francisco case.

TESTING SPECIFIC RESEARCH FINDINGS

Under conditions of high stress, individuals and groups will tend to fixate on one approach to a problem. Yes, the administrators and the citizens did focus on busing as the only tool to achieve integration. To be sure, this narrowing of attention was due to time pressure as well as stress. When the Citizens' Advisory Committee (CAC) began its work, before stress was high, they looked at a wide variety of means to achieve integration. But when the deadline was set, they narrowed down to busing.

Under conditions of high stress, individuals will tend to become rigid in their thinking. Since the administrators largely avoided the problem, this prediction does not apply to this case. When under attack, the planners redoubled their efforts to convince others that their approach was fair, objective, and fulfilled the spirit of the law. The core citizens' group, however, defied this prediction. Members were remarkable in their flexibility of thought and their willingness to revise maps on the basis of new data. In Chapter 11 we will examine more closely how some groups are able to avoid conformist groupthink and encourage flexible thinking even while under stress.

Under conditions of high stress, individuals and groups revert to more primitive cognitive organization (e.g., erratic scanning, a tendency to either/or thinking, seeking less novelty, and rejecting unpleasant messages). The emotionalism and stridency of the board's and the CAC's public meetings indicate the use of more primitive structures. In the CAC meetings, Rev. Kuhn's skills as a facilitator and his insistence that everyone be heard ameliorated the sense of rage and panic some parents felt. In private meetings the core group did not appear to revert to more primitive structures. Members appreciated and dealt with complexity, nuance, and ambiguity, and refused to dichotomize issues in either/or terms. Some weakness was evident, however, in their failure to deal explicitly with the unpleasant possibility of white flight.

A favorable reading of the balance of power between self and problem demands will encourage more active coping responses. Estimations of how Superintendent Shaheen read the balance of power are highly speculative. Seeing himself as a crusader brought in to carry out a dangerous and controversial mission, he did not expect to be around for very long. Citizens, on the other hand, did not have their careers at stake and were enormously confident. They had been successful in past civic efforts; and *no one* knew as much as they did about the schools, the neighborhoods, and the city. Shaheen, it seems, saw the balance of power as unfavorable and was less active in the planning stage; citizens saw the balance of power as favorable and were more active.

The social setting will influence the appraisal process. In the San Francisco case the social setting influenced the appraisal process substantially more than the model predicted. In particular, the case shows the importance of considering the *position or office* that a person holds in relation to the problem and *the stakes* associated with that position. Because their professional reputations and careers were at stake, the administrators found desegregation threatening. With tenure they should have felt secure in their jobs; but Shaheen's proposed administrative reform threatened their security and diverted their attention from the desegregation problem.

Organizations under stress try to increase control. No, this did not happen in the San Francisco case. In fact, Shaheen pushed control and responsibility lower in the organization. This discrepancy between model and reality may reflect a difference in management style or a difference between business organizations and educational systems. Weick calls the latter "loosely coupled systems," highlighting the absence of dense, tight connections in these organizations.[3] Loosely and tightly coupled systems may well respond quite differently to stress. The tightly coupled CAC group exerted a great deal of control over membership and participation in their decision-making.

Under conditions of high stress, groups will emphasize loyalty and good feelings over problem solving efforts. Again the core group did not fall prey to this tendency. Members felt they *had* to confront important disagreements because the problem could be aired in the public arena. If a member was not heard in the core group, she could find an audience at a public meeting or in the newspapers.

All in all, about half of the specific research findings on stress are confirmed in the San Francisco case. More interesting are the ways in which the core group and its individual members escaped the less functional tendencies of groups under pressure. Convened as a temporary problem solving body, the citizens' committee was a very special kind of group, whose reactions might well be expected to differ from those of a longer-term body. In addition, many members of the core group had worked together before the desegregation crisis, and could expect to work together on other civic issues in the future. Thus, in several key respects—notably the balance-of-power reading and the stakes involved—the core group members saw themselves operating under moderate stress, where performance is typically highest. They saw the situation as challenging and thought they were better equipped than anyone to deal with it.

OTHER IMPORTANT FEATURES OF THE CASE

The San Francisco case provides a good illustration of how groups construct and maintain a particular reality through social interaction. Participants colluded in pretending that feelings *did* not count because they *should* not count. In particular, the professional planners steadfastly refused to take account of the likelihood that many white and Chinese students would leave the school system if forced to bus, thereby undoing all the closely calculated racial counts the planners worked so hard to develop. Their technical mentality insisted on using planning tools in a rational, instrumental way.

The final weeks of planning were a time of intense, nearly all-consuming work during which some family relationships faltered and some very special friendships were established. Among the key players two divorces occurred, but it is difficult to know how much this can be attributed to the stress of those weeks. Many families were very supportive while their wives and mothers were off fighting the good fight. Donald Kuhn's wife said her husband was never happier than during this period of chairing the CAC. His strategy of enlisting an aide for continual support and his role as facilitator no doubt contributed to his strong positive feelings. While members of the core group argued with each other in private, they presented a united front to the often hostile outside world. The caring and support they showed each other inspired warm feelings and close friendships that endure to this day. For many of those involved, core group members and others, their participation in the planning process was a peak experience. Several felt a definite "flatness" or letdown afterwards, and one participant noticed a significant drop in creativity and productivity for the following six months.

The imposition of the June 10th deadline contributed to the stress, clarified some uncertainties, and created some new ambiguities. The deadline communicated the judge's seriousness, limited the time frame, and galvanized some people into action. Time pressure then forced participants to set aside secondary issues to concentrate on one main problem. As Weiner points out, the deadline also raised the entry barrier to participation.[4] When first formed, the citizens' group had permeable boundaries and was determinedly egalitarian. After the deadline was imposed, and the core group formed, real involvement in the planning process required an extraordinary time commitment and extensive knowledge of San Francisco. In effect, the deadline restricted community participation in planning for desegregation to a highly active few.

Several other features of the case seem important for our understanding of how people deal with ambiguity and will be examined more closely in later chapters. One such feature is the tremendous increase in the use of personal and informal procedures during the crisis. Anthony Downs has noted this as a tendency of bureaucracies:

> Whenever an organization's environment is changing rapidly in an unpredictable fashion, its formal rules of behavior normally lag behind the conditions in which it finds itself. Organizations operating in rapidly changing, highly uncertain environments tend to rely heavily on informal structure and procedures.
>
> Some informal devices spring up as means of implementing the organization's goals by filling gaps in the formal rules and adapting those rules to fit peculiar situations.[5]

Loosely coupled systems such as school districts are especially likely to employ informal procedures. In the San Francisco case, members of the CAC were chosen on the basis of personal friendship and acquaintance. Several core group members, in particular, were close friends of school board members and were in frequent, informal contact with them. The plan for desegregating San Francisco's schools was in effect created by a small, informal group that met over meals in each other's homes. The formal system was overwhelmed by other problems during this period, and informal connections were developed to carry the load.

This reliance on informal procedures depended on, and in turn fostered, the development of a network of people committed to desegregation, who actively exchanged information and favors. Crossing organizational lines and including full-time and part-time members, the network proved invaluable as a means of coping with the constraints on public discussion of desegregation.

Working in a chaotic, pressured environment is unsettling, and symbols often seem to offer some comfort. In the San Francisco case busing, neighborhood schools, parental control, computer programming, and even desegregation itself came to be emotionally loaded symbols, expressing deeply felt values and fears; for better or worse, they often blocked the possibility of more subtle discussion. The point is that strong feelings, once aroused, cannot be dealt with on a purely rational basis; chaos can only be managed if its symbolic and emotional aspects are taken into account.

LESSONS FROM THE SAN FRANCISCO CASE

One of the most important lessons of this case is that you cannot plan rationally in an irrational situation. That is, managers and planners cannot afford to disregard the irrational or the less-than-completely-rational elements in a situation. The attempt to be clear, logical, comprehensive, unemotional, and impersonal in reaching conclusions need not be abandoned; but it must be responsive to the lack of clarity inherent in multiple conflicting goals and paradoxical, symbolic, and emotionally intense issues. A planning formula—a mechanical sequence of steps to be taken—will not work. The most detailed blueprint is useless when uncertainty governs the building materials, the workers, the permits, and the funding.

Many people involved in this case encountered particular difficulty because they assumed, at least implicitly, a rational planning approach. They were tripped up, surprised and hurt when irrationality and arbitrariness played a large role, even though their own behavior was less than completely rational and consistent. To create a fixed point against which to work, some individuals hardened arbitrary guidelines into performance standards. Others turned to the scientific and objective magic of computer allocation.

As the mapping chapters emphasized, people often strain to accept definitions that promise to relieve threats to self-esteem, the anxiety of incompleteness, concerns about not being in control, or the threat of meaninglessness. Chaos and ambiguity are potential threats to an existing map and the order it provides, but they may also represent an opportunity for creative change.

The crux of the matter is how to use the opportunity. Should you maintain the map largely as it is, or suffer the "little death" required to establish a more complex and adequate picture than that represented by the original map? A severe stress reaction can undo the whole operation. (Recall the dynamics of a downward spiral.) Managers must do all they can to move from high perceived stress to the middle range where performance is highest. You can regulate your own emotional responses to some extent by taking some action, acting to discover goals, ordering part of the world over which you have control. Breathing exercises, meditation, humor, and emotional support from friends all help. In the first century A.D. the Greek Stoic philosopher Epictetus summed it up nicely, "It is not the things themselves which trouble us, but the opinions that we have about these things.''

An ambiguous problem often demands a radical shift in how we understand the world. If the stress in the situation is energizing rather than overwhelming, we may be able to create a new map. But how can an ambiguous problem be reframed? What, if anything, can be done to increase the chances that you will be able to escape the limits of the current paradigm? How does one jump up a level and redefine the problem in a more productive way? To answer these questions we will examine the creative process in the next three chapters.

Chapter 8

The Creative Process

Although often studied, creativity remains an essentially elusive and mysterious phenomenon. Writers of ancient Greece and Rome sought inspiration from the muses, and poets and researchers of modern times can share that feeling. Present-day managers, too, must grapple with how to respond creatively to the stresses caused by the disruption of their conceptual maps.

Psychological research on creativity has burgeoned since 1950, yet no single theory dominates the field. Creativity remains an essentially elusive quality that cannot be satisfactorily described by linear logic. The joy of creativity is that it leaps, dances, and surprises in ways that baffle and astound, delight, and amaze the purely logical in us. It is a stranger from a strange land, and a merry dancer to boot. No wonder the ancients prayed to the muses—who could know when or how they would respond to the call?

Most commentators agree that creativity is not a single point of inspiration. There may be moments—like that which inspired Archimedes' bathtub "Eureka!"—when elements of the solution suddenly click into place. But an examination of the entire thought process almost always reveals periods of strenuous, sustained mental activity before and after the moment of inspiration. Most investigators agree that thinking creatively is arduous physical work. Bruner, for example, tells of an author who obtains clearance from his doctor before throwing himself into the vigorous demands of writing a new novel.[1]

Almost all writers on the subject have seen the central features of creativity as antinomies or paradoxes. Something about the creative process involves integrating apparent opposites held in tension with each other. Ἀμτί means against and νόμοσ is the Greek word for law; antinomy, taken from these roots, means a contradiction between two laws, both of which seem equally necessary and reasonable. For example, creativity is often said to stem from "detached involvement," that is, when a person is simultaneously immersed in and psychologically distant from a problem.[2] Immersion is necessary for intimately knowing the ins and outs of the problem, and distance is necessary for seeing new possibilities.

This chapter focuses on creativity in ambiguous situations: how does creative thought transform fuzziness into something that can be handled and acted upon? We will seek an answer in a synthesis of the research literature on creativity, the reports of writers and artists, and some common-sense observations. Unlike some writers on the subject, I assume that creativity is widely distributed in the managerial population; even if conditions have hampered its growth, creative thinking can be restimulated.

CONDITIONS THAT FAVOR OR BLOCK CREATIVITY

Although the essence of creativity may ultimately remain a mystery, researchers have identified several conditions that favor its appearance. First and most importantly, people should be passionately engaged by their subject. In one of the best books on writing that I know, John Trimble makes the following his strongest recommendation:

> Pick a subject that *means* something to you, emotionally as well as intellectually. As in romancing, so in writing: you're most effective when your heart is in it. If you can't say of your topic, "Now *this* is something I really think is important," you're a fool to write on it, and you really don't need me to tell you.[3]

The same advice applies to managers working on business problems. Small problems don't intrigue, and they don't demand much creativity either. The bankers in Chapter 2 were excited about pioneering the first large-scale use of electronic banking in their region, and the results of their efforts were creative indeed.

Next, managers as creative thinkers must be immersed in the problem. This might seem an easy condition to satisfy, but the work of Mintzberg reminds us that a manager's attention is typically frag-mented among many competing ideas, concerns, and opportunities.[4] Geared to acting and keeping things moving, managers often fail to reflect deeply about their major ill-defined problems and so may not be immersed in a problem in a way that engenders creativity. Com-plicating the matter, creativity requires detachment as well as involvement. When a new framework of thought is needed, the problem-solver must avoid too narrow a focus, which would reduce the chances of seeing a new combination of ideas. In contrast to specific goal-directed thinking, an approach of "serious play" is more likely to allow new ideas to pop up anywhere among the materials of the problem.

According to Maslow, a creative thinker gives up conscious con-trol and allows himself to be dominated by the task rather than being dominated by ego-needs to rationally control it.[5] In this way, the creative attitude gives "permission" for thoughts to delve into the world of the poetic, the mythic, the primitive—the breeding ground for new thought combinations and new paradoxes. It's easy to see, then, the difficulties of applying creativity to many business situa-tions. To make the time to immerse oneself in an ambiguous problem and to give up trying to control a situation completely is a tall order for busy and aggressive executives. Those who are trying to create a new map must remove themselves, at least part of the time, from the bombardment of new stimuli and the pressure for immediate action.

Just as some conditions seem to foster creativity, others block or hinder it. First, a negative or nonsupportive atmosphere discourages creative ideas. For example, evaluations that raise hurt or defensive feelings hinder creative responses. Creativity seems to engage the intellectual and emotional sides of a person in rich interplay. If an evaluation knocks the emotional legs out from under a person, or sends him or her spinning in circles of self-doubt, hurt, or anger, the intellectual capacity to deal with nuance and complexity will soon be brought down.

A rigid separation of work and play also blocks creativity. We have already mentioned the need for serious play to deal with am-biguous problems. Ed Gordon, the research scientist on the High Technology project in Chapter 3, was a grand master at serious play. Colleagues kidded him about how much he enjoyed "playing in his [laboratory] sandbox." Work was such fun for Gordon that he thought nothing of pursuing his projects on his own time if company funding was not available. A spirit of play seems to relieve tension and allows one to acknowledge possible risks without being overcome by them. Play also taps a person's emotional side and energizes intellectual leaps, all of which is very useful for creatively attacking problems.

Another block to creative thinking is the tendency of groups to treat reality as defined by hard facts only. We have seen that each person's "reality" is in part a social construct. If a group is rigidly limited by common sense perceptions, members remain locked into familiar ways of patterning and understanding events. In our culture businessmen are praised for being pragmatic, tough-minded, and in control. Such attitudes devalue the sensitivity of the intuitive side in each of us and, research suggests, tend to decrease creativity.

Group dynamics also underlie another factor that works against creativity—conformity. Especially when a group feels under attack, members may band together and become intolerant of divergent thinking. Groups do not have to be conformist in their thinking, however. Maier and Hoffman have shown that the leader's attitude toward divergence is critical. Leaders who convey the attitude that divergent thinking is "troublesome" tend to have less effective problem solving groups than those who treat it as an opportunity for creative synthesis.[6]

THE QUALITIES OF A CREATIVE PERSON

In the 1950s and 1960s, a popular topic for research was the "traits" that distinguished especially creative people from the rest of the population. Twenty years of research, however, produced little that was useful—for example, in identifying which creative people to hire into your firm—and so the approach has fallen from favor.

A basic flaw in that research, I believe, was the assumption that writers, poets, and research scientists had certain distinctive personal traits that explained their creativity. The traits were viewed as inherent, stable aspects of personality that a few people had but most did not. In contrast, I take the view that creative capacity exists in everybody. Recasting the earlier research on traits, this chapter will view creativity as an interactive process between the person and surrounding conditions. We will explore what human qualities can be stimulated to produce more creative thinking.

Most studies of creativity report that courage in one form or another is highly important.[7] Sometimes this quality is described as ego strength, other times as stubbornness, independence, or a kind of arrogance. For creative persons, acceptance by others seems a minor consideration. Remember Lieutenant Simms fighting for the adoption of continuous aim firing in the Navy (Chapter 2). His bantam rooster personality made him willing to challenge and goad superior officers who could not appreciate the wisdom of the new system. Simms did not have a comfortable life with his fellows, nor, one suspects, did they find it easy to live with him. But his courage and ego strength shine through.

As we have seen, groups need a common map to function effectively. A creative person, in contrast, needs the strength to withstand a group's desire to maintain using a map already in place. This fits with Crutchfield's finding, possibly a tautology, that those who tend to conform are less creative. The extreme conformist has lower ego strength, is less able to cope with stress, and desires to avoid uncertainty and ambiguity at any cost. Such a person, according to Crutchfield, seeks strong anchors and can usually find a group willing to provide them in terms of established beliefs.[8] Being creative requires the courage to resist social pressures and to risk being alone. At the same time, a creative person often displays a kind of humility with regard to the problem—he or she shows a willingness to bow to "rules not of his own making."[9]

Creative people have often been found to possess high tolerance for ambiguity. In fact, in creative periods they seem to *prefer* ambiguity. I saw this most clearly in an organizational simulation I ran with MBA students.[10] For this game, the class was organized into five-person teams. Without announcing the fact, I had chosen teammates according to their test scores on tolerance for ambiguity. The team lowest in tolerance for ambiguity settled into work immediately, established a hierarchical organization, and made the most money of any team in the first two periods of the simulation.

The team highest in tolerance for ambiguity seemed to consist of many of the "mavericks" in the class. After great difficulty in deciding where to start, they eventually settled on trying to counterfeit the game money! In essence, they tried to transform a simulation designed to be rather stable and well-ordered into something more challenging and interesting for themselves. In my judgment, these students would be the hardest to manage of any of the teams in the simulation, but they were also the people I would most want working with me on a messy, ambiguous problem.

Creative people prefer ambiguity, disorder and assymetry; but the need for disorder is not anarchic. In one study more creative Air Force officers showed a positive liking for phenomenal fields where all is not in a good, geometrical kind of order. They expected that the apparent disorder would eventually yield to an order whose principle of organization could not at present be ascertained.[11] Rogers has also noted a creative person's delight in eventually bringing order to apparent chaos.[12]

The Myers-Briggs test of personality types has some interesting implications about creativity. Seventy-five percent of the general population show a preference for sensation; that is, knowledge that is built up through information received through the five senses. But 100 percent of architects, 93 percent of research scientists, and 90 percent of writers show a preference for intuition; that is, knowing developed through imagination and seeing the situation as a whole.[13] This is particularly interesting because the Myers-Briggs instrument was constructed according to a Jungian view of personality. Jung believed that both intuition and sensation are present in every person although one trait usually dominates. So while intuition may never replace sensation as the dominant way of knowing in a hard-nosed, facts-oriented person, the intuitive faculty can be strengthened through exercise. In fact, a person's growth and development proceeds by reconciling such opposites, according to Jung. This suggests that being more complex is desirable for creativity. The difficult trick is to combine in oneself such opposites as playfulness and rigorous discipline, intuition and analytical thinking.

More creative people do show a higher integration of opposites in their nature. For example, on the Minnesota Multiphasic Personality Inventory, a comprehensive personality test, creative men score higher on the scale measuring feminine interests than less creative men do.[14] Integrating the oppositions within the self enables a person to acknowledge the oppositions in the surrounding world.

Creative persons also use what Freudians call the primary process. This is the realm of imagining, where thinking is nonlogical and moves according to mechanisms common to dreaming. But creativity is more than proliferating new ideas. One must also select among the ideas and work hard to transform the primary process imaginings into something useful. Professor Sidney Parnes discovered this through his experience teaching a four–semester course designed to stimulate creativity in students at the State University College at Buffalo. From the start the program was successful in stimulating students to generate new ideas, but few ideas were ever translated into completed projects. Over the years the program has been modified to put greater emphasis on instilling judgment in students in order to balance the proliferation of new ideas.[15] Impulse without the discipline of judgment and hard work is never likely to amount to much, especially in a managerial setting.

We begin to see, then, a constellation of qualities that fit together, sometimes in paradoxical combinations, to foster creativity:

- self-confidence and courage in resisting pressures to conform
- humility in bowing to rules not of your own making
- ability to tolerate disorder and ambiguity
- use of intuition
- integration of opposites in the personality
- willingness to work hard
- disciplined impulse

THE CREATIVE PROCESS

How are these qualities used in the creative process? What steps are taken in generating new ideas or new approaches to a stubbornly ill-defined problem? It is useful to think of the process as occurring in several overlapping and interacting phases, as diagrammed below:

UNCONSCIOUS SCANNING   INTUITION   INSIGHT   LOGICAL FORMULATION

Each phase has its own character, demands, and dilemmas. The first two phases are the most complex and require the most attention. As we shall see, some phases require certain parts of the self to play a stronger role than others.

Unconscious Scanning.   This initial phase is the hardest to describe because it occurs outside conscious awareness. Yet most who have studied creativity agree that the unconscious is a crucial, although necessarily mysterious, source of "effective surprise." To borrow John Fowles's metaphor, the unconscious can be likened to the green chaos of an untamed woods. Boundaries are blurred, trees seem to meld together, the silences and the spaces interconnect in a way that antedates words, classification, scientific or logical understanding. According to such a view, the woods and the unconscious should be seen whole and are "irrational, uncontrollable, incalculable."[16] The unconscious is also a place of fantasy and play in which the mind connects, puns, condenses, and symbolizes in surrealistic and dream-like ways. Such a woods may have rules, but they are not the rules of logic or systematic inquiry.

Anton Ehrenzweig, an art teacher versed in Gestalt psychology and psychoanalysis, argues that logic is too slow-moving and requires more precision than is possible in a world of complex and fuzzy boundaries.[17] Pointing to experiments on subliminal perception, he argues that unconscious vision scans more widely and gathers more information than conscious attention ever could. Because unconscious scanning does not differentiate between figure and ground, and is comprehensive rather than detailed, it can handle open structures with blurred boundaries. The process, if effective, is not completely open-ended, but is guided by the individual's interest and sense of relevance.

Both Fowles and Ehrenzweig deplore the tendency to rush in and name, classify, and measure wildness. On the other hand, classroom teaching and pragmatic approaches often emphasize the need for precision and clarity of boundaries. Here is a world and a faculty that operates best with blurred boundaries and playful impressions. The unconscious can cover a lot of ground quickly, not just tolerating but *using* fuzziness and disorder to find surprising combinations. As Novak summarizes the matter, "Precision is often useful, ambiguity is often creative."[18] In the early stages of problem finding, ambiguity, blurred boundaries, and open structures foster creativity.

Some authors have gone so far as to suggest that most of what we call thinking occurs outside of the conscious stream.[19] If you include the inference-making quality of mind that we discussed in the mapping chapters, such an argument does not seem far-fetched. Artists and others who are practiced in delving into the unconscious have often testified to its importance. Amy Lowell, for example, did not know how she or anyone else wrote a poem:

> What I do know about them is only a millionth part of what there must be to know. I meet them where they touch consciousness, and that is already a considerable distance along the road of evolution.[20]

For unconscious scanning to work, the mind must be immersed in the problem materials. In one of the more interesting experiments on the creative process, researchers presented fine art students with a table of objects and asked them to create a drawing. Those who produced the most original drawing (as judged by a panel of experts) handled more objects, explored them more carefully, and chose to work with the most unusual objects.[21] The more creative students became familiar with their materials in ways that would be difficult to capture in words. They spent more time in the problem-finding or problem-formulation stage. In contrast, managers often feel impelled to move immediately to *solving* a problem.

Managers' most common failing in responding to an ambiguous problem is to settle on an approach prematurely because they are impatient to act. They may think they are being pragmatic, data based, and task oriented in moving so quickly to goal-focused thinking. But most of the evidence on creativity, especially with regard to ill-defined problems, argues that one should tolerate the frustration of disharmony and take time to "play" longer with the problem materials.

Intuition. The second phase of the creative process, intuition, shares some characteristics with the unconscious scanning phase, and bridges the unconscious and the conscious realms. A useful way to see how this phase proceeds may be to look at an outstanding example of creative work—Alfred Sloan's development of the decentralized divisional structure for General Motors.

Sloan's autobiography gives a lengthy account of how he formulated this structure, which has been so widely copied in business. At the time, Sloan was 45 years old and executive vice president of fledgling General Motors:

> At the close of the year 1920 the task before General Motors was reorganization. As things stood, the corporation faced simultaneously an economic slump on the outside and a management crisis on the inside.
>
> The automobile market had nearly vanished and with it our income. Most of our plants and those of the industry were shut down or assembling a small number of cars out of semifinished materials in the plants. We were loaded with high priced inventory and commitments at the old inflated price level. We were short of cash. We had a confused product line. There was a lack of control and of any means of control in operations and finance, and a lack of adequate information about anything. In short, there was just about as much crisis, inside and outside, as you could wish for if you liked that sort of thing. . . .
>
> Confidence and caution formed my attitude in 1920. We could not control the environment, or predict its changes precisely, but we could seek the flexibility to survive fluctuations in business.
>
> The immediate future of the automobile market was, to say the least, uncertain. However, we believed in the future of the product as well as of the economy. I mentioned this because confidence is an important element in business; it may on occasion make the difference between one man's success and another's failure.
>
> In the great expansion in General Motors between 1918 and 1920, I had been struck by the disparity between substance and form; plenty of substance and little form. I became convinced that the corporation

could not continue to grow and survive unless it was better organized, and it was apparent that no one was giving that subject the attention it needed. . . .

In the midst of this welter of thought and attempted action, and a half year before the actual economic and management crisis began, I drafted the "Organization Study" and circulated it unofficially. It became a kind of "best seller" in the corporation all during 1920; I received numerous letters from executives requesting copies of it, so many, in fact, that I found it necessary to reproduce it in quantity.

Sloan quoted from the report:

The basis upon which this study has been made is founded upon two principles, which are stated as follows:

1. The responsibility attached to the chief executive of each operation shall in no way be limited. Each such organization headed by its chief executive shall be complete in every necessary function and enable[d] to exercise its full initiative and logical development.
2. Certain central organization functions are absolutely essential to the logical development and proper control of the Corporation's activities.

This does not need much interpretation. It asks first for a line of authority, co-ordination, and the retention of the effectiveness of the then prevailing total decentralization. But looking back on the text of the two basic principles, after all these years, I am amused to see that the language is contradictory, and that its very contradiction is the crux of the matter. In point 1, I maximize decentralization of divisional operations in the words "shall in no way be limited." In point 2, I proceed to limit the responsibility of divisional chief executives in the expression "proper control." The language of organization has always suffered some want of words to express the true facts and circumstances of human interaction. One usually asserts one aspect or another of it at different times, such as the absolute independence of the part, and again the need of co-ordination, and again the concept of the whole with a guiding center. Interaction, however, is the thing, and with some reservation about the language and details I still stand on the fundamentals of what I wrote in the study. Its basic principles are in touch with the central problem of management as I have known it to this day. . . .

The actual forms of organization that were to evolve in the future under a new administration—what exactly, for example, would remain a divisional responsibility and what would be co-ordinated, and what would be policy and what would be administration—could not be deduced by a process of logic from the "Organization Study." Even mistakes played a large part in the actual events, as I shall show.[22]

Sloan and other General Motors managers faced a messy, disordered, and economically bleak situation in 1918–20. He perceived the disorder as a challenge rather than a threat, however, and approached the problem with a deeply felt conviction that the future belonged to the automobile.

Sloan recognized an organizational problem/opportunity that others missed, and he found the right elements to move from disorder and crisis to laying the foundation for a modern industrial giant. Key to his efforts, and to our understanding of the intuitive phase of creative thinking, is the contradictory tension between the first two principles of his organizational study. Sloan implies that at the time he was not fully aware of the contradiction between decentralized divisional operations and centralized corporate control. In retrospect, he notes, "I am amused to see that the language is contradictory, and that its very contradiction is the crux of the matter." Many creative ideas seem to arise from just such essential contradictions, which often characterize the early phases of the creative process.

Psychiatrist Albert Rothenberg has studied creativity through experimental research and by interviewing artists and scientists over many weeks about their current work. He finds that "janusian thinking lies at the heart of the most striking creative breakthroughs. . . . " Just as the Roman god Janus was usually depicted as having two faces, looking both forward and backward at the same time, (making him an apt doorway ornament) janusian thinking conceives two or more opposites or antitheses *simultaneously*, either as "existing side by side, or as equally operative, valid, or true."[23] Sloan's thinking about GM's organizational problem is a good example of janusian thinking.

Rothenberg says that janusian concepts appear early in the creative process and must undergo further elaboration and transformation. And so it was with Sloan's new organizational structure. The actual forms of organization evolved over time, were not logically deduced from the principles of the study, and sometimes resulted from mistakes. Rothenberg also points out that the selection of which opposites to bring together is key. Who can say how Sloan was able simultaneously to embrace those two opposing principles? Once formulated they became widely accepted in the organization. The popularity of the report—it became a "best seller"—attests to its compelling reasonableness and hints at Sloan's persuasiveness with other General Motors managers.

Further testimony to the key role played by contradictory tensions comes from Arthur Koestler, a novelist, biographer, and writer. He says creativity occurs when two contexts unexpectedly and explosively collide in a person who is not level-headed, but "multi-level-headed." A reasonable person, being level-headed, deals with only one context at a time; he or she inhabits an objective, rationally consistent world.[24] In contrast, a person in creative moments lives in two contexts at once and tries to bring them together in creative invention. Sloan had had experience both as the head of his own small business and as a member of the executive committee of pluralistic GM, and could imaginatively perceive in two contexts at once. Instead of forgetting the lessons of autonomy he learned from running his own business when he joined the GM corporate hierarchy, he positioned himself in the doorway, facing in two directions at once, and formulated a new management structure and policy.

So far we have noted two important characteristics of the intuitive stage of the creative process: an ability to combine two contexts, even though they may seem to be contradictory, and a sense for which combinations will be productive. The chances for a productive combination are enhanced if one can tolerate frustration and disorder—hence the significance of being able to accept ambiguity. Divergent problems offend the logical mind, so a person behaving logically moves to clarify matters.[25] More likely than not, he or she will let one context become primary and fall back upon a familiar and level-headed way of handling a situation. But for ill-defined, divergent problems that require creative thinking, the person who can accept both sides and tolerate disorder stands a better chance of finding a productive combination when scanning through the materials. One also needs a sense for which combinations can turn into something useful. Sloan began working on the organizational problem when it was receiving little attention from other managers at General Motors. In the electronic banking example in Chapter 2, the new president had a sense that the time was right for electronic banking, even though for others the shiny promise of EFTS had dulled after more than eight years of anticipation.

Metaphoric thinking can be most helpful when looking for productive combinations. Metaphors, analogies, puns, and imagery follow symbolic, artistic, dream-like rules rather than those of logic. They offer the delights of surprising combinations and stretch the limits of language (as Sloan seemed to want to do in stating his principles). Metaphors capture feelings, and in the murky world of divergent problems, feelings are as important as thoughts and chains of logical reasoning. In fact, at this early stage, it may not be possible to separate the two. As our discussion of stress showed, in highly ambiguous situations a person's values play a large role and are often signaled by feelings. In the example of Chapter 2, managers preferred the risks of starting their own electronic banking system to the horror of becoming the "captives" of another bank's system. That metaphor said something very important about their values and they acted in accordance with their strong feelings.

Metaphors and their near relations contribute to the creative process in three ways. First, they condense a great deal of experience and feeling into an economical symbol or phrase which honors the brain's easily overloaded capacity. Second, metaphors can move thinking out of rutted channels by suggesting new combinations. They playfully take up connections that linear logic might reject or take years to realize. Third, metaphors often serve to bridge the conscious and unconscious realms. They can become the route by which the efforts of unconscious scanning cross over into conscious awareness. They can be stretched out, joked with, turned on their heads, added to, and eventually transformed into something logic can develop more fully.

For these reasons, practical attempts to foster creativity emphasize the cultivation of metaphoric thinking. Work by Gordon, Prince, Adams, Osborne, and others gives ample proof that a nonevaluative atmosphere and a deliberate seeking of metaphors can stimulate their production.[26] Many of these methods, such as synectics and brainstorming, use a group setting, feelings, interpersonal support, and stimulation to encourage metaphoric thinking.

At this stage one must relax and give up the effort to control and consciously think through everything. Unconscious attention roams widely and interacts at points with conscious attention. One develops hunches, metaphors, and intuitions, which should be pulled into conscious attention and explored more thoroughly.

Both unconscious scanning and intuition need time to work. In both phases, the mind must operate with a certain looseness, with attention roaming over a diverse range of materials. You are less likely to see new combinations if you are highly goal-focused or insist on precision early in the process. A diverse set of materials for thought, deep immersion in the problem, and an embrace of essential contradiction all seem to aid unconscious scanning and intuition. Intuition is a mode of thinking that a manager can develop and foster through intelligent practice.

Insight.   The third phase of the creative process is insight. Sometimes insight comes in a sudden flash but ordinarily hard work is the rule both before and after the magic moment. The appearance of insight is unpredictable, and it is not clear that anything can be done to hasten its approach, beyond fostering the general conditions conducive to creativity. Insight often comes during a moment of dispersed attention while the mind is seemingly not focused on the problem to be solved.[27] Then, all of a sudden, some ideas fit together. Buckminster Fuller has suggested that the new idea generally fades away in about eight minutes. With inspiration so evanescent, many writers are careful to have notebooks or pads of paper easily available in their living and work spaces. Others have found that keeping a record or notebook of ideas is an effective way of capturing occasional insights. From time to time the journal is searched for ideas that may build into a significant new insight.

Logical Formulation.   Of course, the creative process does not end with a moment of revelation. From the vantage point of a new insight, one should be able to see new evidence. Because there is more to seeing than meets the eyeball, a new insight should direct the discovery of new "facts." Furthermore, the insight must be tested, extended, and perhaps restructured as evidence accumulates. Like most managers, a new insight has no automatic authority. It must be strengthened, the dead ends eliminated, the weeds and underbrush cleared, and more direct and economical ways found to state the argument. In Bruner's terms, the insights of the wild, intuitive, nonlogical left hand must be tamed by the logic and precision of right-hand ways of knowing.

This kind of transfer and transformation is captured by the distinction some sociologists make between the context of discovery and the context of justification. The creative part of sociological and indeed other scientific work takes place mainly in the context of discovery, where the unconscious, intuition, and insight are at work in ways I have described. When findings are publically presented, however, these creative insights must be proved. Therefore, in writing up their research, scientists logically test and examine their own work, connect it to the work of others, and invite criticism and additions from other members of the community. This procedure is only a more formalized and therefore more visible version of a process that must occur in any social institution.

Similarly, in a business organization, the insight of an individual or small group must frequently be recast to gain wider acceptance. Clearly, the spread of a new idea does not depend entirely upon its logical structure. We have already seen that the first adoption of EFTS by the bank president was *not* based on logically indisputable evidence. However, an insight does need to be stated in terms that will be understood. Sloan's organization study, for example, emerged from thinking through an insight to the point at which it could be publicly presented in reasonable, persuasive arguments. The report was written with an eye toward what would be acceptable within the organization, to other managers, and to the GM president.

We are all potentially creative. By understanding the environmental conditions that favor creativity, and the steps through which the creative process characteristically moves, managers may be better able to transform that potential to a reality.

Chapter **9**

The Evolution
of Charles Darwin

As in our examination of mapping and stress, we can test our under-standing of creativity by applying the conceptual framework to a specific case. Here we move into dangerous waters. Because most accounts of creative work are retrospective, one must suspect that the artist, inventor, or entrepreneur has inadvertently done what we all do—made sense of chaotic happenstance in light of subsequent events. This difficulty is avoided by laboratory experiments that ask a person to record his or her thought process while working on a puzzle. But from our perspective these experiments have at least two disadvantages. First, participants in the experiments typically try to solve a puzzle, and a puzzle is logically distinct from a mess. Second, in comparison with the managerial situations that concern us, the puzzle is generally trivial, requiring only 10 to 30 minutes to solve. Another major difficulty in finding a "test case" for creativity is that much of the creative process occurs in the unconscious and is there-fore not likely to be part of any private or public record. We can only hope for fragmentary traces of the early parts of the process.

Fortunately, we have a case that goes a long way toward meeting these objections. In the middle of the nineteenth century, Charles Darwin created a new map showing how life on earth came to exist in its current forms. His theory of evolution through natural selection represented a profound change in how man viewed his world. It was a messy problem and not just a puzzle, for it represented a paradigm shift and a revolutionary break in scientific thought. Perhaps more importantly for our purposes, Darwin's method of intellectual capital-building was to keep notebooks in which he recorded his thoughts nearly day by day. Thus, we have a running account of the issues, questions, and observations he was making long before he consciously began to develop his theory of evolution. Along with ideas that eventually proved fruitful, his journal records stray thoughts, dead ends, and mistaken ideas. We are also most fortunate in having an excellent study of these journals by psychologist Howard E. Gruber. The case in this chapter draws heavily from his 1974 book *Darwin on Man: A Psychological Study of Scientific Creativity* as well as from the primary sources of Darwin's journals, notebooks, and letters.[1]

Darwin's experience is fascinating as one of the most significant intellectual achievements of modern times. It is especially useful for our purposes because the need to develop a new paradigm resembles the problem faced by a manager coping with ambiguity. Given our special interest in the creative process, the reader should ask: how well does the evidence of the Darwin case fit the proposed model of the creative process?

- Did Darwin immerse himself in the project?
- How did he become aware of the problem in the first place?
- Was he dominated by the task?
- Did he show detached involvement and, if so, what involved him and how did he detach himself?

Although evidence is likely to be scarce, check for clues to his unconscious scanning process. Look for paradox, antinomy, and janusian thinking.

In all fairness, we cannot expect Darwin's creative process to show all these characteristics. That would assume that creativity works the same way in every individual. But it is likely to be educational to test our ideas about creativity against the events of a specific case.

Darwin's search was replete with mistakes and happy accidents, overlooked the obvious, encountered both generosity and meanness of character, elicited marvelous flexibilities, and ran into unaccountable rigidities of thought. To some extent it is an account of how Darwin educated and formed himself to do his life's work. Hard work was rewarded, but the rewards were mixed. This is a story of how a young man with a modest conception of his own abilities—but with a thirst to make a mark—trained himself to be a discoverer, gained confidence in his distinctive abilities, and wound up formulating one of the most important theories of modern times.

DARWIN'S EARLY YEARS

Charles Darwin was born into a wealthy family at Shrewsbury, England in 1809. In his *Autobiography*, written in his old age for his children and grandchildren, he recalled that, "As a little boy I was much given to inventing deliberate falsehoods, and this was always done for the sake of causing excitement."[2] Because his mother was an invalid, much of his early education was taken over by his sister, Caroline, who was nine years older. Of this experience Darwin wrote:

> She was too zealous in trying to improve me; for I clearly remember after this long interval of years, saying to myself when about to enter a room where she was—"What will she blame me for now?" and I made myself dogged so as not to care what she might say.[3]

When Darwin was eight, his mother died, and he began attending a local day school which, in the tradition of the first half of the nineteenth century, was oriented toward studying the classics in the original Greek and Latin. He did not do well in his schoolboy studies; both his father and his teacher considered him below average in intelligence. Helping his older brother Erasmus conduct chemistry experiments was far more interesting to young Charles than his school lessons and was probably his earliest exposure to science. As a small boy, Darwin was an avid collector of "all sorts of things, shells, seals, franks, coins, and minerals."[4] He was also fond of natural history, the family estate being extensively planted in fruits and flowers.

Darwin's father, a respected physician who had himself hated medicine at first, strongly urged Charles to become a physician. Bowing to his father's wishes, Charles entered Edinburgh University. In his second year he became so nauseated by the operating room that he determined he would never become a physician. Although Charles was lukewarm in his religious beliefs, his father then proposed that he should attend Cambridge and become a clergyman. From the perspective of old age, Darwin judged his academic studies at Edinburgh and Cambridge to have been a waste of time. Still he appears to have put his time outside of class to good use. Companions and teachers at the university deepened his passion for natural history, and he was especially fond of collecting beetles. At Edinburgh he paid for some lessons in taxidermy and made friends with the curator of a local museum of natural history. As an undergraduate, Darwin attended meetings of several societies, such as the Plinian Society, most of them devoted to the study of natural history. He also went on geological field trips with a Professor Grant and probably learned some rudiments of geology.

In fact, Darwin managed to have a great deal of informal contact with several of his professors. The most important was John Henslow, a young professor of botany at Cambridge. The two became friends, and Darwin often accompanied Henslow on long walks and field trips, frequently staying for dinner with the Henslow family. Some of these dinners and walks were shared with distinguished visiting intellectuals, and Darwin was allowed to join in the conversation.

From contacts through Henslow, his reading, and other sources, Darwin became conversant with the intellectual currents of the time in natural history. The gradual evolution of life forms over time was considered a possibility by some, but the evidence was flimsy and no one could say how the process might work. Darwin finished his studies at Cambridge in 1831 with no firm idea of what he would do. His father worried that he would not amount to anything and at least one of his professors thought there was a risk Darwin would turn out an idle man.

Darwin spent the summer of 1831 encouraging his friends, including Henslow, to make a field trip to the Canary Islands. He also accompanied Professor Sedgwick, who later became a bitter opponent of his theory of evolution, on a geological field trip through northwestern Wales. Upon his return he found a letter from Henslow.

Henslow had recommended Darwin for a position as a gentleman naturalist on a map-making and surveying expedition that would sail around the world. (His wife had persuaded Henslow not to make the voyage himself.) The naturalist was to share meals with, and be a companion to, the ship's captain, Robert FitzRoy. A man of exceptional early promise, and from the right sort of family, FitzRoy had been given command of the expedition at the young age of 26. He would personally pay the costs of including the naturalist in the voyage, which would take two years or longer. Henslow urged Darwin to take advantage of this rare opportunity.

Darwin was tremendously excited, but his father ruled it out as a wild scheme. Fortunately, Darwin's maternal uncle was able to persuade Dr. Darwin that such a voyage could be a maturing experience and not out of keeping with the pursuits a country parson might later follow as an avocation. Charles had a favorable interview with FitzRoy, in which each was impressed with the other, and the voyage was agreed upon.

THE VOYAGE OF THE BEAGLE

In a rush of activity Darwin assembled scientific tools, gear, and books for the voyage. He had a sense that this could be an important new beginning. In a letter to FitzRoy asking about the details of equipping himself for the voyage, Darwin closed by writing, "What a glorious day the 4th of November [the original sailing date] will be to me! My second life will then commence, and it shall be as a birthday for the rest of my life."[5]

The enthusiastic naturalist resolved to make better use of his time than he had at the university. In his diary he wrote:

> If I have not energy enough to make myself steadily industrious during the voyage, how great and uncommon an opportunity of improving myself shall I throw away. May this never for one moment escape my mind and then perhaps I may have the same opportunity of drilling my mind that I threw away whilst at Cambridge.[6]

The H.M.S. *Beagle* was a small ship—90 feet long and 25 feet wide at the beam—and carried 74 people. After delays caused by the need to refit the vessel, poor weather, and then the sailors' Christmas hangovers, the expedition sailed from England on December 27, 1831.

For two and a half years the Beagle moved up and down the southeastern coast of South America, measuring and charting. Darwin made inland trips of one to three weeks to explore regions now part of Brazil, Uruguay, and Argentina. He was a keen observer and the range of his interests was wide. His account of the expedition, written in 1837 and published in 1839, remains one of the best travelogues ever written. *The Voyage of the Beagle* is filled with telling, lucidly expressed observations on the animals, plants, people, and geology of the lands he visited. He saw with a newcomer's enthusiasm and reported with the discipline of a trained observer.

Much of Darwin's exploration was devoted to questions about geology, a field of study alive with new questions and making exciting advances. At Henslow's recommendation, Darwin had brought along a newly published geological text by Lyell, the first part of what would be a four-volume work. The leading geologist of his day, Lyell argued that the earth's crust was continually changing. There was a strain, soft-pedalled by Lyell, between an earth created in six days according to the Bible, and a geological process of formation stretching over thousands of years. All along the coast, Darwin found evidence to support and extend Lyell's work. As he became more familiar with geological thinking and evidence, he came to believe that the earth might well be millions of years old—much older than most intellectuals of his day thought.

On one inland excursion to delta cliffs cut by a river through the Argentinean pampas, Darwin found some extraordinary fossils: the shell of a gigantic armadillo-like creature, the tooth of a prehistoric horse, and the teeth of elephant-like animals. These animals were all extinct, raising interesting questions in Darwin's mind about the geographical distribution of animals in the new world.

Fossils that were near relations to present-day animals also confronted Darwin with questions. Why had these animals become extinct? FitzRoy saw this as evidence for the great flood described in the Bible. Darwin was not so sure.

During this time Darwin kept up a lively, though distance-delayed correspondence with Henslow. With all that he was seeing and wondering about, he regretted his inadequate training. He sent back fossils, other specimens, and long letters of description and asked for books and advice from his old teacher. He worried that he wasn't asking the right questions, and that he might miss something important. Henslow was continually encouraging and supportive. He gladly assumed the considerable task of receiving Darwin's many crates and sent along advice, books, and news of Darwin's classmates and friends. Henslow also read portions of Darwin's letters to the London Geological Society and praised his work to professors in geology and natural history. One of these readings so impressed Professor Sedgwick that he told Dr. Darwin that his son was going to do important new work.

Darwin's letters home during this time showed a new maturity and a growing confidence in his work. He found he had a passion for being a naturalist. Guided by a far-ranging curiosity he became an extremely hard and diligent worker. Periods of intense observation ashore were followed by periods aboard ship of organizing his collection, writing up his notes, and reflecting upon what he had seen.

After several attempts, the *Beagle* rounded the tip of South America and began working its way up the west coast. While the ship was anchored off the south Chilean coast, Darwin and an assistant went ashore to collect specimens, and were caught in a major earthquake. Darwin wrote in his diary:

> An earthquake like this at once destroys the oldest associations; the world, the very emblem of all that is solid, moves beneath our feet like a crust over a fluid; one second of time conveys to the mind a strange idea of insecurity, which hours of reflection would never create.[7]

When Darwin and FitzRoy later reached the epicenter of the earthquake, they were awestruck at the tremendous waste and destruction. Darwin wrote, "Nothing, not even the wind that blows is so unstable as the level of the crust of the earth."[8] The apparently unmovable, solid earth beneath one's feet turned out to be not so fixed after all.

Darwin's earthquake observations led him to develop a highly original theory on coral reef formation—before he ever saw a coral reef. When in the following year the *Beagle* reached the reefs and atolls of the South Pacific, Darwin verified and extended his views by careful examination of living reefs. His theory told him what to look for. What is even more interesting is that his theory of coral reef formation is structurally similar to the theory of evolution he developed several years later.[9]

Darwin's relationship with FitzRoy, given the close quarters and some significant political and philosophical differences, was generally good. FitzRoy generously provided a servant to aid Darwin and remained patient as Darwin's growing collection crowded his already squeezed little ship. The two men held differing religious views: FitzRoy strongly believed in a literal interpretation of the Bible and he urged Darwin to use Biblical passages to understand observations of natural history. For the most part, Darwin avoided direct confrontations with FitzRoy, but a couple of discussions led to fierce arguments. Within a few days these were patched over with apologies. For Darwin these discussions may have clarified his own predisposition to seek natural rather than supernatural explanations in natural history. The idea of someday becoming a clergyman faded into background.

In September 1835, the *Beagle* stopped for a month in the Galapagos Islands, located on the equator about 500 miles off the coast of South America. The archipelago consists of ten principal islands, whose volcanic soil attests to their recent geological formation. Desert-like, they are sparsely vegetated except for the highlands which scrape moisture from the clouds. The ship stopped at various islands, and Darwin continued his collecting and observing. One indication of his industry is that in this short visit he collected 193 of the 235 species of flowering plants eventually identified in the archipelago.

Darwin found the land physically unattractive, but he noticed some intriguing oddities in the animal and plant life. All the animals were exceedingly tame and showed no fear of man. The species of local finches seemed related to, but different from, species on the American continent. And the islands were home to several species of giant tortoises, which sailors stored in the hulls of their ships for fresh meat. Toward the end of their stay, FitzRoy and Darwin had dinner with the acting governor, who remarked that he could identify which island any tortoise came from by its shell. Darwin was surprised, but did not at first realize the significance of this remark. In *The Voyage of the Beagle,* he noted:

> It has been mentioned, that the inhabitants can distinguish the tortoises, according to the islands whence they are brought. I was also informed that many of the islands possess trees and plants which do not occur on the others. For instance the berry-bearing tree, called Guyavita, which is common on James Island, certainly is not found on Charles Island, though appearing equally well fitted for it. Unfortunately, I was not aware of these facts till my collection was nearly completed: it never occurred to me, that the productions of islands only a few miles apart, and placed under the same physical conditions, would be dissimilar. I therefore did not attempt to make a series of specimens from the separate islands.[10]

In fact he had already mingled together the collections from two of the islands. Fortunately, FitzRoy had kept better records of his observations, and he generously shared these with Darwin.

When he looked with a keener understanding, the distribution of species of plants and birds also seemed to differ island by island. In particular, the finches caught his attention. Dull in coloration and music, these little black and brown birds were, in fact, "the most singular of any in the archipelago."[11] Either on the islands or on the voyage home, Darwin noticed a gradation in beaks among the different finches. He wrote:

> I have stated, that in the thirteen species of ground-finches, a nearly perfect gradation may be traced, from a beak extra-ordinarily thick, to one so fine, that it may be compared to that of a warbler. I very much suspect, that certain members of the series are confined to different islands; therefore, if the collection had been made on any *one* island, it

would not have presented so perfect a gradation. It is clear, that if several islands have each their peculiar species of the same genera, when these are placed together, they will have a wide range of character. But there is not space in this work, to enter on this curious subject.[12]

Depicted below are four major steps in the gradation of finch beaks.

Darwin was reluctant to leave the Galapagos, remarking ruefully, "It is the fate of every voyager, when he has just discovered what object in any place is more particularly worthy of his attention, to be hurried from it."[13] The series of chronological reckonings had to be completed, however, and so the *Beagle* headed across the Pacific toward home.

The most arduous work behind them, in warm waters and pushed steadily along by trade winds, the morale of those aboard was high. Darwin worked intently at cataloguing and writing up his notes and thinking about what he had seen. Somewhere along this leg of the voyage, he began to doubt that species were immutable. In an undated ornithological notebook, probably written in 1836, he wrote some clipped notes to himself:

> In each Isld. each kind is *exclusively* found: habits of all are indistinguishable. When I recollect, the fact that the form of the body, shape of scales & general size, the Spaniards can at once pronounce, from which Island any Tortoise may have been brought. When I see the Islands in sight of each other, & possessed of but a scanty stock of animals, tenanted by these birds, but slightly differing in structure & filling the same place in Nature, I must suspect they are only varieties. The only fact of a similar kind of which I am aware, is the constant asserted difference between the wolf-like Fox of East & West Falkland Islands. If there is the slightest foundation for these remarks the zoology of Archipelagoes—will be well worth examining; for such facts would undermine the stability of Species.[14]

While far from a theory of evolution through natural selection, this represents a major departure from the established thinking of his time, and a break in the set of beliefs with which Darwin began the voyage.

As a natural historian, Darwin was taught, and continually saw, that species were adapted to their particular environment. As a geologist, he learned from Lyell and saw evidence throughout South America that the earth's crust was continually changing. Yet species were supposed to be immutable from the time of their creation. The creative tension between these observations helped Darwin move toward restructuring his beliefs, but the new theory that would explain these contradictions still remained beyond his grasp.

After the Galapagos Islands, the *Beagle* visited Tahiti and Australia, rounded the Cape of Good Hope, and arrived in England on October 2, 1836.

Darwin returned home from the five-year voyage a much more mature and confident man of 26. The absolute necessity of tidiness in cramped quarters had taught him to be very methodical. He had also learned "good-humored patience, freedom from selfishness, the habit of acting for himself, and of making the best of everything"—in short "the characteristic qualities of a greater number of sailors."[15] The few emotional quarrels with FitzRoy confirmed for him the folly of direct clashes, which he sought to avoid in later life. By now Darwin was thoroughly committed to the study of natural history. With some aid from Henslow and from books, he had largely taught himself to be a scientist and a discoverer.

Looking back on the voyage in his *Autobiography*, Darwin proclaimed it "by far the most important event in my life . . . I have always felt that I owe to the voyage the first real training or education of my mind."[16] In addition, thanks to Henslow and others, he was already recognized in London's natural history societies as someone doing important work.

FORMULATING THE THEORY OF EVOLUTION, 1837–1838

Back in England, Darwin was extremely busy. He had collected enough specimens to fill a small museum, and these had to be sorted out. Experts already busy with other work had to be persuaded to study the new specimens. Reports on the zoological and geological findings of the voyage were prepared under Darwin's editorship and eventually filled eight volumes. During this time, Darwin was invited to address the "great guns" (Darwin's words) of the London Geological Society. The address was well received, further bolstering

Darwin's confidence. His popular account of his travels, *The Voyage of the Beagle*, was written during this time. That it became a best seller pleased Darwin enormously.

Nine months after returning home, Darwin began keeping an important series of notebooks. As he reports in his *Autobiography*, "In July I opened my first notebook for facts in relation to the *Origin of Species*, about which I had long reflected."[17] In his old age, Darwin painted a picture of himself as working in a strictly deductive manner according to the canons of science of his day, piling up facts until they were overwhelmingly convincing in favor of evolution. The notebooks, however, present a far different picture.

The notebooks were small (approximately 4" x 6") and well made, with leather bindings. They were personal notebooks in which Darwin recorded his private thoughts, musings, and questions over a two-year period. Until he later developed a more flexible system of filing, keeping notebooks was one of Darwin's main methods of building intellectual capital. Because of the frequent entries and their private nature, the notebooks are a valuable guide to the development of Darwin's thoughts. Because they were written at the time, rather than recalled through the interpretive lens of memory, the notebooks are a more reliable indicator than the *Autobiography* of how Darwin worked on his theory of evolution. But the notes are not easy to follow. They present a "pandemonium . . . in which many different processes tumble over each other in untidy sequences —theorizing, experimenting, casual observing, cagey questioning, reading, etc.—[that] would never have passed muster in a methodological court of inquiry among Darwin's scientific contemporaries."[18] Yet this is how Darwin actually worked.

Most of Darwin's time in the summer of 1837 was spent writing *The Voyage of the Beagle*. The notebooks were a part-time activity, work on a subject that "haunted" him (Darwin's own word). The work began with a rush of enthusiasm; and, as Gruber observes, "the opening pages of Darwin's first transmutation notebook are written in an expansive, confident mood. Darwin thinks he has a theory that will deal with the origin of life, the causes of variation and heredity, *and* the transmutation of species; he does not even consider separating these issues."[19] He began work on a very broad front, attacking many problems at once. This mode of operation is just the opposite of the severe delimiting of attention so often recommended to scientists working on a scientific puzzle. But then, of course, Darwin was working on a problem without an accepted paradigm. The reach of his attention is impressive, even astonishing. In the first few pages of his notebooks, he considers the geographical distribution of species, observations of Galapagos animal life, the cause of change, and the pampean fossils, among other things.

On the theory-building side, Darwin began with vague notions of "monads" as spontaneous generators of life. By September, monads had proven a weak and insufficient idea, and they disappeared from his notebooks. During this initial period, however, he also developed one of the images most important for his later theory—namely, that all forms of life constitute an irregularly branched tree.

The first drawing of the tree of life in his notebooks was a vague, indistinct sketch. Darwin was searching for some way of understanding the discontinuities he and other natural historians observed among existing life forms. He was also trying to account for the extinction of various species such as those represented by the fossils he discovered in the pampas. He wrote in his notebook in a clipped, personal style of notetaking:

> Organized beings represent a tree, *irregularly branched*; some branches far more branched,—hence genera.—As many terminal buds dying, as new ones generated. There is nothing stranger in death of species, than individuals.[20]

And then a few pages later he wrote, "The tree of life should perhaps be called the coral of life, base of branches dead, so that passages cannot be seen."[21] This image or model began to grow in Darwin's thinking, and 11 pages later it was redrawn with a much more definite shape and with more detail.

Of the time Darwin spent on the transmutation question in late 1837, most was devoted to searching for causes of the origin of life. He read journals on plants and animal breeding intensively, and he questioned breeders on hybridization at length. Darwin was particularly curious about the wide variety of pigeons that could be bred, and eventually he joined two clubs of London pigeon breeders. His search for the origin of life and for heritable variation was not productive. For the next nine months or so the theoretical development of his ideas remained on a plateau. Like several of the searches he conducted, this one did not reach the goal Darwin had in mind when he began. The pigeon research did have the important effect of familiarizing him with artificial selection, however. Notebook entries written in February 1838 hint at the analogy between selection as practiced by domestic breeders and selection in nature, although Darwin is not yet making deliberate, conscious use of this connection.

Then, during May, June, and July there is almost nothing about selection. Darwin seems to have lost the thread of his investigation.[22]

Sometime during this period, Darwin began to experience periods of illness that would eventually limit the number of hours he could work in a day. Some researchers think he had contracted a malady now called Chagas's disease from an insect bite in South America. Other researchers suggest that his illness was a form of hypochondria, derived from his violation of his authoritarian father's wishes and the religious and intellectual beliefs of his time. In spite of the illness, Darwin kept a busy pace.

During this two-year period Darwin, who much preferred the rural life, lived in London, which he disliked heartily. He and Lyell began to spend a good deal of time together. Lyell admired Darwin's geological work and generously praised his efforts. However, as a result of a local geological excursion, Darwin published an article that turned out to be a serious misreading of the evidence. Toward the end of the two years, he began debating with himself whether to give up some of the time that could be devoted to science in order to enjoy the comforts of being married.

In April 1838, Darwin noted to himself the persecution of the early astronomers. He could appreciate the potential dangers that new theories, such as the one he was working on, held for their expositors. Still, with persistence and courage, he continued to search through the evidence he had and to collect new evidence that might help him understand "the species question."

Slowly and most reluctantly, Darwin gave up the search for causes of the origins of life and of heritable variation. He never solved these problems. Instead, showing another kind of courage, he somewhat uneasily accepted them as unexplained premises and moved his thinking to an area where the available tools and evidence allowed him to make progress.

In July 1838, Darwin made a rambling, hard to follow entry in his notebook that deserves inspection:

> Now that I have a test of hardness of thought, from weakness of my stomach I observe a long castle in the air, is as hard work (abstracting it being done in open air, with exercise etc, no organs of sense being required) as the closest train of geological thought.—The capability of such trains of thought makes a discoverer, & therefore (independent of improving powers of invention) such castles in the air are highly advantageous, before real train of inventive thoughts are brought into play, & then perhaps the sooner castles in the air are banished the better.[23]

Darwin seems to be saying that speculation and abstract theorizing are every bit as demanding as reasoning closely connected to concrete evidence. Speculation is like building castles in the air because it is not connected to objects observable through the senses. He mentions two ways in which speculations are useful—they make one a discoverer and they improve one's powers of invention. At 29 years of age, Darwin imagines himself becoming a discoverer; but he reminds himself that imagining comes before, and must eventually be transformed, into a "real train of inventive thought."

In August 1838, Darwin dreamed of returning to Shrewsbury, his birthplace and family home. He had become stagnated in his work, and the dream may suggest a desire to return to a refuge where he might obtain help.

By September, Darwin began feeling he was making progress again. He wrote to Lyell about "the delightful number of new views which have been coming in thickly and steadily,—on the classification and affinities and instincts of animals—bearing on the question of species. Note-book after note-book has been filled with facts which begin to group themselves *clearly* under sub-laws."[24] One can easily sense the rush of enthusiasm and Darwin's excitement in seeing some patterns and groupings beginning to emerge.

Eight days later, Darwin had a remarkable dream in which someone is being executed, all the while remaining witty, not running away, and so facing death like a hero. At first the person is to be hanged; then the facts of the dream change and the person is to be decapitated. As in many dreams, events occurred in a confused manner and the ideas rushed one upon another. The dream may mean several things, but one good possibility is that Darwin is the person about to be executed, and he wants to show courage and wit. As Gruber indicates, the reference to hanging recalls a fragment of Darwin's earlier medical education, in which the lecturer showed that it was impossible to recover from hanging because of the loss of blood.[25] The transition from hanging may indicate Darwin's ambition to do something that will outlast his death. The dreamer feels he is doing something important for which he may well be punished, but the important work will outlive the punishment.

On September 28, 1838, Darwin read Malthus's *An Essay on the Principle of Population* and at last saw a way to construct his theory of evolution. He had previously read about natural selection in various other authors, but had always seen it as a conservative principle, one that weeded out life forms maladapted to their environments. With Malthus's vigorous expression of the idea, Darwin saw the other face of natural selection—the possibility that it might be a creative force in the evolutionary scheme of things. Here was the mechanism Darwin was looking for to explain how variations in life forms originated.

Reading Malthus also led Darwin to reappraise the superfecundity of nature that he had so frequently observed on the *Beagle* trip. In one sense Darwin "knew" that nature generated far more seeds, eggs, individuals than could be supported in the long term. But until he embraced natural selection as a creative as well as a conservative principle, he did not appreciate the significance of this superfecundity. Combined with natural selection, nature's prolific breeding capacity provides the necessary condition for the development, over immense geological stretches of time, of so many variations of life forms. Here then is a theory that tied together many disparate observations and offered a new explanation for the origin of different species.

As the pieces of Darwin's theory fall into place, he records no great hurrah of achievement or completion. The moment is recorded in his usual notebook style, with metaphors, analogies, and some insertions. The even tone of a relentless explorer and questioner continues through this passage. Elsewhere, Darwin sometimes marks an insight with single or even triple exclamation points, but none are found in the crucial passage here.[26] As Gruber observes:

> Darwin had come to the summit. After a hard climb, the summit is not a simple achievement. It is no longer clear which way is up or down. Getting down is still a problem, and other peaks have become visible. Nor is the summit a sharp point, but rather a broad field with subtleties and ambiguities all its own.[27]

A dream Darwin recorded the following month strongly suggests that, even with the major pieces in place, he felt he had a lot more work to do on his theory of evolution. He writes:

> Octob. 30th. Dreamt somebody gave me a book in French I read the first page & pronounced each word **distinctly**. woke instantly but could not gather general sense of this page.—Now when awake I could not picture to myself reading French book quickly, & running over imaginary words: it appears as if the mind had dwelt on each word separately, neglecting time, & general sense, anymore than connected with general tendency of the dream.[28]

Darwin has read part (the first page) of the book of nature and can understand the specifics but the sense of the whole eludes him. The notebook entry also suggests the difference between the alacrity with which he understands the French words (perhaps observations of nature) when asleep, and the laboriousness with which he approaches the same task when awake.

DARWIN DELAYS PUBLISHING HIS THEORY

Darwin now had a theoretical explanation and a great deal of evidence for the theory of evolution through natural selection, but he did not publish. Arguments have raged among scholars as to why, having formulated the theory in 1838, Darwin waited 6 years before telling his closest scientific friend and then another 20 years before publishing the theory. Certainly part of the explanation is that Darwin feared persecution for his materialistic and evolutionary views. Observation provided ample evidence that proponents of such views would be heavily censured. Furthermore, Darwin saw his scientific peers, especially Lyell, trimming the exposition of their views to be less offensive to the temper of the times. Darwin's temperament and health also played a role. He preferred to avoid arguments whenever possible, and his illness had already taken time away from his scientific work. He resented this lost time, and he probably foresaw that controversy would cost him still more. Finally, Darwin's characteristic style of scientific writing in many areas was to accumulate evidence and ideas for years. Methodical in the extreme, he liked to get enough distance from his own work to enable him to see it as someone else's, and criticize and revise it himself before publishing.

Darwin continued to amass evidence supporting his theory. He sent out a detailed questionnaire to animal breeders and continued his omnivorous reading. During this period, 1838–39, he made changes in the proofs of *The Voyage of the Beagle*, pursued his geological work, and continued his editorship of the geological and zoological records of the *Beagle* expedition. He was a busy scientist with a growing reputation.

During this time, Darwin also resolved his internal debate about marriage, and in 1839 he married Emma Wedgwood, the daughter of his favorite uncle, the one who had supported his participation in the *Beagle* expedition. Three years later, Emma and Charles Darwin moved to a spacious country house sixteen miles from London. Emma was a caring and supportive wife throughout his life. They had ten children, seven of whom survived to adulthood.

In 1842, Darwin allowed himself "the satisfaction of writing a very brief abstract of my theory in pencil in 35 pages."[29] This private sketch used artificial selection as an analogy for how natural selection worked. Two years later he wrote an expanded but still private version of his theory in 230 pages.

The first person to whom Darwin confided his new theory was his friend Joseph Hooker, the leading botanist of his day. In an 1844 letter laced with interruptions, parenthetical thoughts, and exclamation points, Darwin wrote that conveying the news of his theory was "like confessing a murder."[30]   The vividness of the image suggests he understood the violence his new theory would do to the conceptual maps of others. Darwin was quite aware of what he had accomplished and wrote out instructions to his wife on how his essay should be published in the event of his death.

Darwin kept up a discussion with a few trusted friends on the "question of species" and showed them his essay of 1844. Several colleagues, including Hooker and Lyell, urged him to publish. At last in 1856, having finished eight years of intense work on barnacles, Darwin began to write up his new theory. He outlined a *magnum opus*, spent two years writing, and was halfway through when he received a letter from Alfred Wallace.

Wallace was a fly-catcher, currently collecting in the Malay archipelago. The two men had previously exchanged letters in which each advised the other he was writing a major book dealing with species. As part of his manuevering for scholarly position, Darwin told Wallace he had been working on this question for 20 years. Wallace's letter of June 1858 was accompanied by a paper describing a theory of evolution through natural selection; he asked Darwin if he felt the paper had merit, to pass it along to Lyell.

Dismayed that someone else had articulated what he had come to think of as "my theory," Darwin asked Lyell and Hooker what to do. With their help, it was arranged that the reading of Wallace's paper at the next meeting of the Linnaean Society was accompanied by excerpts from Darwin's 1844 essay and a letter from Darwin to Harvard biologist Asa Gray. These written works were then jointly published by the Linnaean Society. Surprisingly enough, neither the Linnaean meeting nor the publication aroused much response. Some who might have been outspoken were perhaps quieted because of the support given the papers by Britain's most eminent geologist (Lyell) and her most eminent botanist (Hooker). Later, in reviewing the year's scientific work, the president of the society lamented that, scientifically speaking, it had been a dull year with no striking advances.

The independent development of evolutionary theory by Darwin and Wallace shows some remarkable parallels. As conceptual background, both had been impressed and informed by Lyell's geological thinking, and both had incidentally been avid beetle collectors. For both, Malthus and the evidence of an archipelago were crucial stimulants to forming a new theory. An archipelago provided the closest approximation to a natural experiment on evolution. Islands were near to each other yet separate, so that different species could develop and then be recognized for both their distinctiveness and their relatedness. In addition, it appears likely that the exchange of letters between the two men, in which each announced his intention to write a big book on the origin of species, spurred them on.

Darwin set out at once to write a shorter version of the *magnum opus* on which he had been working. Despite the limitations imposed by his illness, Darwin completed his book in thirteen months. *The Origin of Species* was published in 1859. A printing of 1,250 copies sold out immediately, and the storm of controversy began.

DATES IN DARWIN'S FORMULATION OF THE THEORY OF EVOLUTION THROUGH NATURAL SELECTION

Year	Age	Event
1809		Born in Shrewsbury, England
1825–27	16–18	Attends Edinburgh University to study medicine. Joins Plinian Society.
1827–31	18–22	Attends Christ's College, Cambridge to study for the clergy. Befriended by Professor John Henslow
1831–36	22–27	Voyage of the H.M.S. *Beagle*
		1832–35 —travels along South American coast —develops a theory of coral reef formation
		September–October 1835 —spends one month in Galapagos Islands
1837	28	Begins notebooks on transmutation of species Formulates a first theory of evolution Talks with plant and animal breeders
1838	29	Reads Malthus Formulates theory of evolution through natural selection
1842	33	Writes private sketch on evolution, 35 pages
1844	35	Writes longer essay on evolution, 230 pages
1856	47	Begins writing his *magnum opus*
1858	49	Receives letter from Alfred Wallace
1859	50	Publishes *The Origin of Species*

Chapter *10*

Commentary on the Darwin Case

Chapter 8 laid out a conceptual framework for understanding the creative process. How useful is that framework in illuminating Darwin's theory of evolution through natural selection?

First, it seems quite clear that Darwin's thinking about evolution did not proceed in a straight line. His thoughts loop; he takes off in mistaken directions, fails to appreciate the significance of some piece of evidence, or follows the thread of the argument for a while and then loses it. His experience reveals a creative process that is gradual, determined, and patient. The closest thing to a sudden insight of the "eureka" variety occurred when Darwin read Malthus on September 28, 1838. But that revelation would not have been possible had not many less exciting moments paved the way, and would never have achieved a logical and publicly acceptable form had not much hard work followed.

Each problem area for Darwin was a "partially independent system" that developed unevenly and according to rules of its own. When he was stymied in one place, he turned to work on another front for a while.[1] In close juxtaposition he turned over in his mind a multiplicity of observations and questions about London pigeon breeders, the Galapagos finches and tortoises, geological changes, and the geographical distribution of species. His search through this wide range of materials derived coherence from the firm sense of purpose that guided him from the outset.

Darwin boarded the *Beagle* believing that species were immutable. Geological and biological observations during the voyage caused him to reexamine his beliefs. His mistake of mixing together the specimens from different Galapagos Islands showed him how incorrect and dangerously misleading the notion of immutability was. By the time he opened his first transmutation notebook in 1837, he already believed that species were changeable, and was seeking facts and arguments that would explain and prove this belief. He looked upon existing evidence in a new way and began a voracious search for additional evidence.

At this point Darwin was guided by a belief (although not yet a *judgment*) that species were mutable. That belief influenced how he directed his attention, where he was willing to place his bets (his limited time), and what arguments appealed to him even before he substantiated their validity. Unlike some notions of correct scientific methodology, our model of the creative process allows a place for such premonitions, or beliefs in advance of proof. The Darwin case strengthens our position that a lot of thinking occurs before conscious awareness, and that the guidance of beliefs and intuition is a crucial element in the early stages of creative thinking.

The fact that Darwin was largely self-taught influenced the way his thought developed. He did not believe he learned much from the classical curriculum of the colleges he attended. From work outside the classroom, from Henslow, and on the *Beagle* voyage, Darwin trained himself to be a discoverer.

Darwin would persist in pursuing something he thought important even in the face of disapproval by authorities. If at all possible, however, he preferred to avoid direct clashes—as seen in his behavior toward his father and FitzRoy, and in the timing of the publication of his theory of evolution. He worked prodigiously hard on the tasks he defined for himself, both on the *Beagle* and afterwards. Even an obsessive worker like FitzRoy was impressed. The self-training on the *Beagle* also schooled Darwin to be very methodical, perhaps too methodical at times. After he had written two private essays on his new theory, he began what he expected to be a short study on barnacles. In fact, it was eight years before he completed that study and returned to full-time work on his theory of evolution.

As he developed the theory, Darwin's thinking underwent several important shifts, as cogently summarized by Gruber:

1. After making no progress for eight months in accounting for the origin of life, Darwin dropped the problem from consideration.
2. Darwin struggled to rearrange important elements in his thinking, in order to develop a more plausible structure for his theory and one that fit the evidence better. Important shifts included recognizing that not all changes in nature were adaptive and making variation a major premise of his argument rather than a conclusion.
3. While reading Malthus, Darwin realized that natural selection had a creative as well as a conservative side.
4. This led Darwin to see the great fertility of nature as an important element in evolution that worked together with natural selection.[2]

Let us now consider how well the changing structure of his thinking is described by the framework of Chapter 8.

TESTING THE MODEL

Our model of the creative process comprises four overlapping phases:

UNCONSCIOUS SCANNING   INTUITION   INSIGHT   LOGICAL FORMULATION

In the first phase of the creative process, a person is immersed in materials of the problem and dominated by the task. The unconscious scans the material, getting a sense of the spaces and interconnections of the whole, without dwelling on details or logical rules.

There is no doubt that Darwin was immersed in the materials of the problem and that he was dominated by the task. As he said, it "haunted" him for years. It is very difficult, of course, to assess the character of his unconscious scanning process. The dream about reading the French book shows a concern both for detail and for constructing a sense of the whole. On the Galapagos Islands, Governor Lawson's remark about the distinctiveness of the tortoise shells did not sink in at first. Darwin was immersed in the evidence of evolution from the archipelago, but he needed to see the evidence in a new way. By whatever process, eventually he did appreciate the significance of the tortoise shells and then began trying to sort out his collection of plants and finches to see if they were distinct island by island. Thus, Darwin moved through all four phases—scanning, intuition, insight, and logical formulation—while still at the beginning of his creative thinking about evolution. The evidence of the case suggests that our model, intended to capture the looping and overlapping quality of the creative process, may nevertheless err in presenting an unrealistic image of straightforward progress. Although it may be useful to distinguish phases in order to characterize the main activity of a given period, the activities of other phases will also probably be present to some extent.

The model's second phase, intuition, was said to be often characterized by janusian thinking—the simultaneous acceptance of two seemingly contradictory thoughts. Frequently, we avoid the problem of contradiction by moving from one framework to another in sequence. In janusian thinking, however, the two frameworks are allowed to collide.

The Darwin case shows two important instances of contradiction, one of which is janusian. The first contradiction was the concept of immutable species perfectly adapted to their environment and the recent discovery that the geological world was ever changing. This contradiction was not truly janusian, however, since it was eventually resolved by Darwin's acceptance, reluctantly achieved, of the notion that species do change. The second major contradiction was janusian in character. Darwin's reading of Malthus showed him that natural selection was both creative and conservative. The solution did not lie in determining which of the two opposing principles to reject, but in understanding how both could be true at the same time.

One cannot know in advance which contradictions will be resolved by rejecting a belief and which will lead to janusian thinking. Words lag behind our intuitive sense that a contradiction may be paradoxical and true in a janusian sense. But the rule of thumb for the creative thinker is clear: "follow that contradiction."

Some of Darwin's intuitions were mistaken and others were not directly productive. For example, he spent eight months trying to discover the origin of life before abandoning the question. With similar success, he pursued an intuition regarding the causes of heritable variation. Nevertheless, even mistaken paths of inquiry provided important by-products for his thinking.

Metaphorical thinking is characteristic of both the intuition and insight phases of creativity. Analogy, imagery, oxymoron, and metaphor can condense a great deal of experience and move thought out of rutted channels. Edward Manier, a philosopher, has closely examined the use of metaphorical thinking in Darwin's early notebooks and in his published work. He finds that Darwin used a great many metaphors and analogies in making the central arguments of his theory of evolution. These expressions, such as natural selection, struggle, and check, were ambiguous, and Darwin was much criticized when he used them in *The Origin of Species*. Yet he persisted in using analogies and metaphors in successive editions of the book. Metaphors lay at the heart of his reasoning and argument, for they built the framework from which the evidence could be viewed. Manier further points out that "the succinct management of ambiguous themes can be the source, not of confusion and chaos, but of real leverage in the process of scientific discovery." The ambiguity of metaphors, perhaps continuing the imprecision of unconscious scanning, allows some continuity between the old and the new theory. Manier's point is that Darwin deliberately managed the ambiguities of his analogies and metaphors to skillfully advance his own discovery process and to communicate and persuade others of his results.[3]

The third phase of the creative process, insight, cannot be rushed and often seems to occur in moments of dispersed attention. The evidence of the Darwin case supports both of these points. First, as already noted, the insights leading to the building of the theory seemed to accumulate very slowly. Second, one of Darwin's major insights stemmed from his reading Malthus for amusement one afternoon—after he had already completed the day's work.

Darwin's experience also suggests that it is a mistake to think of insight occurring as a single incident or a single moment. Darwin had several major insights during the two-to-three-year period in which he formulated his theory. More than one insight was required because he was attacking partially independent problems—an insight into one problem did not necessarily mean progress in solving a related issue.

The work of modern biological researchers also indicates that the discovery process does not hang on a single moment of insight. While interviewing Francis Crick, who with James Watson formulated the double helix structure of DNA, Horace Judson commented that discovery "seemed curiously difficult to pin to a moment or to an insight or even to a single person."

> "No, I don't think that's curious," Crick said. "I think that's the nature of discoveries, many times: that the reason they're difficult to make is that you've got to take a series of steps, three or four steps, which if you don't make them you won't get there, and if you go wrong in any one of them you won't get there. It isn't a matter of one jump—that would be easy. You've got to make several successive jumps. And usually the pennies drop one after another until eventually it all *clicks*. Otherwise it would be too easy!"[4]

The framework of Chapter 8 argues that the creative process does not end with the insight phase. Creative work has to continue through the fourth phase, in which the insights, arguments, and evidence are woven together in a logical and publicly acceptable form. If anything, Darwin seems to have overemphasized this phase. Methodical in nature and fearful that his theory would not be well accepted, he delayed public presentation of his work for 20 years—and then acted only under the spur of Wallace's paper.

Darwin's rather restrained response to the Malthusian insight testifies to his keen appreciation for the work required to transform creative insight, as does his notebook reverie about building castles in the air. "Such castles in the air are highly advantageous," he writes; but they must soon give way to a "real train of inventive thoughts."[5] The slow, tortuous quality of the creative process recalls a line from Albee's play, *The Zoo Story*—"Sometimes it's necessary to go a long distance out of the way in order to come back a short distance correctly."[6] That can serve as a good short description of the pursuit and refinement of creative insight.

Overall, the Darwin case provides considerable evidence in support of the four-phase model of creativity described in Chapter 8. Darwin's experience makes it clear, however, that the process does not develop in a straight line from discovery to justification. During the early stage of the process, a discoverer may move rapidly through the activities of all four phases, as a small loop within the larger cycle of the overall investigation. In any phase of the cycle, the activities of other phases are likely to play at least a small part.

A major lesson of the Darwin case, only loosely related to our model, is to be skeptical about "facts." FitzRoy saw the same facts as Darwin but reached far different conclusions. To FitzRoy, for example, the differences in the beaks of the Galapagos finches seemed "one of those admirable provisions of Infinite Wisdom by which each created thing is adapted to the place for which it was intended."[7] Darwin of course took a different view, but he needed to revise his theoretical suppositions in order to "see" the facts before him.

Some contemporary discoverers seem to be consciously aware of this issue. Francis Crick, for example, reflects on how he and Watson discovered the helical structure of DNA while other scientists had been misled by the data:

> The point is that evidence can be unreliable, and therefore you should use as little of it as you can. And when we confront problems *today*,

we're in exactly the same situation. We have three or four bits of data, we don't know which one is reliable, so we say, now, if we discard that one and assume it's wrong—even though we have no evidence that it's wrong—then we can look at the *rest* of the data and see if we can make sense of *that*. And that's what we do *all the time*. I mean, people don't realize that not only can data be wrong in science, it can be *misleading*. There isn't such a thing as a hard fact when you're trying to discover something. It's only afterwards that the facts become hard.[8]

His co-worker, Watson, made the same point in discussing how young scientists should be educated:

You say you have to know all these facts—well, clearly, the facts, some of them, that you learn are wrong, so if you take them too seriously you won't discover the truth. You could say that if you become too imbued in the ideas and talk about them too long, maybe your capacity for ever believing they're false would be burned out.[9]

This is a remarkable point of view, and one that runs contrary to common-sense views of the discovery process. Facts, because they are theory-laden, can be misleading.

Because some facts may turn out to be misleading, and because the creative process is tortuous, looping, and inefficient, a discoverer needs a substantial amount of uninterrupted time to work on a problem. The wealth and position of Darwin's family was very helpful in this regard. In addition, he received a government grant of £1,000 to examine and catalogue the *Beagle* material. Darwin therefore could devote himself for two years solely to these materials and the questions they raised for him. It is not well known, but Alfred Sloan called in sick for a month in order to write his "Organizational Study" for solving General Motors' crisis. James Watson makes a similar point: "It's necessary to be slightly underemployed if you are to do something significant . . . I was very underemployed when we solved the structure of DNA."[10]

Along with enough time, the creative process requires several kinds of courage. To set off on a voyage around the world, to live in cramped quarters, to sign on as a naturalist when he had only a minimum of relevant education, required considerable courage, and Darwin felt stressed before embarking. For the first time in his life, he experienced pains in his chest as the departure date was repeatedly postponed. But he did not see a doctor because he feared being advised not to go on the voyage. Aboard the *Beagle*, he never became accustomed to the rolling motion of the ship and was often seasick.

His inland travels required stamina and a willingness to face unknown dangers. Working on his theory, he persisted in addressing questions that other thinkers of his day had touched upon and then backed away from.

Exploring without a map can bring the traveler to the terror of unmeaning, but the discoverer finds the courage to push on. Darwin's 20-year delay bespeaks the opprobrium he rightly guessed his views would bring upon him and his family. Other notable scientists of the day, including Lyell, trimmed their arguments and theories to be more acceptable. Although reluctant to go public, Darwin was courageous and bold when his hand was forced. Courage and confidence, along with some periods of doubt and depression, run through his process of creativity. He seems convinced that, like the character in his dream, he will be able by wit and luck to escape the hangman.

To sum up, the Darwin case suggests two principal modifications of our model of the creative process. First, the evidence suggests that the four phases interact in more complicated and dynamic ways than we originally suggested. Specifically, creative thought does not proceed in a straight line from discovery to justification, but loops back and forth. Second, a thinker—and thus a manager—often faces a network of problems. Each problem is semi-independent of the rest, follows its own rules, and develops at its own rate, yet interacts with other problems in the network.

IMPLICATIONS

Looking back over what has been said about the creative process raises a disturbing thought: managers may be temperamentally ill-suited to be creative. Managers choose a type of work that rarely rounds to an aesthetically pleasing whole, work in which quiet moments hardly ever occur naturally. Much of what a manager does trains him or her in ways of behaving that are inimical to creative thinking. A manager is expected to solve problems and to be attuned to the facts, action-oriented, and focused on goals. A good manager is supposed to rely more on the empirical evidence of his senses than on intuition. The nature of the work influences the type of person who is attracted to management, and vice versa. Managerial work is fragmented and frequently interrupted. Many managers would rather not be alone and thinking by themselves; instead they prefer to be in contact with others who are capable of getting things done. These are all marvelous qualities. But they exist in tension with a human being's other potentials.

In many managerial settings, the opposing attributes—namely, those associated with creativity—have not been much exercised. Managers are often solving unambiguous puzzles, and creativity would be more unsettling than useful. One executive told me with a smile, "I don't want any Picassos in my organization," meaning that creativity would be disruptive in his business. As managerial problems become more ambiguous, however, the need for creative thinking grows.

What guidelines or techniques for stimulating creativity are implied by our discussion? The first set of recommendations has to do with the general relationship between a manager and the problem. When attacking a poorly defined question, a manager should immerse himself or herself in the materials of the problem. At the same time, this immersion should be a detached involvement. The manager as a problem-framer should try to find ways to see the materials from a distance, through different lenses, from different points of view. Drawing on a diverse range of experiences, either within yourself or among co-workers, is often helpful. Seek out people who do not share your set of assumptions.

Early in the process one should avoid negative evaluation, accept paradoxes, and look for essential contradictions. Recognize and exploit the opposing tensions and seeming contradictions within the self. Truth always extends beyond what words can say. Confidently acknowledging the limitations of language allows one to more readily accept seeming verbal contradictions in the ways order can be brought to an ill-defined problem. Remember that part of Sloan's solution for his company's crisis hinged on an articulation of two basic and contradictory principles for organizing.

Interestingly enough, physical fitness and moderate physical activity seem to play a role in stimulating creativity. Body and mind are intertwined in a way that can help build a robust and vigorous imagination. A study at Purdue University showed that flabby professors and university administrators increased their creativity during a six-month program of exercise and leisure sports activities.[11] This parallels findings that physical fitness increases one's ability to cope with high levels of stress. The whole person, physically and mentally, seems to be involved in creative thought; and moderate, regular exercise helps to keep the whole person invigorated.

The second set of recommendations for stimulating creativity has to do with the specifics of sitting down to work. Find a quiet place and time, free of interruptions. Begin perhaps with some wordless activity, a breathing exercise from yoga or meditation, designed to put you in a state of relaxed awareness. Words seem to distract the unconscious mind and give more control to right-hand ways of knowing; yet new ideas often begin in a region beyond the verbal. So you might give yourself a period of time during which it is "all right" to think without using words.

Be receptive to what the unconscious tries to push over into consciousness. The poet William Stafford describes this as a vital element in his own creative process:

> When I write, I like to have an interval before me when I am not likely to be interrupted. For me, this means usually the early morning, before others are awake. I get pen and paper, take a glance out the window, (often it is dark out there), and wait. It is like fishing. But I do not wait very long, for there is always a nibble—and this is where receptivity comes in. To get started I will accept anything that occurs to me. Something always occurs, of course, to any of us. We can't keep from thinking.[12]

So jot down your ideas without evaluating them for the moment and without trying to control the process. See what visual images the mind conjures up. Pay special attention to metaphors; play with them. Use analogy, antinomy, and imagery to leap out of existing channels of thought and see new possibilities. Treat metaphorical thinking as a guide to what the unconscious mind is dreaming about.

The next suggestion may seem outside conscious control but it is not: learn to dream. In the words of John S. Morgan, consultant and writer on creativity:

> The most fertile region for new ideas is the borderland between sleep and full awakening—a sort of marshy shore where discipline still operates but not with sufficient firmness to hamper the dreamlike fluidity of imagination.[13]

One can strive for the same relaxation of control in order to consciously generate new ideas. Another route is to deliberately disrupt routine ways of thought, and dialectical thinking as well as the dream world can be helpful here. You might work with the antitheses of your starting assumptions, and explore *as if* those assumptions were true.

To help a group be more creative, many process facilitators emphasize the need to listen carefully and respond actively to each other's images. The group can use notes, drawings, or a tape recorder to record the ideas that bubble up. Group members should not worry about precision at this point, but instead work with blurred boundaries and a certain looseness of attention. At all costs, defer a tight focus on specific goals. Give imagination room to play by treating the woods of the unconscious as a whole.

After some period of intuition and paradoxical thinking, the manager/problem-attacker should begin to do some sorting. Start playing with combinations that feel promising. Be especially alert to essential contradictions, for they may become the source of janusian thinking. If possible, one should alternate periods of direct engagement and indirect attention to the problem. Sleep on it, and come back to it another day.

The last set of recommendations has to do with the personal qualities that seem to enhance creative efforts. Persistence and tenacity are obviously important, since the appearance of a new insight is unpredictable and cannot be rushed. Courage and commitment to the problem are also vital. Courage is needed to accept the possibility of failing, and this is difficult in a success-oriented culture. Another part of courage is being hopeful, tolerating disorder while believing that ultimately some new principle of order can be found.

It should be clear by now that I am not outlining a how-to course in the usual sense. Results are not guaranteed in the same way they are with good craftsmanship. Creativity is more like fishing than cabinet making, since the design and the plan do not exist beforehand. You can go fishing, follow correct techniques, and still catch no fish.

We began this section wondering if many managers aren't fine puzzle-solvers, but less adept at creative discovery. Such an orientation would be no great handicap if business problems continued to be more puzzling than messy. However, the evidence seems to be that more and more managers face ill-structured, complex, and shifting problems. The entrance of new technologies, increasing economic interdependence, sudden government regulation or deregulation, population shifts, the enfeeblement or resurgence of value frameworks—these can all cause new and messy problems for managers. The list proliferates and I leave details to the futurist. But the trend is abundantly clear. Managers will face increasingly more complex and ambiguous problems. Where there is no paradigm or where the conceptual map is blurred, managers will need more creative thinking.

Chapter 11

Conclusion

The long journey is nearly completed. Ten chapters are behind us with one more to go. This concluding chapter sums up the main evidence, looks across the cases for common patterns, and specifies managerial implications for managing change and ambiguity. Let us begin by returning to the issue of how best to define and understand ambiguous administrative situations.

WHAT MAKES THESE SITUATIONS SO TROUBLESOME?

We began in Chapter 1 with a list of characteristics that might theoretically be expected to define uncertain, shifting, and ambiguous situations. After each major case, I offered my subjective ratings on how troublesome each characteristic was for participants. Now we can add ratings for the two major cases in the appendices and collate the ratings. Table 11.1 summarizes my ratings for the five cases: the response of General Motors to foreign competition and the oil shock (Chapter 1 and Appendix B); the electronic banking case (Chapter 2 and Appendix A); the high technology VIS case (Chapter 3); the San Francisco desegregation case (Chapter 6); and the Darwin case (Chapter 9).

The column totals rank the ambiguity of the five cases and generally seem reasonable, especially in naming the San Francisco case as the messiest. The real interest of the task lies in the row totals which

TABLE 11.1.   Troublesomeness of Characteristics in Five Cases

Characteristics	GM	EB	Hi Tech	SF	Darwin	Total
1. Nature of problem is itself in question	***	**	***	***	*	11
2. Information (amount and reliability) is problematical	**	***	**	**	*	10
3. Multiple, conflicting interpretations	**	*	**	*	**	8
4. Different value orientations, political/ emotional clashes	**	**	***	***	***	13
5. Goals are unclear, or multiple and conflicting	**	*	***	**	*	9
6. Time, money, or attention are lacking	*	*	**	***	*	8
7. Contradictions and paradoxes appear	**	**	**	***	**	11
8. Roles vague, responsibilities unclear	*	*	*	**	*	6
9. Success measures are lacking	*	*	*	**	*	6
10. Poor understanding of cause-effect relationships	*	*	*	**	*	6
11. Symbols and metaphors used	**	***	*	**	***	11
12. Participation in decision making fluid	*	*	*	**	*	6
TOTAL	20	19	21	27	18	

*** = very troublesome   ** = moderately troublesome * = slightly troublesome evaluate how troublesome each characteristic seemed to be for participants. The range of values suggests that some problem attributes were typically less important than others. Specifically, the items with the lowest row totals, which all happened to total to six, were:

participation in fluid decision-making	6
success measures are lacking	6
roles vague	6
poor understanding of cause-effect relationships	6

A recent examination of university governance suggested that a significant source of ambiguity was fluid participation, i.e., continual shifts in which players were active.[1] In the situations we examined, however, fluidity of participation was not a significant factor. There was an occasional surprise, but the base of key players stayed largely and predictably the same. Similarly, a lack of success measures was not a problem. With the possible exception of the San Francisco case, multiple measures, generally accepted by major participants, were available and were used to score the game. Along these dimensions, then, the managerial environment may be significantly less ambiguous than the academic realm.

Nor were vague definitions of roles and responsibilities a significant source of ambiguity in these five situations. In the San Francisco case it was not entirely clear whether basic responsibility lay with the board, the superintendent, or the associate superintendents. But managers in all the other cases seemed able to avoid the pitfall of unclear responsibilities, and this dimension, therefore, was not nearly as troublesome as some others.

Another surprise is that poor understanding of cause-effect relationships did not engender more problems for managers in these situations. Managers apparently did not expect problem connections to be explained as causes and effects; instead they engaged in a qualitatively different kind of thinking. They searched for meaning in a multiply influenced situation, knowing that there were likely to be black holes, quarks, black boxes, and anomalies. In an ambiguous situation you accept from the start that, although you can make progress, you will not completely understand the problem. Cause-effect thinking is too simple and too linear to help in these more complicated, ambiguously formulated problems.

Those items that received the highest row totals pinpoint the characteristics that seemed to trouble managers the most:

The most difficult situations are those in which conflicting parties to the problem have different value orientations, making political/emotional considerations paramount. Political processes come to the fore, rationality is less in evidence, and emotional responses are heightened.

The other four most troublesome characteristics are interrelated aspects of the problem of information, broadly interpreted. As I worked through the evidence of these specific cases, I found I had to enlarge my concept of how information problems contribute to ambiguity. At first I expected that decisionmakers would be either starved for information or overwhelmed by too much data. But the evidence strongly suggests that having the right amount of information is not as critical a problem as being able to judge its significance and reliability. Recent thinking about complex information processing has been much influenced by information overload experiments. But a simplistic extrapolation from these experiments may be misleading. Thinking in terms of channel capacity suggests that the remedy must be to widen the channel, install valves to regulate the flow, and/or build reservoirs to accept the spill-over. But the information component of these complex cases is more aptly characterized by asking "what information do you notice?" and "how do you interpret it?" The most significant informational problem for these managers was to find the right problem to address and to structure the related information search and information processing in a productive way.

The interrelationship of information and action is no different for managers than for other human beings: an individual sees an event, interprets it using existing categories, takes action, gets feedback on results, and takes additional, corrective action if necessary. Including the feedback cycle, a manager twice circles a stable orbit, as can be seen in Figure 11.1.

Even though the ideas may be complex, the actions a subtle set of if/then contingencies, and the events a rich array of specifics, the pilot can be put on automatic when stimulus and response are habitual. Psychologists and philosophers agree that much (and some would argue *all*) human behavior is nearly automatic.

FIGURE 11.1.

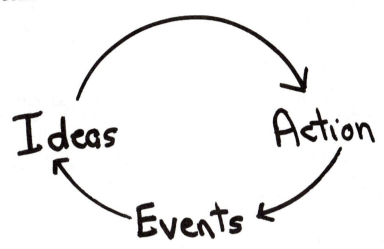

The essence of the situations we have been studying is that managers' action cycles have been destabilized. The definition of the fundamental nature of the problem is vague and shifting. Consequently, information is incomplete and of dubious reliability, and events are not easily categorized. Contradictions then appear as symptoms and signposts. They call attention to the clash of values, logical inconsistencies between two frameworks, or the presence of false or misleading facts. The old and the new bump against each other, and contradictions identify the points of highest friction. Once an action orbit has begun to wobble, events are sure to outpace logical thinking. Managers are then tested on how skillfully they use the next set of adjustments—employing metaphors, symbols, and negative thinking to regain a stable orbit. Some new way of framing the problem has to be conceived and tested.

The discussion of specific cases has suggested some ways in which managers can handle the stress of ambiguous situations and creatively formulate a more adequate map. A general review of these cases suggests two further lessons for management: the value of informal procedures (the use of core groups and networks) and the need for a new understanding of managerial control. These common patterns are especially important because the cases explored in this book were deliberately chosen to be very different from each other. The situations vary significantly in the sources of ambiguity and change, the nature of the task, the types of people involved, the amount of control managers have over the situation, and so on. Patterns that emerge from such a diverse sample must reveal something powerful and fundamental at work.

CORE GROUPS AND NETWORKS

In ambiguous situations where standard operating procedures no longer work, the evidence of this study suggests that managers often turn to informal procedures, especially the use of core groups and networks. The San Francisco schools case is the most obvious example of the value of a core group—a few people frequently meeting face-to-face to attack a common problem—and a network of contacts. Table 11.2 summarizes the role of these informal procedures in four cases, answering three questions in each case:

1. Did a core group exist?
2. To what degree was a network of contacts used?
3. If a core group or a network did exist, how effective was it in reducing uncertainty and responding positively to change and ambiguity?

A core group made a key contribution in two of four cases. Of the two that lacked a core group, one (the Darwin case) was not a managerial situation; the other (the high tech case) suffered the consequences of a defective core group. A network was used to a significant degree in three out of four cases, and again the case making limited use of networks paid a price for that omission.

The people associated with the high technology project were capable and sophisticated, yet management made several serious mistakes in commissioning the team. In the first place, many members were assigned only part of their time to this project, and some only became involved at a relatively late stage of the project's development. Fundamental questions about the nature of the research project, whom to sell to and how, were never resolved. Members did not have enough time together to learn to function as a *group* and to develop a common map. To become a group, members need frequent, face-to-face communications to develop practical skill in understanding the diverse worlds of other team members.[2]

In the San Francisco case the core group arose out of the necessity of responding to a court-imposed deadline. Members selected themselves, and excluded those who would slow them down. They

TABLE 11.2. Scorecard on Core Groups and Networks in Four Cases*

Case	Core Group Exist?	Network Used?	Effective?	Remarks
Electronic Banking	Yes	Yes	Yes	Highly effective use of core group, several task forces, and network.
High Technology Project	Mixed	Limited	Mixed	Defective as a group because marketer and business manager not full time. Part time involvement limited use of contacts.
				Did force a company decision on whether to continue funding project.
San Francisco Schools	Yes	Yes	Yes	Highly cohesive core group was embedded in active network.
				Constructed plan within severe time constraints, but busing led to "white flight."
Darwin	No	Yes		Not a managerial or administrative situation.
				Network of personal and written contacts very active during the two years in London when theory was formulated.

* There is some evidence that GM turned to increased use of informal contacts to cope with problems associated with foreign competition and the oil shock; and they did take the highly unusual step for GM of setting up a technical project center which cut across divisional lines. We do not have sufficient information, however, to be able to rate the GM case along with the others on these points.

began to work with available data, even though it was incomplete, fuzzy, and sometimes incorrect. Although not open in membership, the core group was democratic in its internal operations. Members developed a high level of trust and confidence in each other, engendering strong internal debates. Several members were skilled at deflecting flare-ups and restoring a sense of mission. Equally important, core group members were embedded in a network of contacts with influential people in the government, the legal profession, community groups and the educational system. They used their contacts to send and receive messages to shape the context for desegregation planning.

The core group in the electronic banking case shared the toughness and intensity of the San Francisco citizens committee members in many ways. The banking core group comprised ego-resilient people who could withstand being pushed hard by the new president, deal with his contradictory demands, restore his confidence when necessary, and still complete the task. They were willing to use judgment and intuition when logic had run its course. Like the San Francisco core group, they did not pay much attention to rank, and everyone felt free to offer his views and to question "expert" opinions. Members avidly sought information from outsiders, such as consultants, other bankers, professional association reports, and equipment vendors, and wove this data into their decision process. Key to successful implementation was the way the president linked the core group to important officers at the different banks through a series of task forces.

In sum, the evidence of our cases suggests that managers in ambiguous situations should employ informal procedures such as core groups and networks. If standard operating procedures fail to cope with increased turbulence, managers can activate networks, beginning with contacts they already have and then creating new links to deal with the specific topography of the current problem. At the center of this skein of old and new connections, one generally finds a small, intensely interactive group that lends vitality and direction to the whole.

Our earlier discussions of stress and creativity help explain the value of networks and core groups in turbulent situations. First, a close, cohesive group gives people the emotional support of others sharing a common fate, reduces their sense of isolation, and helps them feel more powerful. The net effect, or the network effect, then is to bring stress within a manageable range. Second, a group can comprise a diversity of intellectual resources which provides more chances for the janusian thinking that feeds creativity. So a core group embedded in a network is responsive to both the intellectual demands and the emotional stress of change.

In an effective core group, candor, trust, and empathy are high; individuals are willing to work very hard, employing both logic and intuition, hard and soft data, hunches and judgment, to direct the search for new information and to patch or to leap over the gaps. Internal disagreement is constructive, allowing group members to go through cycles of diverging and converging, in part because they share a common map of the situation. They agree on the fundamental nature of the problem although they may express the problem in different ways. An effective core group is also connected to a large network of contacts, and enjoys easy, rapid, and informal communication with outsiders on a variety of topics relevant to the group's work.

To establish such a body is a tall order—no wonder creative, fresh-thinking groups are so rare. Still, managers can enhance their chances of putting together an effective core group by being aware of the personal qualities that this study suggests are likely to prove helpful in managing ambiguity. Table 11.3 summarizes the traits a manager should look for in choosing core group members.

THE CONCEPT OF CONTROL

The cases we have examined suggest that managers need to think about control in a new way. The manager is often metaphorically portrayed as the captain at the helm of the ship. The captain charts the course, issues orders to keep the sails trim, and efficiently uses wind and current to maintain the course. The crew understands the dangers of not following orders and accepts a very visible hierarchy that places the captain at the top, in charge of their collective destiny. To a manager in a confusing, changing situation, the captain imagery is romantic and appealing—and misleading and dangerous.

Consider the evidence. In the San Francisco case neither the superintendent of schools, nor the mayor, nor even the federal judge had a "crew" willing to acknowledge the moral and legal authority of a leader in charge of everything. The 67-member Citizens Advisory Committee dithered, the superintendents provided only flimsy direction, and the judge felt harassed by events beyond his control. The citizens who took responsibility for planning were able to influence, but not control, events. In the high technology case, the business

TABLE 11.3. Personal Qualities of Potential Core Group Members

Preference for ambiguity, variety	Used to be described solely as *tolerance* for ambiguity, but actually it goes beyond tolerance. Is in some sense a delight in new combinations, and in partially blurred and disordered situations. Most useful when accompanied by what Barron found in more creative Air Force officers: a taste for unusual kinds of order.
Humble courage	Confidence that no one else could attack the problem so adroitly while acknowledging that the problem is, in one sense, bigger than the problem-attacker and imposes its own demands.
Patience and persistence	Situations are often so changing and changeable that effectiveness requires a long-time perspective and bull-dog determination to use occasions as they pop up to bend events to your will.
Humor that oils	Humor that recognizes the stress and at times the absurdity, irony, and paradoxical character of the situation as opposed to hostile, attacking humor.
Optimism and confidence	Usually born out of past successes. Can encourage others, keep everyone's stress levels in most productive range. Sloan, Crozier, the high technology project members all mention it as key quality. Was key ingredient for San Francisco citizen's group.
Willing to work intensely	The small number of players in the core group means that each must be willing and able to work long, hard hours.

manager was appointed a captain of sorts. But he had to keep several bosses happy, including the principal scientist who was formally one of his crew. William Crozier, the CEO of BayBanks, also worked extremely hard to control the introduction of electronic banking, but he tried to keep the levers of power out of sight and to foster more responsibility among the players. The man he appointed to chair the core group, William Fish, said you could not run the group with a tight rein. As in the core group of the San Francisco case, procedures were democratic, influence flowed to expertise, issues were confronted, and disagreements aired— a *modus operandi* quite different from that of a well-trained, smoothly functioning crew.

Another manager whom I have observed provides a clue as to what control means for a manager in an ambiguous and changing situation. Ken Binder is a project manager for a thriving architectural firm on the East Coast. Some of the firm's construction projects, particularly urban renewal projects involving multiple agencies, take on the ambiguous and messy character we have been studying. Such projects have chewed up other project managers in the firm to the point of seriously endangering their physical and mental health. The company prefers to assign Binder to any politically complicated project, since he seems especially skillful at bringing order to chaos. Although he works hard and can be bone-tired after a crisis period, Binder's style of managing change and disorder allows him to survive the pressure.

Ken Binder has many of the skills and attitudes we have been discussing. He is able to keep cool under pressure and to map new situations. He has a fine sense of humor and he stays in touch with a network of people from past projects. He keeps careful records, documents important agreements and milestones that have been reached and devises scheduling systems when appropriate. But, most important, while he tries to tack down everything that can be tacked down, he acknowledges that there are times when he will have to let the situation go its own way. He has learned to wait until later to re-gain directional control. This kind of control, which might be de-scribed as "assertively going with the flow," is reminiscent of the simultaneously loose/tight controls critical for the early stages of creative thought.

A novel by Richard Adams captures the paradoxical nature of this concept of control. The story concerns a young, tidily correct ceramics dealer who owns his own shop in a small English town. While on a business trip to Copenhagen, his regular predictable world is knocked askew when he falls in love with, and marries, a beautiful German woman. Several months later he is still trying to understand the changes she has brought into his life, and he writes:

> I recall an old man, a friend of our family, once telling that what he remembered most vividly about the 1914–18 War was the frightening realization, upon reaching the front, that here all lifelong assumptions—the safety and predictability one had always taken for granted and come to rely upon—did not apply. . . . That great area of life dominated by Aphrodite—the area of sexual passion—is very similar; or so it has often seemed to me. What is it like? Is it like a deep wood at night, through which virtually everyone has to pass; everyone that is, who lives to grow up. There are no generally accepted rules. . . . if it were not for Aphrodite, none of this would happen. There would be no

forest: a plain, perhaps, or mountains, with dangers of their own; but not the dark forest by night.[3]

So too for the managers of change. They must learn how to make their way in the dark forest by night, where there are no generally accepted rules. Letting go at times, giving up the captain's stance—this, of course, represents a marked departure from traditional concepts of good management. But effective management in turbulent times requires new ideas.

RECAPITULATING THE BASIC ARGUMENT

We live in a world of transition, where change and ambiguity are facts of management life. Management training and management textbooks, however, tend to assume a world of stability and continuity. When the times become discontinuous, managers must find new tactics and new ways of thinking. The body of this book has reviewed and synthesized research on how people think in new situations, how they respond to the challenges of change, and what conditions stimulate fresh thinking about fundamentals.

By examining several real-life situations, or cases, we've explored several themes. First, one's cognitive map of any situation is the starting point for much else that happens. The map influences what information is gathered, how it is evaluated, and what is seen as important. The new CEO in the electronic banking case made a major contribution by remapping the bank's problem. Instead of thinking in terms of the "computer problem," he formulated the question as one of strategy and marketing, a much more productive mapping, as time and events proved. Problems of change and ambiguity call for more supple and often more complex ways of thinking. Throughout the book we have seen that linear descriptions of changing situations don't work.

The chapters on mapping showed how mapping develops relationships among models, evidence, facts, and assumptions. We saw that reality has subjective and objective faces. If the environment is turbulent, subjectivity becomes more prominent and the balance of mental activity tips toward nonlogical processes. We also saw how members of a group interact to create a social reality—fragile in the beginning but tenacious when grown. A common pitfall for managers is to try to short-circuit this cumbersome, anxiety-producing process. Managers should spend enough time on mapping to be sure they are addressing the right problem. In a group someone should be specifically appointed to monitor the tendency to settle prematurely on a solution.

From the outset, I have argued that managing fundamental change involves managing the ambiguity that necessarily accompanies such change. Now we can sharpen that argument. In a time of fundamental change human beings cannot think through all the complex interconnections and consequences of even a limited number of alternatives. The future is too uncertain, too multiply influenced, to allow such a detailed, comprehensive approach. Camus pointed out that man is not smart enough to be rational. Man is also too smart to be totally unambiguous.

A major lesson for managers seeking to improve their mastery in complex, changing situations is to appreciate the necessity and usefulness of ambiguity. They must endure the discomfort of allowing some contradictions to remain unresolved. Too often people free themselves from a dilemma by focusing on one side and ignoring the other. While producing short-term relief, one-sided attention tosses away a valuable indicator of where remapping is needed.

Ambiguity is valuable because it can protect options for the future. Decisions, goals, and symbolic slogans, if fecundly ambiguous, are open for reinterpretation depending upon future needs. Ambiguity is a promissory note on the future that can be redeemed in various currencies. At other times it allows people to receive an important, unwelcome message at their own speed. In the high technology case, the ambiguous "decision" of the December meeting forced people to work out the details for themselves. Judge Weigel used a similar tactic in the San Francisco case, delivering his ruling but remaining stubbornly uncommunicative about interpreting its meaning. He was not in the business of telling school administrators how to run their school district beyond ruling on what the law required.

The study of Darwin's creative process revealed how metaphors and symbols, because of their essential ambiguity, can bridge unconscious and conscious ways of knowing. The skillful use of ambiguous metaphors lay at the heart of his thinking, possibly because the metaphors tried to make sense of unconscious scanning. BayBanks' adoption of the slogan "something better" shows how ambiguity, used cleverly, can sidestep conflicts and suggests continuity between old and new ways. For the young staffers, "something better" meant a strong commitment to a new and innovative common product, while the older bank presidents could read it as a continuation of personal service and of each bank's commitment to its local community. In short, ambiguity is a necessary component of managing complex change. Rather than fight it at every step of the way, the challenge for executives is to appreciate the ways in which it can be put to good use.

Since ambiguity raises stress levels for many people, however, managers must try to keep stress within productive levels. We return to the inverted-U curve relationship between stress and performance:

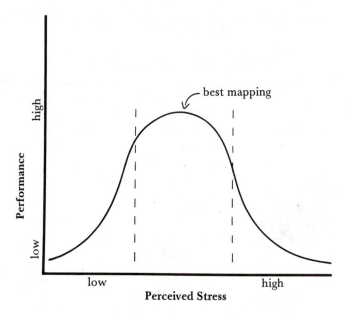

The best mapping and the most creative thinking are likely to occur when stress is in the middle range. Since it is the *perception* of stress that determines performance, managers can work to influence how people appraise the situation. The aim is to have them see the situation as challenging, rather than threatening, and therefore in the middle range of perceived stress. Managers can influence each of the two main factors that affect people's appraisal of a stressful situation. The first factor is the balance-of-power reading, how well the individual feels his resources match the demands of the situation. Obviously, expanding resources of time, money, and staff can help diminish extreme levels of stress.

The second factor is how the disruption and consequent changes touch the individual's core values. This relationship is more subtle and complex. Table 11.4 may help draw out the continuum of intra-psychic and interpersonal possibilities. At the left side of the continuum a person welcomes change; at the right side he or she strives to maintain the continuity of existing relationships.

TABLE 11.4. Change and Continuity in Core Values

Change ←——————————→ Continuity			
Some rearrangement or stretch among core values is possible, even exciting.		It is very important that core values appear to remain intact, with unvarying relationships to each other.	
Order and stability are boring. Creating new combinations is the challenge. Asymmetry and more complicated kinds of order have appeal of their own.		Things should be clear and precise, terms defined, everything in its place. Order and symmetry are the classical virtues.	
positive expression	*negative expression*	*positive expression*	*negative expression*
creative maverick street smart	doesn't get things done undependable hard to focus	common sense judgment solid and stable	stolid unimaginative rigid
Implications for managing		*Implications for managing*	
Manager should give subordinates scope to roam within some guidance.		Manager should shield subordinates from full chaos.	

Both tendencies can be at work within the same person. A manager observes which seems to predominate at a particular time and tailors his or her response accordingly. Regulating stress involves helping subordinates deal with their own tensions by making them feel powerful, by instilling a sense of purpose and confidence as the group undertakes remapping.

Mapping anew, or significantly revising an old map, calls for fresh thinking. So the recommendations for mapping meld with those for fostering creativity. To protect against the self-sealing quality of maps, a manager should find and support the loyal opposition. He or she should stimulate disagreement by conducting a dialectic and by occasionally introducing perspectives from outside the group. A fresh viewpoint often exposes the weakest links in the chain of logical reasoning, namely the underlying assumptions. General Motors unwittingly achieved this broader perspective when provoked into electing outsiders to its board. Although perhaps unsettling a first, the outside views broke the insularity of top managers' beliefs and better prepared them to respond to the turbulence of the auto market in the 1970s.

For creativity to flourish, the manager or the core group should become immersed in the material of the problem (again underscoring the importance of full-time commitment), while striving for detached involvement. The problem must be alive and meaningful to the players, but they must be psychologically able to view it as if from a distance. To some extent group members should be skeptical of "facts." Our examination of the creative process showed that facts are theory-laden. If the theory is incomplete or mistaken, as must be the case when you are experiencing map troubles, then the facts can be wrong or at least misleading. Similarly, a guideline for the group is, "Follow that contradiction." Contradictions, paradoxes, and ironies provide ways of tapping into janusian thinking and of identifying false facts and misleading theoretical constructs.

If the work requires a great deal of creativity, being slightly underemployed is an enormous help. Darwin clearly had time to create a new map, as did William Crozier when he was a bank vice president without portfolio and could choose his own projects. Alfred Sloan used a variation of this when he called in sick for a month so he could think through and write up the decentralized divisional structure for General Motors. Creative thinking takes time, and off-site retreats for the core group are one way to provide it.

We have emphasized the need to use both right-handed and left-handed ways of knowing. When a manager encounters map trouble, he or she should not expect thinking to proceed in straight, logically defined ways. The intuitive thinking of remapping is more likely to loop, to curl back over itself, and to leap in order to progress. One should not try to impose a logical template on this early stage of the creative process; rather, the template is applied to the *result*, the insight, which must be translated into a logical, persuasive argument. Likewise the group must give its members "permission" to use beliefs and hunches to guide the collection and interpretation of evidence.

All in all, working on a poorly structured problem, you should take an iterative, experimental, learn-as-you-go stance. This sometimes entails acting before you are certain, in order to gain more information. Especially in messy situations, a map is a sketch that carries you into the unknown; you can't expect to know it all before-hand.

SKILLS AND VIRTUES IN MANAGING AMBIGUITY

Managing change and ambiguity calls for a set of skills, attitudes, and personal virtues different from that used in managing stable, well-defined situations. Table 11.5 describes the main skills and attitudes that this research study has shown to be helpful in coping with poorly structured problems.

TABLE 11.5.   Managerial Skills and Attitudes for Coping with Poorly Structured Problems

Problem-finding	Combination of judgment, intuition, and logic that enables a manager to key in on the right problem. Contains elements of being able to frame a problem in several different ways and to choose among them. Overlaps with map building.
Map-building	Ability to generate one or more ways of conceptualizing a problematic situation. Involves relating organizational and personal values and identity to the demands of the situation.
Janusian thinking	Shorthand for comfort with acknowledging and constructively using seemingly contradictory beliefs. Since this is often at the heart of creative thinking, provides important skill for building maps of a poorly structured problem.
Controlling and not controlling	Posture of assertively going with the flow. Knowing which things can be influenced when. Knowing when to let events follow their own head. A manager of ambiguity needs to know when to act like the captain of the ship and when to ride the river.
Humor	Humor that helps regulate stress and encourages unusual juxtapositions, rather than biting, sarcastic, denigrating humor.
Charisma	Ability to stir enthusiasm, commitment, and confidence when in troubled waters. Defines purpose for people in terms of superordinate goals. Heightens people's sense of their own power and their willingness to take risks.

Humor was not explicitly identified as a management skill in our discussion of specific cases. But managers in pressured situations often use humor to help them cope. One of Darwin's dreams, for example, is of the hero who remains witty while facing death; he eventually escapes death through his wits—a pun and another form of humor. The high technology research team used gallows humor to lighten their disappointment at the project's demise. Several managers told me that one of the key qualities they look for in selecting project members is a sense of humor.

Humor may well lie at the heart of our approach to the contradictions of change. In the cases we studied, humor served to relieve tension, put events in perspective, make fun of the high stakes, reaffirm the common fate of the group, or honor a central paradox or contradiction. Humor was a safety valve for the self-regulation of stress levels and at times renewed people's enthusiasm for the project. The type of humor constructed upon sudden and unexpected juxtapositions of opposites keeps people loose and playful even when stakes are high. As a form of creativity, such humor may well engender a climate hospitable to other forms of creativity as well.

My research identified several other skills that were useful to particular managers, although not to the majority. In a given situation, one of these skills might be crucial:

- Problem bracketing
- Channel switching
- Dialectical reasoning
- Nonverbal communication
- Summary memos
- Public recordings

Problem bracketing (the term is psychologist Howard Gruber's) is the ability to set aside a fundamental issue that cannot be immediately settled. In the meantime the manager works on problems that seem more likely of success. Undisciplined bracketing, of course, poses the danger that important, seemingly intractable issues will never be seriously addressed. The manager should return periodically to the bracketed problem to see if events have created new possibilities and if the problem will now yield to renewed attack.

Channel switching is the ability to shift attention from one problem to another rapidly and completely. Ken Binder, the architectural project manager, was a master of channel switching. Amidst a whirl of telephone calls, visitors, meetings, and reports, he could immediately and easily tune into any sub-problem in any of his four to six projects. Such adroit switching was impressive to behold—in fact it left the observer a little dizzy—and made for solid connections to his clients and to members of his team.

The third skill is *dialectical reasoning*. A manager does not have to be able to conduct the dialectic according to the formal sequence outlined in Chapter 2; in fact, for most important situations a skilled outside facilitator should run the dialectic. But the spirit of the dialectic, being able to pose counter-arguments and counter-assumptions, can be quite valuable in uncertain situations. As BayBanks was formulating its strategy for introducing ATMs, Crozier often engaged his staff in dialectical arguments. He would push his people hard, challenging their arguments with the strongest counter-arguments he could devise. No feelings were spared. Both he and his staff knew that long-term success depended upon constructing the most solid arguments possible and knowing, even better than the opposition, where the weak spots were.

Nonverbal communication is useful for conveying deniable, ambiguous messages and messages about feelings. In the high technology case, top management conveyed their disposition through nonverbal means instead of making a clear-cut declaration. Nonverbal communication is also important for building understandings that go beyond what words can capture. Such messages can engender trust when group members feel in touch with and can rely on their sense of other members' feelings and their point of view. Feelings are a primitive, direct indicator of how a person matches the evidence of a particular situation or proposal to his or her core values and assumptions. Several of the most effective managers in complex change situations were skillful in using nonverbal communication to tap into this facet of problem-attacking.

Some managers find it useful to write *memos that summarize* a discussion and identify key questions and issues. Ken Binder is masterful at quickly writing concise summaries of agreements to date; and Crozier called for periodic written reports from his staff. Because new maps of reality are fragile, group members under pressure may snap back to the old standard view. I have seen groups fight spiritedly over an issue and painfully reach an agreement, only to find four months later that no one is sure what was decided because no one wrote it down.

Finally, I have found that *recording* on chart pads or chalkboard the key points and issues from a group's discussion serves several valuable functions. Especially for poorly structured problems, public recording aids everyone's memory, keeps discussion on track, and allows for rapid correction of misunderstandings. Most importantly, public writing seems to externalize ideas, putting them "out there," perhaps aiding the detached involvement useful in creative thinking.

LEVERAGE POINTS FOR EMPLOYING THESE FINDINGS

In thinking about how to employ these findings, a manager should remember the great variation in how people respond to the stress and challenge of change laced with ambiguity. Some people run for cover, delegating problem-solving in order to avoid involvement, as the school administrators did. Others remain protectedly insular. Some people see only part of the turbulence and deny the rest. They seek to impose order by defining the problem according to an existing model or map. The professional planners in San Francisco and some of the bank presidents chose this approach to tidy things up. Some will persevere, as Darwin did, and courageously face stunning contradictions, ultimately working through to a remapping, but then temporize before going public. Having bravely faced one kind of conflict, they try to avoid another. Others wade into the work of change, concerned and excited. They will do their best under trying circumstances; win or lose, they know a new set of problems will follow whatever victories they achieve.

Sometimes a modest amount of effort, applied in the right way, can pay disproportionately large dividends. These are the areas where the manager should try to exert control. Table 11.6 summarizes and briefly comments on these leverage points.

The question of deadlines deserves some elaboration. The dynamics of deadlines are most clearly seen in the San Francisco case. A federal judge ordered the school system to prepare a complete desegregation plan in six weeks. People were willing to neglect family and friends and work around the clock because the cause was important and the deadline demanded immediate action. People narrowed their focus, pruned away related problems, were willing to forego challenges to underlying assumptions, and became impatient with nuance or indecision.

Deadlines should be used judiciously, of course. A prematurely imposed deadline could cut short the gestation period for remapping and set people busily working in the wrong direction. The tradeoffs are clear. By imposing a deadline, you give up the exploration of alternative futures, skepticism about purpose, and the appeal of

TABLE 11.6. Leverage Points

Selecting people to the core group	Rules of thumb: the more creativity you need to solve the problem, the more heterogeneous and unorthodox group members should be. However, you don't want more diversity than necessary. Since the core group is to be small, there are complex tradeoffs in choosing among background, experience, personal problem-solving style, etc. See Table 11.3 for personal qualities helpful in coping with ill-defined problems.
Framing the problem	Initial presentation of problem is very important. Should include spirit of experimentation and convey expectation that will go through several iterations. Try not to frame problem within confines of one expert field. Make problem definition a part of the charter of the group.
Setting timetable and standards	Easy to underestimate the time needed to construct a new map, but thinking through one or two sequences of tasks and associating them with dates is usually very helpful. Also group needs to know how polished, logical, and finished a product is needed. Scheduling forces consideration of these standards. Chief danger here is to kid oneself about what can realistically be accomplished to a chosen standard within time constraints.
Setting deadlines	Deadlines set important processes in motion: shedding secondary problems, focusing on most promising materials, etc. Most likely to be helpful for parts of the problem, rather than the whole. Proceed with care, temptation is to set deadlines prematurely.

worthwhile and connected objectives. You gain focused commitment, drive, eagerness for action and results, and a forceful convergence of efforts.[4] The manager of change must be sensitive to the task, the people, and surrounding pressures to know when it is time to begin narrowing focus.

CONTINUING YOUR LEARNING

In Chapter 1, I argued that most management education programs, concentrating as they do on conveying well-defined analytical techniques, are a poor classroom in which to learn about managing change and ambiguity. Until programs are developed for managing change and ambiguity, what can you do on your own? The first step is learning to recognize ambiguity and contradiction. This could involve reviewing the cases in this book, and reading novels, histories, and biographies that capture these aspects of life. A valuable exercise would be to follow an unfolding problem in the news. (For example, in 1974 the oil embargo would have been a good choice.) Clip stories from newspapers for a year or two, build your own file, and write monthly summary memos. After enough time has elapsed that events are beginning to develop a shape, look for an extended critical analysis and compare it to your own understanding as shown in the memos.

At the same time, you should also work to recognize internal ambiguity. Keeping a journal can help you track your own experience. I suggest using a two-column format. One column records events that anyone in the situation would see, and in this sense is a public account. The second column records thoughts and feelings, including what embarrassed, worried, or excited you about the situation. Reviewing such a journal from time to time can help you identify your personal patterns in coping with change and ambiguity.

Many people find a support group an effective mechanism for exploring these personal issues. The climate and atmosphere the group develops is important, and a skillful process facilitator is invaluable. Group members can bring in work experiences, journal excerpts, and summary memos for discussion.

A final possibility for speeding up your learning is to look for someone to coach you. The coach could be a mentor within your organization or an outside consultant. The coach must understand complexity and ambiguity in organizational settings and be able to construct dialectics between your own starting points and their opposing tensions. He or she should be skilled at empathetically understanding your point of view, but not afraid to challenge that view and to ask you to consider opposing points.

The development of these skills and virtues is a tall order because it is so intricately related to personality. Recent research has established that adult development proceeds through stages that cannot be leapfrogged. Like the process of organizational change, human growth in these areas takes years. The difficulty is that managers have to manage even while trying to develop some of the requisite skills.

There are several things you can do in the short term. A key consideration in choosing staff should be to add relevant skills that you lack. For example, Crozier chose Fish for his patience and diplomatic skill, and Curtiss for his marketing know-how. Next, the manager who knows his own weak sides can ask his staff for help in correcting his tendencies. To a limited extent, judicious use of consultants can shore up change skills on a project, but you don't want to overdo this. Finally, in the long term, I believe that managers can improve their own personal skills if they are willing to make a serious commitment over a number of years.

The world of managers and administrators is becoming more complex, interconnected, unsettled, and ambiguous. My aim in the book has been to develop usable managerial frameworks suited to this turbulence and change. To behave as the captain of the ship or as a purely rational decision-maker will not suffice. These approaches work for well-defined problems, for managing on a clear day and a calm sea. My central argument is that poorly structured problems *are substantively different* from well-defined ones. The processes used to attack the two are quite dissimilar, and disaster awaits the manager who mistakes one for the other. The book has been devoted, therefore, to changing the way managers think of themselves and their work—diminishing some traditional functions, such as directive control, and enlarging others, such as creative conceptualization.

To sail more turbulent seas, the manager must be more like a discoverer, a Darwin, who is still learning and changing. Many managers recognize that the nature of the game has changed, that change and ambiguity pervade their work lives. My goal has been to explore what the new demands mean for managers, and how they can cope effectively. Managers may have to revise the expectations they have of themselves and others. Just as there is no free lunch, there are no blueprints. Managers in changing, ambiguous situations are going to have to figure it out as they go along. The process of managing change is not like constructing a cabinet or a building; it is far more interesting.

The philosopher Bergson says there is no such thing as disorder, but rather two sorts of order, geometric and living. The really important and challenging problems in management are poorly structured, messy, cross-cut by value differences, and characterized by contradiction and paradox. Trying to impose geometric order on such a blooming, buzzing confusion is a critical mistake. We have been searching for ways to bring living order to this tangled growth. While the full development of needed skills and personal qualities may take years, it is a worthy journey. My wish is that we could travel, explore, and invent that path with humble courage and persistence. We are all sailors on a voyage, and explorers in the dark forest at night.

The Electronic Banking Case

In June 1974 William Crozier, 41, the newly elected CEO of Baystate Corporation, faced a difficult set of problems. The recent performance of the bank holding company had been good, but Crozier was concerned about the future. Interest rates, it appeared, had peaked and were heading down. Some of the company's banks had begun to surface bad loans on the books, which meant sharply higher provisions for losses. Inflationary cost increases and a recession threatened profits. Moreover, Baystate faced a loss of market share. Savings banks and several small independent banks were aggressively marketing NOW accounts. Customers liked these interest-paying checking accounts and were transferring their money to banks that offered them. Responding to this competition effectively would be costly and was complicated by Baystate's established practice of letting its 12 member banks act independently on most matters.

"The organization is killing its banks with autonomy," Crozier remarked to Bill Fish, formerly a president of a member bank and now with the holding company. "We're not doing all that we *can* do at this point in time."

"You've worked here ten years," Fish quietly replied. "You understand the organization's strengths and weaknesses. The company bought into what you wanted to do in electing you."

"Individually, the banks don't have the leverage to deal with the changes necessary," continued Crozier. "By themselves they can't exploit the benefits of their collective size through joint marketing or computer systems. The power of the company is being dissipated."

Baystate enjoyed a long and proud, if somewhat conservative, New England banking tradition. Its deposits in 1974 totalled $1.6 billion, making Baystate the third-largest banking company in Massachusetts. Its greatest asset was the state's largest branch network, 173 locations with extensive coverage in the greater Boston area in particular. The holding company had always operated with a low profile. Consequently, most customers, and indeed some bank employees, were not aware of its existence. They thought mainly in terms of the Harvard Trust Company, the Norfolk County Trust Company, or the particular member bank where they did business or worked.

Unlike most holding companies, Baystate Corporation was not built around a single large bank; instead Baystate comprised 5 large banks and 7 smaller ones. Each of the 12 banks enjoyed a tradition of autonomy, having its own board of directors, president, and senior officers. Holding-company management had cultivated this independence, believing it developed highly motivated affiliates.

The holding company was the majority stockholder for each member bank, and thus controlled basic policies. Holding company executives, for example, actively participated in selecting bank CEOs and could veto the appointment of bank directors. They handled most operating matters through gentle persuasion, however. Changes rarely came about without a clear consensus. Even then affiliates could, if they chose, only nominally support group policies without much fear of near-term reprisal. Thus in 1974, perhaps one-third of the banks favored increasing commonality among the banks, but most favored continuing past policies that had brought success.

An earlier effort to realize economies of scale by centralizing computer operations at Baystate had failed. In the early 1960s the Baystate banks held equal shares in the Baystate Computer Center, BCC, which provided data processing for the banks. The banks, particularly the larger ones, vied for dominance in BCC affairs. The system did not work well and three of the largest banks pulled out and set up their own computer facilities. These moves weakened BCC and increased unit costs for the remaining banks. By 1973 there were five data centers within Baystate. Cooperation in joint programming and for joint purchases of software was limited. Consequently, little hardware and few software programs were compatible.

Over the years many similar efforts had fallen apart, or produced suboptimal results. Baystate's board of directors, regardless of the level of earnings, found these failures confusing and frustrating, and the problem of centralization had been an important issue in Crozier's election as CEO. In 1973, the current president was near retirement, and the two senior vice presidents were engaged in a civilized competition for his job. Crozier's rival favored continuing the decentralized policies and administrative structure that had brought the banks to their present position. This point of view, widely favored among the bank presidents, argued: "We are doing well. Why change to something else?" Crozier, in contrast, had spent the previous ten years as a staff generalist at the holding company and was convinced that the banks needed to centralize. Since day-to-day operations were handled by the banks, some staffers such as Crozier had time to generate their own projects. Although the wages were low, Crozier was free to investigate a wide variety of issues such as acquisitions and minority share exchange. In 1973 he put together a confidential white paper on computer operations at the holding company which signaled what he would do if elected president of Baystate.

CROZIER'S WHITE PAPER AND ELECTION

"Concerning Computer Operations and Other Important Related Matters" was distributed on November 26, 1973 to the board of directors of Baystate. In this white paper Crozier restructured the computer operations problem. Past efforts to solve the problem had failed, he argued, because

> Computer operations have, more often than any other area, been the ground upon which power struggles have been fought within the corporation; thus they have attained, as with other major battlefields in history, a sizeable symbolic meaning.

As a starting point, then, Crozier argued that "a direct frontal assault on the matter might not only be unwarranted but unwise." To solve the problem, the report began by talking about fundamental issues of business strategy and by transforming the computing problem into a marketing problem.

The report argued that banking was no longer a local business: changes in the marketplace dictated that banks compete on a metropolitan, and maybe even statewide, basis. Baystate should therefore take "a more homogenized view" of selling financial services in the greater Boston market, including:

• construction of an overarching group identity

- development of group-wide marketing programs
- intensified use of the Baystate distribution network
- group-wide TV advertising

In short, Crozier said that to compete in the changing marketplace, Baystate would have to operate as a coordinated banking system.

After acknowledging the tradition of consultation rather than direct orders to member banks, Crozier's report moved to computer operations. He documented the incompatibility of the various data-processing systems in use by the banks and statistically analyzed the cost of such duplication. Any move to centralize computer operations, the report acknowledged, would run into heavy resistance unless there was an important, clearly understood, and widely accepted rationale for change. "Such a rationale is available by focusing priority attention on marketing opportunities and problems. If we are going to present a more unified marketing approach," Crozier wrote, "it will require greater standardization of services, procedures and practices." The report concluded by recommending that a task force be appointed to work on corporate unity and identity "without crippling local identities." The board approved that recommendation in January 1974 and a consulting firm was hired to interview bank executives and make recommendations about developing commonality of identity among member banks.

In June 1974 the board of directors of Baystate Corporation named Crozier the new CEO. "The first phone call I made after I was elected was to Lee Barnes (of McKinsey & Company)," Crozier said later. "I told him the board of the holding company had decided on me and thus, in essence, to centralize operating policies. I, of course, knew McKinsey's ability and reputation. But more important, I knew Lee from my days in Section A at the Harvard Business School, knew how he thought and trusted him completely. He had a strong background in data processing and was an extremely attractive, high-minded man."

Crozier saw his job as bringing out of the organization what it was capable of and doing it in a graceful way. People could not be treated in a high-handed, rude, or insensitive fashion. He continued discussions with top executives of the holding company about the white paper and its implications for the banks. In addition he worked to shape the conclusions of the identity study that was nearing completion. The consultants had interviewed 27 bank officials, mainly presidents and vice presidents of the banks. By now most bank officials favored some commonality of identity, but did not agree on how it should be done. A small but strident minority wanted no change in the status quo. Members of this group said:

> "We are investment-oriented, not marketing-oriented."
>
> "A common identity would be great for the small banks, but would hurt the large banks."
>
> "I will not sit at a table to attempt to create commonality of product. It doesn't work."

The chief consultant said he had never seen such strong opposition to centralization in the many banks he had previously studied. He had therefore planned to recommend changing to a common name and identity at a gradual, measured pace. Crozier favored an accelerated pace, however. One of his young, aggressive staff met with the consultant and gradually convinced him to recommend a far speedier change to a common name and identity.

Crozier also organized a small group to look into electronic funds transfer systems, or EFTS, to preempt the fledgling efforts already begun by some member banks. He wanted to avoid costly separate and uncoordinated efforts, and he wanted innovation to come from the holding company.

EFTS IN 1974

EFTS had been around for seven or eight years, but had not lived up to its early promise. In 1974 systems were still rudimentary, confined mainly to Docutel cash-dispensing machines in quite limited formats. Further clouding the outlook for EFTS, most consumers seemed to have a marked preference to interact with human tellers. As Bill Fish, recruited from a member bank to the holding company staff, expressed it, "EFTS couldn't quite get over the rim of reality." Having been touted for so long without delivering much, electronic systems had receded to the background for many retail bankers.

Crozier himself was skeptical whether EFTS would ever prove out economically. He believed in sound analysis, and yet "you couldn't get any hard numbers on EFTS." No one could prove that the new technology was anything but a huge expenditure of money with, perhaps, flimsy marketing payoffs. Still, a technology that offered the possibility of lowering operating costs and improving service, two perennially troublesome areas for banks, could not be ignored. So Crozier's instincts were to investigate, without depending too much on EFTS.

The first report on EFTS was written by staff members Donald Isaacs and Richard Finlayson. Dated November 22, 1974, the report examined the potential of automated teller machines, or ATMs. These machines could perform a range of teller functions and were ordinarily located in or near existing bank buildings. ATMs ranged from Docutel cash-dispensing machines already being used in other regions of the country to interactive on-line terminals that allowed a variety of transfers, deposits, and payments.

The report enumerated the benefits (ten), the drawbacks (seven), and questions about cost justification for ATMs. Research indicated that a good marketing effort was crucial for an ATM program because customers had to be sold on the idea. Isaacs and Finlayson surveyed banks in other regions of the country and were struck by how decisions on ATMs had been made:

> The tendency has not been to take a scientific approach to the purchase of equipment and the measurement of program success. ATMs have been purchased and marketed for a variety of reasons ranging from the whims of the chief executive to the fact that they looked like a good idea or seemed like a nice gimmick. Furthermore, even after installation, usage data were quite scarce.

The report noted that ATMs were early in the product life cycle and therefore quality should improve and prices drop in the future. A major consideration was how much flexibility it was economical to buy in an ATM system. This issue could not be resolved because cost data were fuzzy and changing, and because there were three schools of thought on how to allocate costs. In concluding, the authors recommended continuing to accumulate information.

GREATER BOSTON TASK FORCE AND STAFF MEMBERS

Early in 1975, Crozier hired McKinsey and Company and formed the Greater Boston Task Force (GBTF) to oversee the process of change. Along with William Fish and himself he appointed to the task force those who seemed to have the most to lose under the new approach, namely the CEOs of the four largest banks. To help set the course for a new program of cooperation and development among the banks, the GBTF was to study ideas for consolidating marketing and operations presented by a team led by McKinsey and Baystate staff.

Supplementing these efforts were the loosely connected activities of several key staff members. Most of these staffers were young, full of energy and new ideas. Marketing know-how was supplied by Trumbull Curtiss, on loan from one of the banks for two days a week. Intense and aggressive, Curtiss, 34, knew what sold; but his aggressiveness could sometimes offend more traditional bankers. He exuberantly played the role of a cheerleader who gets people excited about change.

Perhaps even more impatient than Curtiss was Don Isaacs, who had recently joined Baystate after earning a master's degree at MIT. Isaacs, 27, could quickly become restive with those not able to keep up with him intellectually. He was a very competent technical person, whose background in data processing, computer operations, and management would be helpful in the investigation of new technology.

Balancing this youth and fire was William Fish, who headed the Baystate team on the McKinsey project. A consummate diplomat in his late 40s, Fish rode herd on the young pups whose eagerness might otherwise undo the project. He tempered Curtiss's sometimes unconventional behavior and was a buffer between Curtiss and Isaacs on the one hand, and Crozier on the other. In addition, Fish was greatly admired and respected by the bank presidents. He had served recently as president of the Massachusetts Bankers Association in a particularly controversial period during which the association was restructured. He was one of them and could be trusted not to recommend wild-eyed schemes.

Other important contributors at different times were Richard Finlayson, who advised on buildings and facilities, and Crozier's assistant Ilene Beal, who helped in gathering and analyzing data.

The consultants from McKinsey were to assist the GBTF by defining a strategy to improve Baystate's position in consumer banking. They were also to establish requirements for computer systems development, and to examine what services were needed to support the new strategy. In discussing the committee Crozier remarked to Fish, "We have to do it from the outside and with the best. If we don't do it that way someone inside will think he is smarter and undermine our plans." Crozier later remarked that it was noteworthy that no inside computer hand was ever invited to participate in any part of the process.

McKinsey's first report appeared in March 1975 and identified EFTS as an important opportunity for strengthening Baystate's position in the retail market. Their next report argued that Baystate's main competition would come not from other commercial banks, but from thrift institutions offering NOW accounts. To meet this threat, Baystate needed to differentiate its services from those offered by thrift institutions. ATMs were one way to accomplish this aim.

The interaction between McKinsey consultants and the members of the GBTF resembled an ongoing seminar or workshop. The consultants employed the logical, rigorous analysis that Crozier favored. The six month period of learning gave top bank executives a chance to voice their objections, to ask questions, and to modify the consultants' analysis on the basis of the bankers' superior local knowledge. The same issue could be talked through several times, over and over again if necessary, and an executive did not have to "decide" at a single meeting. The consultants' outside perspective lent additional weight and authority to positions advocated in the earlier white paper. Likewise, because Crozier's position was not fixed, he was learning and being influenced during this time as well.

Afterwards staff members had different views of McKinsey's contribution:

WILLIAM FISH

Often consultants document and support what management has done in concept. That is what happened at Baystate. They did an objective analysis which supported what we had long been thinking about.

DONALD ISAACS

They reaffirmed for us what the economics of retail banking were and the advantage of having our own proprietary product. They also helped us sort out the data and took an aggressive stance for ATMs. They were not laying out a final plan, but a direction.

WILLIAM CROZIER

The watershed event was their study. We had a narrow skeleton and they wrote a report which documented the ideas for the banks. The report provided a tunnel under the river of their discontent, and the tunnel had no leaks. As a practical matter, we overwhelmed the banks with logic.

Crozier's emphasis on logic is apparent in a front-page article on him that appeared in *The American Banker* of April 2, 1975. Crozier was quoted as believing that the banks in Baystate would have to start thinking of themselves as part of a family. Some resistance was to be expected, but Crozier would not be patient with opposition that was not based on intelligent reasoning. Similarly, Crozier said it was not Baystate's style, or his, to try to do anything that cannot be intelligently explained and promoted. Therefore, the staff would have to rely on hard work, information, and smart thinking to support their views.

Commenting on the process of introducing change in the banks, Crozier observed that "It's not fair or smart to drop bombshells on folks." Change would be evolutionary, and his job would be "creating a political atmosphere that will find people not bucking too hard when change actually comes." With its extensive distribution system and historical low profile, Baystate resembled a sleeping giant, and Crozier planned to "wake the giant Baystate up nice and easy."

The article was headlined, "Crozier Welding Baystate into New Force." The following day when he walked into a GBTF meeting, one of the bank presidents remarked, "Oh, the president of the Crozier Welding Company," and nothing more was said. Just as the earlier white paper had announced his recommendations to the directors, the newspaper article broadcast his intentions and, equally important, the new rules for disagreeing, to bank officers and the rest of the organization.

At about this same time, in early 1975, Crozier moved to restructure a group formed by the bank presidents and known as the Advisory Committee. Holding company executives had been able to attend its quarterly meetings. At Crozier's recommendation, however, the board of Baystate dissolved the Advisory Committee and created a Council of bank presidents and key holding company department heads. The Council would be chaired by the CEO of Baystate Corporation, namely Crozier.

The McKinsey consultants issued their final report to the Greater Boston Task Force in May 1975, setting forth the road map for the future of Baystate's retail banking. They recommended a limited ATM program of 10 to 20 machines. Its work completed, the GBTF was disbanded. Crozier and his staff began preparations to ask the Baystate Council, bank boards, and the holding company board for formal approval of the steps necessary to carry out the prescribed program.

STAFF WORK ON THE COMMON NAME

The initial McKinsey study behind them, Fish, Curtiss, Isaacs, and the others continued with product, operational, and identity issues, now at a very intense pace. They were feeling charged up, and worked long hours on many days.

As an outgrowth of the earlier identity study, a top-of-the-line New York firm was hired in March 1975 to conduct a name search and to design a new logo and signage for Baystate. As part of their studies, the design consultants ran a contest among bank employees to help select a new name. The employees responded enthusiastically, submitting over a thousand suggestions. The name chosen was BayBanks. The holding company would adopt the name, BayBanks Inc. Each bank would keep its historical name, but preceded by Bay-Bank (e.g., BayBank Middlesex, BayBank Norfolk Trust). Under the new identity program, which proposed extensive graphic and signage changes, the group would be advertised as BayBanks.

At monthly Council meetings the bank presidents discussed ideas for signage, advertising, promotion. This involvement fostered their commitment to centralization. The executives agreed with the program of graphics involved in the change of name to BayBanks; but to complete this action the board of directors of each member bank had to vote to change its own bank's name.

Holding company officials and staff members made personal visits to the BayBanks. They generally made a 20-minute presentation to the directors, showing the results of the two consultants' reports and the new graphics design. The bank most opposed to the common name was the largest in assets and was also the biggest earner. At their directors' meeting, the usual business was conducted until five minutes before five o'clock, the traditional ending time. The bank president asked the executives from the holding company to make a brief presentation concerning the name change. Then the president said, "Here is the motion *we* would like you to pass." Silence. "All those in favor say, 'Aye.' " In a low voice and through firm jaws the directors said, "Aye." "All those opposed?" Silence. And so it was done.

"In fact," Crozier told his staff, "we could have bombed them into submission. Persuasion with the facts was better, but it took time. Meeting after meeting, cheery and gentlemanly behavior had a better long-term effect." All the banks voted approval, but there was an additional step. Several of the banks were national banks and therefore had to request permission from the Comptroller of the Currency in Washington, D.C. to change their name. Their request sparked a protest from a small bank north of Boston which contended that the new name, BayBanks, encroached upon its name, Baystate National. "I became despondent, I was totally down,"

Crozier said, "because there was so much at stake that could be undone by this protest. We had all the troops lined up and ready to go, and then this delay occurred. We didn't know how long we could hold our own people in harness." Finally, the Comptroller approved the name changes and the commonality program was rolling forward once again.

To introduce employees to the new name and new common product line, while tying into the "Bay" theme, Trumbull Curtiss organized employee presentations at the New England Aquarium. At the end of the work day, 1,000 employees were bused to the aquarium and treated to refreshments and a dolphin show. The new name was announced to an applauding, cheering audience. Two days later a second presentation for another 1,000 employees drew the same enthusiastic response. The parties were important as an emotional signing-on of employees and made it more difficult for disaffected officials of member banks to slow down the bandwagon. In the following weeks, ties, scarves, and silver pins with the new name were distributed to employees.

Because of space constraints, members of the staff group handling the transition were physically dispersed throughout the greater Boston area, which made it difficult to meet often. Through 1975 meetings were intense, but spotty. The group met once a week or more, depending on whether a big issue was in the air. As Don Isaacs described it, "This was so new to us and to the industry. You'd go forward, get hit by something, go two steps back and reconsider basics, and then get moving forward again." Procedures were largely informal and, with no bashful people in the group, discussions were candid and disagreements open. Control was loose and leadership was shared. As William Fish recalls:

> You coudn't have run that group with a lot of control and obtained the results we did. It was completely fluid. By the structure of the group, each of the people reported to someone other than me. Rank has no privileges.

Group members saw their meetings as generally positive, optimistic, and enthusiastic.

Crozier was supportive and encouraging of the direction in which they were heading. At the same time, he was an extremely demanding manager who could roundly criticize someone's efforts privately or in front of peers. He wanted to be absolutely certain that these first projects went perfectly. Often when a group member took a position, Crozier would take the opposite view in order to probe and test the underlying judgments.

One Saturday night in February, Crozier had trouble sleeping. The next day, he called Fish, Curtiss, and Isaacs, and said "I'm uncomfortable with all this. I'd like to get together today at two o'clock." So they met on Sunday afternoon for four hours. It was a challenging meeting in which they looked at key issues and found many weaknesses in each option. There was some yelling as forceful personalities explored arguments back down to basics. Much of the discussion was conjecture since at this early stage facts were few. As a result of this brainstorming, they sketched on a blackboard their current reading of the EFTS options for BayBanks.

Many meetings were suddenly convened in this way. Something would trigger Crozier or another member of the group to summon the others. Their commitment was fueled by the idea that they were going to "beat the savings banks" and, to a lesser extent, the other big commercial banks in town.

As might be expected, operating people in the banks would sometimes hold back on helping the central staff. In response to a request for information they might say, "It's impossible to pull all that together" or "It would take an awful lot of work, you'll have to talk to my boss." So staff would talk to Crozier, Crozier would talk to their boss, and their boss would talk to them. The process was cumbersome and frustrating, and from time to time the group would commiserate with each other over drinks on Friday. Occasionally, a staff member might try too hard to make everyone like the moves toward centralization, and Crozier would admonish, "Don't try to be friends with everyone." At other times a staff member would push someone, who would complain to his boss, who would talk to Crozier. And so Crozier would call and demand, "What are you trying to do? Be nice!"

STAFF WORK ON EFTS

EFTS was by no means a well defined issue in 1975. It was clear that the electronic transfer of funds between accounts was technologically feasible, but no one knew what configuration or application might be best for the BayBanks system. In addition, banking is a heavily regulated industry, and no one could be sure what direction future legislation on the state or the federal level might take. Finally, surveys showed that customers were, at least initially, resistant to using these machines.

The uncertainties raised mixed feelings in the staff. Following Crozier's lead, they wanted to put together a case so strong and so well prepared that the logic and the evidence would compel agreement. Yet for this issue facts were fuzzy and information incomplete.

The banking industry had a bad year in 1975, especially in New England. The economy was in distress, interest rates were down, some banks had problems with bad loans, and it looked as if there would be severe pressure on profits. As Don Isaacs recalled, "In 1975 we had so many things to do, we wouldn't have been working on EFTS; but Bill kept coming back to it. The economics were still soft, and to justify the expense you had to rely a great deal on the 'marketing kick.' " Electronic funds transfer was new to Crozier and to New England, but he was convinced that at a minimum BayBanks needed experience in this sort of newly developing technology. Occasionally, Crozier would question whether they should be spending so much time on EFTS, and staff members would resell him that they were on the right track.

BUILDING SUPPORT FOR EFTS

Gradually, staff interest and excitement about ATMs firmed into a conviction that ATMs were the right move for the bank. The most rigorously trained staff member, Don Isaacs, said, "A person who was equally rational could have reached the opposite conclusions." The argument for ATMs rested on the potential for marketing benefits, the benefits of research and development, and the possibility of cost savings. Although these were not definitively quantified, Crozier could argue that the chances of success were great enough to warrant the investment required. The scantiness of the data, however, dictated that the program begin modestly and feel its way.

In October 1975 Crozier commissioned a study team from one of the member banks, the Valley Bank in Western Massachusetts. Early on the Valley Bank had experimented with EFTS, but their work had been preempted by the Greater Boston Task Force, of which they had not been members. Rather than let them develop further plans on their own, Crozier thought it was logical and politically sound to involve them in the EFTS effort at this point. "The people at Valley think they are ahead of the rest," Crozier told Curtiss. "We've got to get them into the flow of things." Using the results of the McKinsey study, the new group developed a further detailed electronic strategy for the bank.

Their report was fine-tuned by Isaacs and presented to the Council of bank executives. The presentation reviewed the problems and opportunities of EFTS for the bank, including competitors' activities in this area, the most recent research on EFTS, and the major equipment and system choice points. The strategy would be: to issue plastic cards to customers, to begin a pilot program with eight to thirteen ATMs, to install inquiry terminals in each branch, and to monitor competitors' moves.

In February 1976 the Council approved the formation of a project team to develop a detailed plan of action. The EFTS group—Fish, Isaacs, and Curtiss—were the core of the new project team, with expertise added in facilities planning and data processing. Early in 1976, they spent three days with McKinsey consultants listing every task that had to be performed. Then McKinsey took it all and created a beautiful three-color network planning chart on a magnetic board. As it turned out, the chart was hardly used because the project changed continually. The most a project team member would say for the color-coded magnetic board was, "Oh, we'd use it every once in a while to see if we'd forgotten some task." But the chart did not function as a planning/scheduling system.

The project team visited vendors, talked to banks in other regions of the country, and surveyed equipment manufacturers. By July 1976 they were ready with their recommendations to the Council: a full-scale marketing approach to ATMs in nine locations and check verification terminals, or CVTs, for balance inquiries and check approval in every branch. The initial program would cost slightly more than $1 million. When the presentation was finished and before anyone could speak Crozier said, "Well, that was a fine presentation. We can't do anything else but go ahead." The Council gave its approval, and a team was formed to implement the ATM/CVT program.

The final decision on equipment was made in January 1977, and the machines were installed in nine months. Curtiss supervised the development of a new series of employee presentations and an advertising campaign which used radio and television heavily and was accompanied by personal demonstrations at the banks. The ATMs and CVTs were unveiled to the public in the fall of 1977. Customers loved them. Even though at first only a small proportion of the bank's customers were actually using the machines, access to one's money twenty-four hours a day was seen as a great benefit. Along with the name change and clever advertising, the new machines helped the bank holding company become highly competitive again. In three months recognition of BayBanks jumped from 63 percent to 93 percent of the people surveyed. The banks began winning back market share and—thanks in part to the economic recovery from the 1973–75 recession and actions to remedy bad loans—earnings improved rapidly.

LOOKING BACK

Recalling the period 1974–77, several key participants summed up their feelings:

WILLIAM FISH

It was a great time, I tell you. It was one of the most exciting times in my life—sort of like being in the service. You say, "Boy, that was fun," but you'd never want to do it again.

TRUMBULL CURTISS

Why did it work? Crozier was new, very aggressive and had the support of the board. We were all young, except Bill Fish who added tremendous diplomatic skills. And every time we did a major project, we paid Cadillac prices. Everything we did for the banks was A-1 class.

DON ISAACS

At the beginning it was very important to have a success, so Bill held the decision reins tightly in hand. Now we have a track record of success and can afford a mistake and it wouldn't be disastrous. Back then, it would have been.

WILLIAM CROZIER

This period wasn't fun. It was extremely awkward, extremely tense, all the time punctuated by moments of sheer ecstasy. I imagine it's like the staff of a political campaign when they win an election. You can't fight like that all the time. We were glad to have the chance. It was a breakthrough time for the company, when you could spend an enormous amount of energy in a profitable direction.

The personal stakes were high and information on key issues was incomplete. It was not a situation most managers like to be in. Looking back on EFTS and other major decisions at BayBanks, Don Isaacs recalled:

> As a quantitative man, it makes me uneasy to say it, but fundamentally the approach we have followed for every major decision in the last five years is to know that we are headed in the right direction. We know what business we are in and what's consistent with out business. Thank God we know that. And we know our strengths and weaknesses.
>
> Every once in a while I feel a little guilty. We are probably less analytical and too "seat of the pants" than we should be. Can we afford to do it this way? I have read all the stuff on how you're supposed to make decisions. Are we that backward? Or you wonder, "Does it exist any place?" You have a guy like Otto Eckstein, with one of the best economic models around, who has difficulty forecasting with any accuracy three months out. So how much do you rely on analysis?

BRIEF CHRONOLOGY OF EVENTS

November 1973	Crozier white paper urges more centralized marketing
Spring 1974	Consulting firm begins study of corporate identity
June 1974	Crozier elected CEO of Baystate He hires McKinsey
November 1974	Isaacs & Finlayson report on ATMs: potentially significant, many uncertainties, recommend further study Consultants on identity recommend changing to common name and signage
January–May 1975	Greater Boston Task Force formed McKinsey reports to GBTF Firm hired to develop new name Survey vendors of ATMs
April 1975	Article on Crozier appears in *The American Banker*
June 1975	New name is chosen and graphics study is begun

Fall 1975	Challenge to name
October 1975	Valley Bank project team studies electronic banking alternatives
November 1975	ATM presentation to Council by Isaacs and staff
January 1976	Staff report identifies major alternatives in EFTS Planning/thinking sessions with staff
February 1976	BayBank Council approves assembling a project team for EFTS Trips to equipment manufacturers
April 1976	Presentation to employees at the Aquarium
July 1976	Council approves full-scale marketing plan of eight to ten ATMs and CVTs in every branch. Implementation team formed
January 1977	Decision on and installation of equipment
September 1977	EFTS presented to the public

Appendix B

GM's Response to Change, 1956-1981[*]

The first nine months of 1973 were the most prosperous in automobile industry history. Sales exploded despite increasing inflation, price hikes on cars, and recurrent warnings of a gasoline shortage that summer. Then, on October 19, war broke out in the Middle East, and OPEC placed an embargo on oil to the Western nations that lasted until March 1, 1974.

In only a few months the bottom dropped out of the American big car market. At the end of 1973, the Big Three (General Motors, Ford, and Chrysler) had more unsold cars in their inventories than ever before. The economy slumped, and the press proclaimed "profound and lasting changes in the auto industry." The next two years saw recession and a murky, uncertain climb to economic recovery. The auto executives urgently reworked their strategies as the public turned to smaller cars, especially imports.

As the leader, GM was hit the hardest. In six months it lost seven percentage points of market share, and profits and annual earnings also dropped precipitously. The company stopped large car projects in several of its plants. Richard C. Gerstenberg, then chairman of GM, said, "People were wondering . . . is the company going to make it?" [1]

The press charged the industry as a whole with poor planning and

---

*Adapted from a case by E. Mary Lou Balbaky. "GM and Ford: Decision-making in Turbulent Times." Harvard Business School, No. 0-381-172.

lack of judgment. Critics scored the automakers for habitually responding to market fluctuations with quick and easy shifts in the appearance of their product rather than reexamining basic goals and strategies. "The writing was on the wall," *Forbes* wailed, "but Detroit didn't bother to decipher it . . . the Big Three misjudged the trend to smallness." [2]

In fact, the U.S. auto industry had been well aware of the trend to small cars since the late 1950s, and both Ford and GM had essayed various responses, which met an inconsistent reception in the market. The general message Detroit heard was that Americans preferred larger cars. Government policies promoted this tendency by supporting extensive highway construction and inexpensive fuel. From the mid-1960s on, the industry became preoccupied with the pressing technical and financial demands of meeting new safety and pollution control standards. In the face of erratic and confusing signals, auto executives seemed to cling all the more tightly to assumptions and strategies articulated by Alfred Sloan in the early years of the industry.

To maintain demand and profitability in an industry that was cyclical because of its ties to the national economy, Sloan developed the strategy of upgrading consumer preferences. Cars of the same shape and size, made from the same basic metal parts, could be sold with different equipment at very different prices. Thus, each year GM could offer superficially different new models made more expensive through added improvements, different features and styling.

Especially after World War II, the automakers stimulated demand for cars that reflected a consumer's sense of identity and desire for importance. The big luxury car came to symbolize status and success, and sales confirmed Detroit's belief that the industry was giving people what they wanted.

By the end of the 1950s, however, there were signs that the era of the large glamour car was ending. Ford's overdesigned Edsel did not sell well and in the recession of 1958, new car registrations fell to 4.7 million (down 35% from 1955). Imports took an unheard-of 8% of the market (up from 1% in 1955), and two new compacts, the Rambler and the Studebaker Lark, also did well.

American auto executives, used to equating "biggest" with "best," had difficulty accepting the appeal of the small, economical car. As the imports moved toward a 10% market share, however, the Big Three brought out their first generation of compact cars. Domestically produced small cars won an easy victory over the imports, whose market share dropped to 5% in two years.

Secure again, Detroit proceeded to follow the old principles and upgrade the compacts over the next few years. As the compacts grew in size and price, the import market rebounded to 7% of sales in 1966 and 10% in 1968. Elliot "Pete" Estes, president of GM in 1980, remembered the time this way:

> Over the years, we made several passes at going to small cars. We tried it with our compacts in 1959 . . . and the Pontiac Tempest, Buick Special (etc.). . . . The customers didn't like them [and] the Corvair was a victim of bad publicity. . . . It was a disastrous experiment. By 1965 we had to sell the engine plant we were using for those cars. We learned that the more power we put in a car the more cars we sold. History taught us that big was better.[3]

THE SIEGE OF DETROIT

Sales of the compacts were not aided by the hostile indictments of Ralph Nader's 1966 book, *Unsafe At Any Speed*. Nader was personally instrumental in galvanizing Congress to pass the National Traffic and Motor Vehicle Safety Act (MVSA) of 1966, which set mandatory safety performance standards for all new vehicles. The standards included such requirements as seat belts, energy-absorbing instrument panels and steering columns, crashworthiness tests and more protective bumpers. Over the years there were waves of costly recalls affecting all the auto companies. More than 30 million cars and trucks were recalled for the correction of safety defects from 1966 to 1973 and these years were just the beginning of the tide. The quality image of certain American automobiles was severely tarnished.

In addition, the effect of automobile exhaust on air quality became a matter of serious public concern. Under the Clean Air Act of 1963, as amended in 1965, crankcase and exhaust control devices were required on all new cars sold in the U.S. in 1968. Further amendments in 1970 posed even tighter standards requiring a 90% emissions reduction by 1976.

Throughout the late 1960s and early 1970s the auto industry was preoccupied with the difficult technical problems and serious capital investment required to meet the various regulations. To install catalytic converters on all its 1974 models, for example, GM had to build a $100 million plant in three years. Construction was already under way before decisions had been made on many aspects of the converters, including the proper blend of catalysts.

The auto manufacturers repeatedly protested that the standards could not be met in the time allowed, that they were too costly, and that the need for certain requirements had not been adequately demonstrated. GM first claimed that it could not meet the 1976 emissions standards, then found an effective way to do so that actually reduced fuel consumption. As a result, it was lambasted for its early resistance.

THE GM RESPONSE

The GM board of directors had traditionally been composed largely of insiders. After beating back a Nader-inspired attempt to elect outsiders who would speak for the public interest, the company opened its board to people from outside in the late 1960s. Through the efforts of the new board members, GM established a science advisory committee, a public policy committee, and a corporate directions committee for long-term planning. These committees pressed GM to think more about energy and about developing American competition for the foreign imports to help offset the increasing U.S. government trade imbalances. This was a dramatic change. Government officials attributed a good part of the nation's shrinking trade surplus to Detroit's shortsighted thinking about the imports.

In 1968, not wishing to appear blind to the import problem, GM's top management announced the production of the Vega two years before it was to be introduced. In the early 1970s, the science advisory committee urged GM Chairman Gerstenberg into meetings with academics and oil company executives on the energy problem. In July 1972 the board created an *ad hoc* energy task force under David Collier, then GM's treasurer. Collier's group reported back to the board early in 1973 that there was a serious possibility of a gas shortage, which would profoundly affect GM's business. Since early that year, the oil companies had been urging consumers to cut back on gas consumption and dealers were limiting sales. Many people believed that the oil companies were trying to eliminate independent dealers in order to raise gas prices. Few saw the long-term implications of the increasing dependence of the U.S. on the disposition of Arab leaders and other oil cartel members.

GM executives had no clear sense of when these conditions might become a crisis, and they did not have a complete coping strategy worked out. Both GM President Cole and Corporate Vice President John DeLorean had independently tried to get the company to be more aggressive in creating new small cars, but with little success. (When DeLorean resigned in 1973, he charged that GM executives had become "totally insulated from the world.") One executive commented:

> There was a distinct awareness of a conservation—or economy ethic. But our conclusions were really at the conversational level. At that time there was certainly no tendency to go whole hog in emphasizing economy. . . . We were not at all sure sufficient numbers of large car buyers were ready to move to dramatically smaller-lighter cars. We were dreadfully aware of how Chrysler had been gurt by moving too soon to smaller cars in earlier years.[4]

Nevertheless, in April 1973 GM began a modest program to shrink the size of some of their cars. To avoid creating a gap in the product line into which the competition might move, they began by reducing the bulk of the full-sized cars, with the intention of later downsizing the intermediates and eventually making more drastic product changes. In a significant departure from GM's traditional decentralized division structure, a project center was formed to ensure effective coordination of the engineering and development work among the five automotive divisions. Moreover, for the first time in company history, a corporate-wide product plan was devised in place of the usual five-year plans for each division. GM had begun to think in the long term.

THE OIL EMBARGO

In October 1973 the oil embargo was imposed, finding the auto industry totally unprepared. As gas shortages developed, buyers flocked to the imports and the few small American cars available. Although imported cars had experienced three price hikes that year, they quickly captured almost 15% of the total American market. AMC, which made primarily small cars, increased its sales by 50% to almost 5% of the market. Because they offered some small cars, Ford and Chrysler precariously held onto their shares of the market, but GM suffered badly. Its big car sales fell by a stunning 50%. In a matter of weeks, GM laid off 84,000 workers and temporarily furloughed 85,000 more. Fifteen assembly plants were closed briefly to deplete big car inventories while the Vega plant went on double shift. By early 1974, GM's share of the market had fallen to 37.5% from a high of 44.4% just before the embargo. First-quarter profits were at a 26-year low.

No one was certain about the long-term significance of the oil shortage. Many thought the crisis might be temporary, but perhaps recurring in three to five years. Others predicted profound and lasting effects on the automobile industry. In December, the Senate passed an energy conservation bill requiring better fuel efficiency for automobiles for 1978 and a 20 miles-per-gallon minimum fleet average by 1984. Yet *Auto News* suggested that people's desire for big luxury cars was still robust and that this market would remain stable once the panic of the moment subsided.

THE DOWNSIZING DECISION AT GM

Although GM had already launched a modest program to downsize its largest cars, the effects of the gas shortage made quicker action essential. Moreover, decisions about future plans had to be made rapidly because the financing for the product line had to be approved by the board in January 1974.

GM executives generally agreed that the company needed a car smaller than the Vega, with excellent fuel economy, that could be produced as soon as possible. None of GM's domestic designs came close to meeting those requirements. The final decision was to use a GM car that had been designed in Germany and was being produced in Brazil as a successful competitor to the Volkswagen. The car, which was later called Chevette, could be put on the American market in a record 18 months (compared with the usual three years required to move a new car from drawing room to showroom). "We flew a team to Germany to pick up the drawings," recalled Pete Estes. "We even stayed with the metric system to simplify our problems in debugging the car over here."

Under pressure, the ordinarily slow corporate decision process was considerably speeded up. "Essentially, two or three of us agreed on what needed to be done and rammed it through," said Estes. Still, most major questions and issues were discussed informally in order to arrive at a consensus before any of the formal meetings.

Since GM offered models in every price range, many warned that downsizing a given model would damage sales of the next smaller model and so forth. Gradually executives accepted the idea that the exterior dimensions of the whole line had to be shrunk, and a new concept of size had to be sold to car buyers. Instead of "bigger is better," the message was to be "less is more." Estes commented:

> One of the big problems was to get the dealers to realize the full potential of these newly designed cars. We emphasized that the downsized regular car would not sacrifice the interior space, comfort or value of the "regular" car, and was not a compact or smaller car. . . . And there had to be an opportunity for our dealers to maintain profitability.[5]
>
> The consumer is the gut issue. . . . You have to remember that the automobile is the most postponable consumer purchase there is. Our customer doesn't have to buy a car tomorrow, or next week, or for the next four years. . . . So our business stops as soon as the customer loses confidence.[6]

In spite of everything, some at GM still thought that downsizing was the wrong decision and that the big car was by no means through. Others, however, pressed hard for smaller cars, fearing a competitive debacle if GM clung to its old line. Executives even discussed whether the company should drop full sized cars altogether, but the psychological commitment to total market coverage was substantial and the idea was dropped.

In December 1973, the Product Policy Committee finally decided that a drastic change was needed to increase fleet mpg. The previous plan had been to remove about 400 pounds per car. Now the target was 800 to 1,000 pounds. One executive commented on a crucial product strategy meeting held later that month:

> So much of the discussion was really instinct. There were strong feelings, rather than studies or data, that said every division should have small cars in its line. The decision process was highly unstructured.[7]

On January 23, 1974, GM formally announced that it would substantially reduce the size of its cars over the next three years, and that each division, including Cadillac, would have its own small car. The Chevette would be introduced in August 1975. In February the board gave its final approval.

1974: THE ROLLERCOASTER YEAR

1974 was a bleak year for the auto industry, the country as a whole, and the Western world. It was the most turbulent and unpredictable period in post-war auto history. Because of long gas lines and talk of gas rationing, the rush to small cars continued and their market share rose to 48.4% in January.

On March 1, the oil cartel lifted the embargo, but intermittent oil shortages continued and an economic slump set in. Consumer purchasing power and confidence had been badly hurt by the widespread repercussions of the oil shortage and a worldwide recession grew in tandem with double digit inflation. Interest rates soared to unprecedented heights and credit was tight. At the same time, automobile prices were hiked several times to pay for the plant conversions needed to switch production to small cars. Price-sensitive consumers stopped buying.

Overall, 1974 sales of domestic cars were only 7.2 million units, down 24% from 9.5 million in 1973. The sales of big luxury cars, however, began to improve by mid-year as the availability of gas seemed more assured, and the small car market declined. Sales of imports dropped 20% by the end of 1974, although their share of a greatly reduced new car market increased to 15.9%.

By midsummer 1974 Ford and GM were faced with increasing inventories of the small cars they had hurried to produce. Again, auto workers were laid off, adding to the expanding unemployment rate, plants were closed and production shifted to big cars. To reduce their swollen inventories, dealers instituted rebate programs on the small cars.

CRITICISM AND REORGANIZATION

As GM's sales and market share dropped alarmingly, news commentators sharply criticized the company for having no serious small cars other than the troublesome Vega and the Monza. Furthermore, like DeLorean, they accused the company of having become so large and ingrown that it had lost the flexibility to change, or even to see the new demands of the marketplace. Gerstenberg was forced to reply publicly that: "GM is not the insensitive, unchanging giant so many picture it to be. GM is in the vanguard of improving gasoline mileage. . . . But, we don't yet have a fix on what people want."[8]

The securities analysts also seemed to be skeptical that GM had the long-term commitment to achieve a turnaround without losing its high profit margins (6.7% in 1973, compared with 4% for Ford, and 2.2% for Chrysler). In 1974 a Cadillac Coupe de Ville cost only about $300 more to build than a Chevy Caprice, but sold for $2,700 more, yielding a potential extra profit of $2,400. The Vega subcompact netted GM only about $125 per car.

A long-term trend toward small cars also threatened the sales of optional equipment, such as air conditioning, automatic transmissions, and power steering, which returned profits of 40% or more. Small car buyers skipped the options partly because they wanted cheaper, simpler cars, and partly because they didn't need power steering or power brakes with a small car. Another problem was that unlike luxury car buyers, small car buyers were not typically loyal to a company or a line. Thus the market promised to become even more uncertain.

All the auto companies looked for ways to boost profits on their smaller cars, by promoting options on small cars or making them standard equipment, or by offering luxury fuel economy cars at big car prices. Nevertheless, most analysts predicted a sharp decline for the auto industry. With the largest financial and psychological stake in big cars, GM was predicted to be a big loser.

In response to these doomsday reports, GM executives reaffirmed their intention to convert plants and increase small car capacities. Gerstenberg predicted that GM would spend $1.3 billion on retooling in 1974. And in September 1974, GM undertook a major reorganization at the top.

Early in the summer the executive committee had begun seeking successors for Gerstenberg and Cole, who were retiring. The committee took inventory of GM's problems at the same time and presented their observations to a newly created Organizational Review Committee consisting mainly of the outside board members. The review committee recommended a major reorganization that would bring new executives into the upper echelon. Four relatively young men were invited to serve on the board and the executive committee. The reorganization was intended to increase GM's sensitivity to outside events and to make the corporation more responsive to the public and the government. Thomas Murphy, the new chairman, felt that the company had previously seen itself only in business terms and not as part of a broader society. The industry was too crucial to the general economic welfare to allow this isolation to continue.

GM was also concerned with gearing up to enter the international market. Accordingly, Estes, the new president, was freed of substantial responsibilities in order to concentrate more fully on overseas operations and the development of "world cars."

Early in 1974, the Senate had passed a bill requiring cars to achieve 20 mpg by 1984. There was no expectation that the bill would get through the House and its purpose was mainly to warn Detroit that the government could regulate mileage as it had safety and emissions. The Federal Energy Administration (FEA) asked GM what it would do voluntarily to improve fuel economy. A report was produced by a GM task force and a "voluntary fuel economy program" was created in Washington. Through an exchange of letters with President Ford, GM committed itself to an all-out effort to meet or exceed an 18.7 mpg fleet goal (a 50% improvement) by 1980. For the first time in a long time, GM executives felt exhilarated by the challenge.

As the demand for small cars shrank, and the big-car market revived, in the latter half of 1974, industry watchers reported that GM was having second thoughts about its five new divisional small cars, although it continued to develop the Chevette at a furious pace. GM officials declined to comment. Industry analysts began to revise their forecasts of the size of the 1975 small car market and noted that this segment was already becoming sharply competitive. Each of the auto companies announced plans for improved small car models in 1975. "The pendulum may swing back and forth several times before the shares of the market stabilize" an industry source commented. "You have to give GM credit for being prepared to move."[9] GM was going ahead cautiously developing key parts for its new lighter, downsized big cars.

THE ECONOMY RECOVERS—SOMEWHAT

April 1975 was the low point of the recession that followed the oil embargo. Prices were up 11% over 1974 and unemployment had risen to 8%. Probably no industry was harder hit than automobiles. The first quarter of 1975 was GM's worst since 1946, with net income less than 1% of sales.

By midsummer, however, the economy was on its way to recovery. Inflation was still high but had slowed. Auto sales steadily improved after the mid-year, workers were rehired, and each of the U.S. automakers showed a profit in the last quarter.

In December, Congress passed the Energy Act of 1975 which gave consumers another few years of relatively cheap gas. The Energy Act rolled back the price of oil (and thus gasoline) slightly before allowing prices gradually to rise just above the rate of inflation. The bill also converted President Ford's voluntary fuel economy agreements into law and further mandated that each manufacturer meet fuel economy averages of 20 mpg by 1980 and 27.5 mpg by 1985.

In early 1975 the trade media were full of confusing reports about what was happening to the market. On the one hand, the state of the economy and government policies seemed to indicate that the shift to small or fuel-efficient cars was inevitable, and that gas-guzzlers were losing their prestige. Imports' market share reached 18.2% in 1975. At the same time, dealers' inventories showed badly slumping small car sales and a rebounding demand for larger models. By year end, dealers were saddled with very heavy inventories of small cars. GM had a 110-day supply of Vegas in November, compared with a 15-day supply of Cadillacs. Costly rebate programs in early 1975 were required to bring inventories down.

One reason commonly advanced for the resurgence of the large car was that gasoline was once again inexpensive and available. Moreover, some argued that the population most likely to buy small economy cars was hard hit by the recession and inflation and fears of economic collapse and high unemployment. Key observers blamed the softness of the small car market on steeply rising prices rather than a genuine preference for large models. The perceived poor quality of American small cars also seemed to be turning buyers away.

Although *Auto News* reported that the small car market was expanding again in October 1975, it seemed fairly clear that buyers were moving back to larger cars much more rapidly than expected. Intermediate-sized cars were selling better than standard-sized cars, however, and auto dealers predicted that the market was moving to mid-sized models. The media consensus was that the auto industry had panicked in reaction to the oil embargo and had moved too abruptly and too ambitiously into small car production.

THE BIG GAMBLE

Despite these market fluctuations, GM continued to reduce the size and improve the fuel economy of nearly all of its cars. The changeover required was substantial, the risk very great, and the cost enormous, even by GM standards. The initial estimate of immediate costs was $3 billion. GM reduced its quarterly dividend—a move dreaded by all the auto companies—and in March 1975 floated $600 million worth of new debt. This was the largest fixed-income financing ever made by an industrial corporation.

GM's strategy was two-pronged. The Chevette was supposed to capture part of the market for VW-sized cars. Simultaneously, GM hoped to remain dominant in the middle and high end of the market by offering six-passenger cars that were economical to drive and easy to park, such as Cadillac Seville. Economy would not come cheap, however. The Seville cost $12,480, compared with $8,800 for the full-sized Cadillac. GM was trying to break the unwritten law that the cost of a car should be related to its length and width.

In the fall of 1975, GM introduced the Chevette, which was 16.7 inches shorter and 629 pounds lighter than the Vega. After an initial rush to buy, sales fell below forecasts and by February 1976 GM had cut production by 50%. Dealers were not interested in promoting the Chevette when they could sell larger cars with much higher profit margins. Later the *New York Times* referred to the Chevette as "the right car at the wrong time."

Larger American cars made a real comeback in 1976. The small car market continued to stumble and further rebate programs were thought necessary. Imports' market share fell 5 percentage points to 13.2% in mid-1976. Gas was plentiful, disposable income was up, and buyers were wholeheartedly buying mid-sized and larger cars.

THE GREAT COLLISION OF 1977

GM's new downsized cars were due on the market in September 1976 at the start of the 1977 model year. Ford had decided to leave its unaltered big cars in the market as a challenge. A full foot longer than GM's new models, they could not match the improved fuel economy of the GM cars. But would that matter? From July onward, headlines trumpeted the coming big car–economy car showdown:

> GM'S 1977 LINE RUNS AHEAD OF THE PACK: The Big question: Do People Really Want Smaller Cars? (*New York Times*, 7/29/76)
>
> ***
>
> FORD TO PIT BIG CARS AGAINST GM. The Greatest Auto Marketing Battle in 50 Years is About to Get Underway. (*Auto News*, 8/27/76)

GM's downsizing opened up all sorts of possibilities for shifts in consumer allegiances. Not for many years had there been such an opportunity for either Ford or GM to capture market share at the other's expense. The stakes were extremely high. Even a single percentage point of market share could mean a half billion dollars in revenues. GM had a tremendous amount of money invested in its big car names and the long-established customer loyalties associated with them. Ford now saw a chance to gain share in the profitable large car market long dominated by GM—but to do so it would have to risk an end-of-the-decade collision with the federally mandated fuel economy standards. In the interim might lie a substantial opportunity. "Government standards may ultimately doom the full-sized car but we hope to defer that eventuality as long as the customer is voting for it in the marketplace," said William Bourke, executive vice president at Ford. [10]

Both GM and Ford turned out to be winners in the confrontation of 1977 models. Large cars continued to be in high demand and both companies were offering newly restyled models with great fanfare. "The American consumer still has a weakness for whatever Detroit deems the newest automotive style," the *Wall Street Journal* observed. The auto market as a whole was still rising from its 1974–1975 low and showed record profits again. Both Ford's standards and intermediates and GM's new downsized models did well with buyers who wanted big cars.

Those who wanted smaller cars and real fuel efficiency chose the higher-quality foreign imports and felt safer doing so since dealer networks were expanding. Despite repeated price hikes, imports took 18.5% of the market. The losers were Chrysler, and AMC, and domestic small cars in general.

Although sales were good, both GM and Ford had to make many recalls. The U.S. entry of Ford's successful European subcompact, the Fiesta, had to be postponed for several months because it did not meet the 1978 emissions level. Finally, Congress relented and allowed the auto industry to sell 1978 models at 1977 emission levels.

1978—ANOTHER RECORD YEAR

Sales and profits remained very high for both GM and Ford in 1978, and the import market share dipped slightly. Press interpretations of the competitive balance of power were contradictory. Early in the year, *Business Week* reported that sales of GM's second line of downsized intermediate cars were disappointing, in part because they were significantly more expensive than Ford models of comparable size. Ford was thought to have a good chance to gain share at GM's expense.

At the same time, *Fortune* reported that GM's big gamble had paid off. Its new downsized cars were holding their own and GM led the Big Three automakers in terms of fleet gas mileage. Furthermore,

GM's successful turnaround had given the company an enthusiastic sense of purpose and a sharper understanding of the world. They were only beginning to reap the benefits of their internal reorganization and their new point of view, the article predicted.

GM profits for 1978 were over $3.5 billion and a sales blitz late in the year gave the company 61% of the domestic auto market, up from 57% in 1977. Meanwhile Chrysler and AMC were fighting for survival, and Volkswagen had begun building cars in the U.S.

THE MARKET TURNS DOWN

Fuel prices began to rise early in 1979 but the automakers expected car sales to remain largely unaffected as long as fuel supply was not disturbed. They ignored economists' predictions that tight credit, rising inflation, and consumer debt would lead to a sales downturn. By early spring, shortages of gasoline developed in California and gas lines formed again. Auto sales plummeted and—as in 1973—demand shifted abruptly to small cars. Analysts predicted that this time the buying shift would be permanent.

As buyers scrambled to find the most fuel-efficient cars, Ford, and Chrysler in particular, were left awash in full-sized vehicles. Ford offered $1,000 rebates to move its inventories. With "uncanny timing," GM had introduced its new front-wheel drive, fuel-efficient, "X" cars in April. Profits reached record levels and GM took over 60% of the domestic market, raising antitrust worries among some analysts.

By late 1979, the U.S. auto market was in a significant recession, with sales 25% lower than in 1978. "No one had figured on a gasoline shortage and its impact on auto buyers," said one news analyst.[11] Chrysler Corporation teetered on the edge of bankruptcy and was forced to seek loan guarantees from the government. Ford's share dropped from 23.5% to around 21%. The company's domestic operations incurred a $1 billion loss, offset by its hugely profitable overseas business. Imports grabbed a record 23% of the U.S. market.

In December 1979, reviewing the past decade, *Auto News* judged GM much stronger than it had been in 1970, because it had begun downsizing its cars two to three years ahead of its competitors.

Lee Iacocca, president of Chrysler by then, said "I give [GM] credit for making the decision . . . and also for being rich."[12] Ford and Chrysler attributed their difficulties to a lack of financial resources and excessive government regulation. Both felt they had been hurt much more by the government regulations than had GM, which could spread the costs of meeting standards over a larger number of cars.

The extreme downturn in profitable large car sales could hardly have come at a worse time. Because of federally mandated fuel economy, exhaust emissions and safety standards, Detroit had to spend billions of dollars in 1979 to design cars that wouldn't be sold until the mid-1980s. "The industry is beset by pressures that are leading it into uncharted areas. The decade ahead will be a revolutionary period in automotive history," a leading news magazine predicted.[13]

One aspect of that revolution was a turn toward the international market. While Ford had long been established overseas, GM was underrepresented. Downsizing improved GM's access to foreign markets and it began to think of entirely new possibilities for its operations. While the American market was close to saturation, the opportunities abroad were rich. During 1979, GM announced expansion of its existing plants in Europe, Mexico, and Brazil and continued plans for a "world car."

THE AUTO INDUSTRY IN DISARRAY

In 1980, the auto industry was in its worst recession in 18 years. Car sales were down over 20%, and the U.S. automakers together lost a whopping $4 billion. There were tremendous human costs as well. Over 300,000 hourly workers were laid off, 40,000 white collar workers were fired, and an estimated one million workers in the auto supply industries also lost their jobs. GM was able to sell its new fuel-efficient X cars as fast as it could make them, but it could not make enough of them to avoid its first annual loss since 1921—a deficit of $763 million.

Despite the loss, GM prepared to go ahead with a heavy investment program. Reshaping its entire corporate strategy to focus on world technological leadership, it would reverse its decade-long policy of penny-pinching on assembly plant investment. To replace the entire range of GM cars with efficient new ones designed for world markets, the company planned to spend as much as $80 billion by 1990 in the most radical plant modernization in its history. The new plants would include assembly line robots and computer-guided machines and systems. Multinational teams would participate in the design and construction of every new plant so that the company would be globally integrated and open to worldwide ideas.

Meanwhile, some in the industry blamed the government for the sorry state of 1980 sales. Ford officials complained that by holding down gasoline prices, the government had created a false demand for big cars that evaporated when gas prices rose. They also blamed the government for overburdening the auto industry with regulations. In August, *Business Week* pointed out that while the automakers blamed everyone but themselves, it was evident that poor product quality and the bad publicity resulting from product disasters were major impediments in the sale of domestic small cars.

All the manufacturers announced efforts to improve quality. "There is little doubt that the industry finally understands the significance of matching the image of quality that imports enjoy," *Business Week* reported.[14] Analysts were skeptical, however, and *Fortune* pointed out that despite GM's promise of unprecedented reliability, the X cars had suffered many defects.

In 1981 the hoped-for recovery of the auto industry did not seem imminent despite Detroit's new front-wheel drive cars and heavy rebates for larger models. High interest rates, higher car prices and low consumer confidence continued to depress auto sales, although there was some improvement. GM's new "J" cars, which were offered in the late spring, sparked a lot of dealer interest, which was then frustrated by the shortage of the cars. The automakers pressed the new administration in Washington to limit imports from Japan for at least three years to allow the domestic industry to catch up. It was believed that the Japanese would cooperate in some sort of voluntary restraint in the future.

The Reagan administration proposed to ease or eliminate 35 safety and emissions regulations which it believed could save the automakers $1.3 billion over the next five years. The new administration also seemed to be changing the policy of publicly announcing auto recalls in order to avoid "inducing alarm in the public that is unjustified."[15]

The "gamut of woes" facing the industry in 1981 encouraged the Detroit automakers to form ties with overseas companies. GM, however, eschewed any partnerships. "Until 1985," said GM chairman Roger Smith, "GM has everything covered."[16] In August, *Auto News* reported that the U.S. was rapidly becoming a nation of small cars. More than 40% of the automobiles on the road were compacts or subcompacts and by 1985, about 80% of Detroit's output was expected to be small cars.

The auto companies were hoping for extensive overseas sales of their world cars and looked for an explosion of pent-up domestic demand as the economy improved. But no one was making any definitive predictions. "Ten years ago you could tell market change three years ahead, but in today's world, you're really tossing a coin," said a Chrysler sales director.[17]

Notes

CHAPTER 1

1. Herman Melville. *Moby Dick.* New York: Norton, 1967; Joseph Heller. *Something Happened.* New York: Ballentine Books, 1975; Leo Tolstoy, *War and Peace,* translated by Ann Dunningan. New York: New American Library, 1968; and Tom Nicholson, "Iacocca's 'Little Miracle.' " *Newsweek,* August 3, 1981: 64-67.
2. Peter F. Drucker. *Managing in Turbulent Times.* New York: Harper and Row, 1980.
3. Joseph L. Bower. *Managing the Resource Allocation Process.* Homewood, IL: Richard D. Irwin, 1970, pp. 320, 321.
4. Paul Watzlawick, John A. Weakland, and Richard Fisch. *Change: Principles of Problem Formation and Problem Resolution.* New York: Norton, 1974.
5. James D. Thompson. *Organizations in Action.* New York: McGraw-Hill, 1967.
6. Melville Dalton. *Men Who Manage.* New York: John Wiley, 1959.
7. In trying to define these situations more clearly, we face an unusual, and, at times paradoxical, problem. The essence of these situations, at least in the beginning, is their lack of definition. This point notwithstanding, we can learn more about the class of situations even if more precisely defining a particular instance would remove it from the class under study.
8. E. Mary Lou Balbaky. "GM and Ford: Decisionmaking in Turbulent Times," HBS Case No. 0-381-172. HBS Case Services, Harvard Business School, Boston, MA, 1981.
9. Henry Ford II, quoted in William S. Rukeyser. "Detroit's Reluctant Ride into Smallsville;" *Fortune,* March 1969, p. 168.
10. Richard C. Gerstenberg. in "Fresh Thinking Is No Longer Treason in Detroit," *Fortune,* March 1974, p. 21.
11. Joseph Kraft. "The Downsizing Decision," *The New Yorker,* May 5, 1980, p. 152.
12. Andy Rooney. "Sixty Minutes," "A Few Minutes with Andy Rooney: On Following Directions," CBS Television Broadcast, January 27, 1980.
13. Jerome S. Bruner. *On Knowing: Essays For The Left Hand.* New York: Atheneum, 1973.

CHAPTER 2

1. Horace Freedland Judson. *The Search for Solutions.* New York: Holt, Rinehart and Winston, 1980, p. 109.
2. Ibid., p. 109.
3. Peter L. Berger and Thomas Luckmann. *The Social Construction of Reality.* Garden City, N.Y.: Doubleday & Company, 1966.
4. Ibid., p. 109.
5. Chris Argyris and Donald A. Schon. *Theory in Practice: Increasing Professional Effectiveness.* San Francisco: Jossey-Bass, 1974.
6. R.V. Tooley. *Landmarks of Mapmaking.* Text written by Charles Bricker, New York: Thomas E. Crowell, 1976.
7. Roger I. Hall. "A System Pathology of an Organization: The Rise and Fall of the Old Saturday Evening Post," *Administrative Science Quarterly,* June 1976, 21(2): 185–211.
8. John Dewey. *The Quest for Certainty.* New York: G.P. Putnam's Sons, 1929, p. 243.
9. Ibid., p. 223.
10. John D. Steinbruner. *The Cybernetic Theory of Decision.* Princeton: Princeton University Press, 1974.
11. Norwood Russell Hanson. *Patterns of Discovery.* Cambridge, England: University of Cambridge Press, 1965.
12. Stanley Keleman. *Living Your Dying.* New York: Random House, Inc., 1974.
13. Robert Tannenbaum. "Some Matters of Life and Death," Human Systems Study Center, Working Paper 76-2. Graduate School of Management UCLA, April 1976.
14. Stephen L. Fink, Joel Beak, and Kenneth Taddeo. "Organizational Crisis and Change," *The Journal of Applied Behavioral Science,* 1971, 7(1): 15–41.
15. Elisabeth Kubler-Ross. *On Death and Dying.* New York: Macmillan Publishing Co., Inc., 1969.
16. Elting E. Morison. "A Case Study of Innovation," *Engineering and Science Monthly.* April 1950.
17. Donald A. Schon. *Beyond the Stable State.* New York: Random House, Inc., 1971.
18. Thomas S. Kuhn. *The Essential Tension—Selected Studies in Scientific Tradition and Change.* Chicago: University of Chicago Press, 1977; Thomas S. Kuhn. *The Structure of Scientific Revolutions.* Chicago: The University of Chicago Press. 2nd edition, 1970.
19. Ian I. Mitroff. *The Subjective Side of Science.* Amsterdam: Elsevier Scientific Publishing Company, 1974.
20. James G. March and Herbert A. Simon. *Organizations.* New York: John Wiley, 1958.
21. Charles E. Lindblom. "Still Muddling, Not Yet Through." *Public Administration Review,* Nov/Dec 1979: 517–526.

22. Charles Christenson. "The Power of Negative Thinking." Working Paper, HBS 72–41. Boston: Graduate School of Business Administration, Harvard University, December 1972.
23. Chester I. Barnard. *The Functions of the Executive.* Cambridge: Harvard University Press, 1938.
24. Michael B. McCaskey. "A Contingency Approach to Planning; Planning with Goals and Planning without Goals." *Academy of Management Journal.* June 1974, 17(2): 281–91.
25. James G. March and Johan P. Olsen. *Ambiguity and Choice in Organizations.* Bergen, Norway: Universitetsforlaget, 1976, pp. 69–81.
26. Richard O. Mason and Ian D. Mitroff. *Challenging Strategic Planning Assumptions.* New York: John Wiley, 1981.

CHAPTER 4

1. For example, Edward Roberts of M.I.T. has found little protection from patents in his investigation of research activities in a chemical and petroleum company. Personal communication, October 1981.
2. Harold M. Schroder, Michael J. Driver, and Siegfried Streufert. *Human Information Processing.* New York: Holt, Rinehart, & Winston, 1967; William G. Perry, Jr. *Forms of Intellectual and Ethical Development in the College Years.* New York: Holt, Rinehart, & Winston, 1968; Jane Loevinger. *Ego Development.* San Francisco: Jossey–Bass, 1976.
3. Chester I. Barnard. *The Functions of the Executive.* Cambridge, Harvard University Press, 1938, p. 304.
4. Richard L. Daft and John C. Wiginton. "Language and Organization," *Academy of Management Review,* 1979, 4(2): 179–191.
5. Michael B. McCaskey. "The Hidden Messages Managers Send," *Harvard Business Review.* Nov/Dec. 1979, pp. 135–148.
6. Alfred Korzybski. *Science and Sanity.* Lancaster, Pa.: Science Press Printing Company, 1933.
7. Ben Yagoda. "How to Review a Subway Map," *New York Times Book Review,* February 24, 1980, p. 22.

CHAPTER 5

1. Researchers have also conducted a plethora of experimental studies mainly using college students. These laboratory studies are prized for their precise control of highly specified variables. Since ethical considerations limit the amount, type, and length of stress that can be induced, I will make only limited use of these studies and of laboratory studies conducted with animals such as monkeys and rats. Instead I will concentrate upon studies and reports of people in naturally occurring stressful situations. Managers

should find this approach more useful than that of much previous work which treats stress as a general problem in information processing, in which information is characterized as hard bits of knowledge that can be arranged into meaningful patterns. Such an approach not only ignores emotional processes but neglects a key fact of managerial life. In the important situations that interest us, hard facts are often not available, the patterns that give meaning are elusive, and information is subjective, multi-faceted, contradictory—in short, ambiguous.

2. Henry A. Kissinger. "Domestic Structure and Foreign Policy," in *International Politics and Foreign Policy*, J. Rosenau (ed.). New York: The Free Press, rev. ed., 1969, p. 265.

3. Irving L. Janis and Howard Leventhal. "Human Reactions to Stress," in *Handbook of Personality Theory*, E. Borgatta and W. Lambert (eds.). Chicago: Rand McNally, 1968, pp. 1041-1085.

4. S. Stouffer, A. Lumsdaine, R. Williams, R. Smith, I. Janis, S. Star and L. Cottrell. *The American Soldier, Vol. II: Combat and its Aftermath*. Princeton: Princeton University Press, 1949.

5. Douglas T. Hall and Roger Mansfield. "Organizational and Individual Response to External Stress." *Administrative Science Quarterly*, 1971, 16 (4): 533-547.

6. Janis and Leventhal. "Human Reactions to Stress," p. 1051.

7. Harold M. Schroder, Michael J. Driver and Siegfried Streufert. *Human Information Processing*. New York: Holt, Rinehart & Winston, 1967.

8. Mark Zborowski. *People in Pain*. San Francisco: Jossey-Bass, 1969.

9. Abraham Zaleznick, Manfred Kets de Vries, and John Howard. "Stress Reactions in Organizations: Syndromes, Causes, and Consequences," *Behavioral Science*, 1977, 22: 151-162.

10. N.J.C. Andreasen. R. Noyes Jr., and C.E. Hartford. "Factors Influencing Adjustment of Burn Patients during Hospitalization." *Psychosomatic Medicine*, 1972, 34: 517-525.

11. Carl R. Anderson. "Coping Behavior as Intervening Mechanisms in the Inverted-U Stress-Performance Relationship," *Journal of Applied Psychology*, 1976, 61(1): 30-34.

12. Susan Folkman, Catherine Schaefer, and Richard Lazarus. "Cognitive Processes as Mediators of Stress and Coping," in *Human Stress and Cognition*. V. Hamilton and D. Warburton (eds.). New York: John Wiley, 1979, pp. 265-300.

13. Richard S. Lazarus. *Psychological Stress and the Coping Process*. New York: McGraw-Hill, 1966.

14. John J. McDonough. "One Day in the Life of Ivan Denisovich: A Study of the Structural Requisites of Organizations." *Human Relations*, May 1975, pp. 295-328.

15. Zaleznik, et al. "Stress Reactions in Organizations."; Robert L. Kahn, Donald M. Wolfe, Robert P. Quinn, J. Diedrick Snoek, and Robert A. Rosenthal. *Organizational Stress*. New York: John Wiley, 1964.

16. Lazarus. *Psychological Stress*, pp. 117, 134.

17. George E. Ruff and Sheldon J. Korchin. "Adaptive Stress Behavior," in *Psychological Stress,* M. Appley and R. Trumbull (eds.). New York: Appleton–Century–Crofts, 1967, pp. 297–323.
18. Tom Wolfe. *The Right Stuff.* New York: Farrar, Straus and Giroux, 1979, p. 249.
19. Leo Tolstoy. *War and Peace.* New York: Signet Classics (The American Library), 1968, pp. 897–8.
20. Irving L. Janis and Leon Mann. *Decision Making: A Psychological Analysis of Conflict, Choice and Commitment.* New York: Macmillan Free Press, 1977.
21. Irving L. Janis. *Psychological Stress.* New York: Wiley, 1958.
22. Ibid.
23. R. Gal and R.S. Lazarus. "The Role of Activity in Anticipating and Confronting Stressful Situations." *Journal of Human Stress,* 1975, 2: 4–20.
24. David A. Whetten. "Sources, Responses, and Effect of Organizational Decline," *The Organization Life Cycle: Creation, Transformations, and Decline,* J. Kimberly and R. Miles (eds.). San Francisco: Jossey–Bass, 1980.

CHAPTER 6

1. The basic study of the desegregation of San Francisco's public schools is by Stephen S. Weiner. *Educational Decisions in an Organized Anarchy,* unpublished Ph.D. thesis, Stanford: Stanford University, 1972. A chapter by Weiner based on his dissertation appeared in James G. March and Johan P. Olsen. *Ambiguity and Choice in Organizations.* Tromsø, Norway: Universitetsforlaget, 1976, pp. 225–250.
2. Personal interview, Goosby. All personal interviews were conducted by E. Mary Lou Balbaky or the author, May–August 1979.
3. *San Francisco Sunday Examiner & Chronicle,* July 26, 1970.
4. William Cooney, *San Francisco Chronicle,* August 7, 1970, p. 1.
5. Ron Moskowitz, *San Francisco Chronicle,* August 8, 1970.
6. Personal interview, Shaheen.
7. *San Francisco Examiner,* December 18, 1970, p. 1.
8. Personal interview, Shaheen.
9. Weiner, *Educational Decisions,* p. 102.
10. Jim Wood, *San Francisco Examiner,* March 3, 1971, p. 1.
11. Reynold Colvin quoted by Ron Moskowitz, *San Francisco Chronicle,* March 4, 1971, p. 1.
12. *San Francisco Examiner,* March 4, 1971.
13. Personal interview, Shaheen.
14. Jim Wood. "The Reason for Weigel's Ambiguity," *San Francisco Sunday Examiner & Chronicle,* May 9, 1971.
15. Donald Kuhn quoted in Weiner. *Educational Decisions,* p. 153.
16. Elba Tuttle, quoted ibid., p. 169.

17. Personal interview, Lauter.
18. Personal interview, Johnson.
19. Personal interview, Lauter.
20. Personal interview, Kopf.
21. Personal interview, Hanlock.
22. Personal interview, Hanlock.
23. Jim Wood. "Frantic Rush to Integrate S.F. Schools," *San Francisco Sunday Examiner & Chronicle,* May 30, 1971.
24. Personal interview, Johnson.
25. Weiner. *Educational Decisions,* p. 311.
26. Ibid., p. 316.

CHAPTER 7

1. Irving L. Janis and Leon Mann. *Decisionmaking: A Psychological Analysis of Conflict, Choice, and Commitment.* New York: The Free Press, 1977, p. 115.
2. Ron Moskowitz. "San Francisco, California: Where San Francisco Went Wrong," in *The Integration of American Schools* by Norene Harris, Nathaniel Jackson, and Carl E. Rydingsword. Boston: Allyn & Bacon, 1975, pp. 62-71.
3. Karl E. Weick. "Educational Organizations as Loosely Coupled Systems," *Administrative Science Quarterly,* March 1976, 21(1): 1-19. I have shifted Weick's use of the term. He refers to the external connections between two systems. I use the term to refer to the internal connections among elements of one system. As used in this book, loose coupling describes a condition in which the components of a system are weakly related. A tightly coupled system, in contrast, means that a change in one component will have pronounced, and usually immediate, ramifications for other elements of the system.
4. Stephen S. Weiner. "Participation, Deadlines, and Choice," in *Ambiguity and Choice in Organizations* by James G. March and Johan P. Olsen. Bergen, Norway: Universitetforlaget, 1976, pp. 225-250.
5. Anthony Downs. *Inside Bureaucracy.* Boston: Little, Brown, 1967, pp. 63, 64.

CHAPTER 8

1. Jerome S. Bruner. *On Knowing: Essays for the Left Hand.* New York: Atheneum, 1973.
2. J.P. Guilford. *The Nature of Human Intelligence.* New York: McGraw-Hill, 1967.
3. John R. Trimble. *Writing with Style.* Englewood Cliffs, NJ: Prentice-Hall,

1975, p. 4.

4.   Henry Mintzberg. *The Nature of Managerial Work.* New York: Harper & Row, 1973.

5.   Abraham H. Maslow. *The Farther Reaches of Human Nature.* New York: The Viking Press, 1971, p. 4.

6.   N.R.F. Maier and L. Richard Hoffman. "Acceptance and Quality of Solutions as Related to Leaders' Attitudes toward Disagreement in Group Problem Solving," *Journal of Applied Behavioral Sciences,* 1965(1): 373–386.

7.   Maslow. *Human Nature,* p. 7.

8.   Richard S. Crutchfield. "Conformity and Creative Thinking," in *Contemporary Approaches to Creative Thinking,* H.E. Gruber, G. Terrell and M. Wertheimer (eds.). New York: Atherton, 1963, pp. 120–140.

9.   Robert B. McLeod. "Retrospect and Prospect," in *Contemporary Approaches to Creative Thinking,* H.E. Gruber, G. Terrell and M. Wertheimer (eds.). New York: Atherton, 1963, pp. 175–212.

10. Michael B. McCaskey. "Tolerance for Ambiguity and the Perception of Environmental Uncertainty in Organization Design," in *The Management of Organization Design.* R. Kilman, L. Pondy, D. Slevin, (eds.). New York: Elsevier, 1976.

11. Frank Barron. "The Needs for Order and for Disorder as Motives in Creative Activity," in *Scientific Creativity: Its Recognition and Development.* C.W. Taylor and F. Barron (eds.). New York: John Wiley, 1963, pp. 153–160.

12. Carl R. Rogers. "Toward a Theory of Creativity," in *Creativity and its Cultivation,* in Harold H. Anderson (ed.). New York: Harper & Brothers, 1959, pp. 69–82.

13. Donald W. MacKinnon. "IPAR's Contribution to the Conceptualization and Study of Creativity," in *Perspectives in Creativity,* I.A. Taylor and J.W. Getzels (eds.). Chicago: *Adline,* 1975. pp. 60–89.

14. Ibid.

15. Sidney J. Parnes. "Aha!," in *Perspectives in Creativity.* I. A. Taylor and J.W. Getzels (eds.). Chicago: Adline, 1975, pp. 191–248.

16. John Fowles. *The Tree.* Boston: Little, Brown, 1979.

17. A. Ehrenzweig. *The Hidden Order of Art.* Berkeley: University of California Press, 1967.

18. Michael Novak. *The Experience of Nothingness.* New York: Harper & Row, 1971, p. 39.

19. Susanne Langer. *Mind: An Essay on Human Feeling.* Baltimore: Johns Hopkins Press, 1966; Lawrence Kubie. "Research in Protecting Preconscious Functions in Education," in *Contemporary Educational Psychology: Selected Essays,* R.M Jones (ed.). New York: Harper & Row, 1967, pp. 72–88; Michael Novak. *The Experience of Nothingness.*

20. Amy Lowell. *Poetry and Poets.* Boston: Houghton Mifflin, 1930.

21. Jacob W. Getzels and Mihaly Csikszentmihalyi. *The Creative Vision: A Longitudinal Study of Problem Finding in Art.* New York: John Wiley &

Sons, 1976.

22. Alfred P. Sloan, Jr. *My Years with General Motors.* New York: Anchor Books, Doubleday & Company, 1963, pp. 45-60.

23. Albert Rothenberg. *The Emerging Goddess.* Chicago: University of Chicago Press, 1979, p. 55.

24. Arthur Koestler. *The Act of Creation.* New York: Macmillan Co., 1964.

25. E.F. Schumacher. *A Guide for the Perplexed.* New York: Harper & Row, 1977.

26. W.J.J. Gordon. *Synectics.* New York: Collier, 1961; George M. Prince. *The Practice of Creativity.* New York: Collier, 1970; Alex F. Osborne. *Applied Imagination.* New York: Scribner, 1963; James L. Adams. *Conceptual Blockbusting.* San Francisco: San Francisco Book Co., 1976.

27. Anne Roe. "Psychological Approaches to Creativity in Science," in *Essays on Creativity in the Sciences,* Myron A. Coler (ed.). New York: New York University Press, 1963.

CHAPTER 9

1. Howard E. Gruber. *Darwin on Man.* New York: Dutton, 1974. A second edition will soon be issued by the University of Chicago Press.

2. Charles Darwin. *The Autobiography of Charles Darwin, 1809-1892.* (hereafter referred to as *Autobiography*), Nora Barlow (ed.). New York: Norton, 1958, p. 23.

3. Ibid., p. 22.

4. Ibid., p. 23.

5. Letter written about October 17, 1831. *The Life and Letters of Charles Darwin.* (hereafter abbreviated as *LL*). Francis Darwin (ed.). New York: Appleton, 1911, Vol. 1, p. 187.

6. *Charles Darwin's Diary of the Voyage of the H.M.S. "Beagle."* (hereafter referred to as *Diary*). Nora Barlow (ed.). New York: Macmillan, 1933, p. 14.

7. *Diary,* p. 277.

8. Quoted in Alan Moorehead, *Darwin and the Beagle.* New York: Penguin, 1971, p. 138.

9. Michael T. Ghiselin. *The Triumph of the Darwinian Method.* Berkeley, California: University of California Press, 1969, p. 43.

10. Charles Darwin. *Narrative of the Surveying Voyages of His Majesty's Ships Adventure and Beagle. Volume III, Journal and Remarks, 1832-1836.* London: Henry Colburn, 1839, p. 474. Darwin wrote this book in 1837, but because of problems with the other two volumes, the book was not published until 1839, and afterwards underwent several editions. Hereafter this book will be referred to as *Voyage,* and the reader is asked to remember that it was mainly written in 1837. In subsequent editions this book was titled, *The Voyage of the Beagle.*

11. Ibid., pp. 461, 462.

12. Ibid., p. 475.

13. Ibid., p. 474.
14. "Darwin's Ornithological Notes," Nora Barlow (ed.). *Bulletin of the British Museum (Natural History), Historical Series,* 1963(2): 203-278.
15. *Voyage,* p. 608.
16. *Autobiography,* pp. 76, 77.
17. *Autobiography,* p. 83.
18. Gruber. *Darwin on Man,* p. 122.
19. Ibid., p. 152.
20. Darwin's second notebook, B 21-22. Darwin lettered his notebooks beginning with A and running through E. In early 1838 he opened a second series of notebooks and began the lettering with M. We will follow the usual notation, using the letter Darwin assigned to a notebook followed by his page number(s).
21. Darwin's second notebook, B 25.
22. Gruber. *Darwin on Man,* p. 168.
23. Darwin's M notebook, M 34, 35.
24. *LL,* p. 268.
25. Gruber. *Darwin on Man,* p. 3.
26. Ibid., p. 170.
27. Ibid., p. 172.
28. Darwin's N notebook, N 33, 34.
29. *Autobiography,* p. 120.
30. *LL,* p. 384.

CHAPTER 10

1. Howard E. Gruber. *Darwin on Man.* New York: Dutton, 1974, p. 251.
2. Ibid., pp. 150-174.
3. Edward Manier. *The Young Darwin and His Cultural Circle.* Boston: Reidel, 1978, p. 4.
4. Horace Freeland Judson. *The Eighth Day of Creation.* New York: Simon and Schuster, 1979, pp. 180, 181.
5. Darwin's M notebook, M 34, 35.
6. Edward Albee. *The American Dream and The Zoo Story.* New York: Signet, 1959, p. 30.
7. Quoted in Alan Moorhead. *Darwin and the Beagle.* New York: Penguin, 1971, p. 168.
8. Judson. *Creation,* pp. 113, 114.
9. Ibid., p. 45.
10. Ibid., p. 20.
11. A.H. Ismail and L.E. Tractman. "Jogging the Imagination." *Psychology Today.* 1973(6): 79-82.
12. William Stafford. "A Way of Writing," in *A Writer's Reader,* Donald Hall and D.S.L. Emblen (eds.). Boston: Little, Brown, 2nd edition, 1979, pp.

371, 372.
13. John S. Morgan. *Improving Your Creativity on the Job.* New York: American Management Association, 1968, p. 81.

CHAPTER 11

1. Michael D. Cohen, James G. March, and Johan P. Olsen. "A Garbage Can Model of Organizational Choice," *Administrative Science Quarterly*, 1972, 17(1): 1-25.
2. The problems the VIS people had in forming a core group are all the more relevant when research findings from the management of new technology are examined. Donald Marquis of MIT found that research projects in the Department of Defense and the Department of Transportation have a greater likelihood of success if they are undertaken by a small core of full-time members from the beginning. Similarly, Edward Roberts, also of MIT, found that successful transfer of research projects from the lab is aided by the early appointment of a small, multifunctional task force. Aerospace companies sometimes resort to setting up a "crisis room" where a small team of problem-solvers live around the clock until the problem is solved.
3. Richard Adams. *The Girl in a Swing.* New York: Signet, 1980, p. 148.
4. Michael B. McCaskey. "A Contingency Approach to Planning: Planning with Goals and Planning without Goals," *Academy of Management Journal*, 1974, 17(2): 281-291.

APPENDIX B

1. Joseph Kraft. "The Downsizing Decision," *The New Yorker*, May 5, 1980, p. 134.
2. *Forbes*, "Automotive—The Writing was on the Wall, but Detroit Didn't Bother to Decipher it." January 1, 1974, p. 141.
3. Kraft, p. 146.
4. James B. Quinn. "General Motors Corporation: The Downsizing Decision," The Amos Tuck School of Business Administration, Dartmouth College, Hanover, New Hampshire, 1978, p. 10.
5. Ibid., pp. 9 and 13.
6. Kraft, p. 146.
7. Quinn, p. 12.
8. *Fortune*, "Fresh Thinking is No Longer Treason in Detroit," March 1974, p. 21.
9. Charles B. Camp. "GM Said to be Applying Brakes to Plans for New Fleet of 1977-Model Small Cars," *Wall Street Journal*, August 15, 1974, p. 1.
10. *New York Times*, "Ford Hopes to Gain from GM's Decision to Reduce Models," September 8, 1976, p. 53.

11. Jeffrey L. Sheler. "A Troubled Auto Industry—Impact on U.S.," *U.S. News & World Report*, August 22, 1979, p. 23.
12. Robert W. Irwin. "The View from the Summit. Automaker Chiefs assess the turbulent '70s," *Auto News*, December 17, 1979, p. E2.
13. Sheler, p. 21.
14. *Business Week*, "Driving to Rebuild Ford for the Future," August 4, 1980, pp. 70–71.
15. Jeffrey Mills. "Carter, Reagan Officials Clash over Auto Recalls," *Boston Globe*, August 12, 1981, p. 33.
16. *Business Week*, "Autos, Distress that Won't Go Away," January 12, 1981, p. 53.
17. *Business Week*, "Detroit's New Sales Pitch," September 22, 1980, p. 79.

Selected Bibliography

Rather than repeat all the items listed in the footnotes, this bibliography represents a selection of books and articles for each major section of the book.

GENERAL – MANAGING CHANGE AND AMBIGUITY

Argyris, Chris and Donald A. Schon. *Theory in Practice: Increasing Professional Effectiveness.* San Francisco: Jossey-Bass, 1974.

Landau, Martin and Russell Stout, Jr. "To Manage Is Not To Control," *Public Administration Review*, March/April 1979: 148-156.

March, James G. and Johan P. Olsen. *Ambiguity and Choice in Organizations.* Oslo, Norway: Universitetsforlaget, 1967.

Quinn, James Brian. *Strategies for Change.* Homewood, Ill.: Irwin, 1980.

Watzlawick, Paul, John H. Weakland, and Richard Fisch. *Change: Principles of Problem Formation and Problem Resolution.* New York: Norton, 1974.

Weick, Karl E. *The Social Psychology of Organizing.* Reading, Mass.: Addison-Wesley, 2nd. ed., 1979.

Wrapp, H. Edward. "Good Managers Don't Make Policy Decisions," *Harvard Business Review*, Sept./Oct. 1967: 91-99.

MAPPING

Berger, Peter L. and Thomas Luckman. *The Social Construction of Reality.* New York: Doubleday, 1966.

Boulding, Kenneth E. *The Image.* Ann Arbor, Mich.: Ann Arbor Paperbacks, 1961.

Downs, Roger M. and David Stea. *Maps in Minds: Reflections on Cognitive Mapping.* New York: Harper & Row, 1977.

Kuhn, Thomas S. *The Essential Tension.* Chicago: The University of Chicago Press, 1971.

Polanyi, Michael. *The Tacit Dimension.* New York: Doubleday Anchor, 1967.

Vickers, Geoffrey. *The Art of Judgment.* New York: Basic Books, 1965.

Wilford, John Noble. *The Mapmakers.* New York: Knopf, 1981.

STRESS

Holsti, Ole R. "Crisis, Stress, and Decision-making," *International Social Science Journal,* UNESCO, 1971(23): 53-67.

Janis, Irving L. and Howard Leventhal, "Human Reaction to Stress," in E.F. Borgatta and W.W. Lambert (eds.) *Handbook of Personality Theory and Research.* Chicago: Rand McNally, 1968, pp. 1041-1085.

Kahn, Robert L., Donald M. Wolfe, Robert P. Quinn, J. Diedrick Snoek, Robert A. Rosenthal. *Organizational Stress.* New York: Wiley, 1964.

Kobassa, Suzanne C., Robert R.J. Hilker, and Salvatore R. Maddi, "Who Stays Healthy Under Stress?," *Journal of Occupational Medicine,* September 1979(21): 595-598.

Lazarus, Richard S. *Psychological Stress and the Coping Process.* New York: McGraw-Hill, 1966.

Monat, Alan and Richard S. Lazarus (eds.) *Stress and Coping.* New York: Columbia University Press, 1977.

CREATIVITY

Adams, James L. *Conceptual Blockbusting*. San Francisco: San Francisco Book Co., 1976.

Bruner, Jerome S. *On Knowing: Essays for the Left Hand*. New York: Atheneum, 1973.

Getzels, Jacob W. and Mihalyi Csikszentmihalyi. *The Creative Vision*. New York: Wiley, 1976.

Golde, Roger. *Muddling Through*. New York: Amacom, 1976.

Gordon, William J.J. and Tony Poze. *The New Art of the Possible*. Cambridge, Mass.: Porpoise Books, 1980.

Gruber, H.E., G. Terrell, and M. Wertheimer (eds.) *Contemporary Approaches to Creative Thinking*. New York: Atherton, 1963.

Prince, George M. *The Practice of Creativity*. New York: Collier, 1970.

Taylor, I. A. and J. W. Getzels (eds.) *Perspectives in Creativity*. Chicago: Aldine, 1975.

Index